T0244437

Praise for *The Mentally Strong Leader*

"If you want to build the mental resilience to thrive under pressure and drive change despite obstacles, this book will prove an indispensable resource again and again."
    —**Daniel H. Pink, #1 *New York Times* bestselling author of *The Power of Regret*, *When*, and *To Sell is Human***

"In *The Mentally Strong Leader*, Scott brilliantly highlights the often-overlooked, yet crucial, trait of mental strength in leadership. Drawing from extensive research and real-world experiences, Mautz unveils a proactive approach to leadership that empowers individuals to achieve exceptional results, even in the most challenging environments. With his six mental muscles and a wealth of practical tools, this book provides a comprehensive guide to cultivating mental fortitude. *The Mentally Strong Leader* is a must-read for anyone aspiring to become an exceptional leader."
    —**Dr. Marshall Goldsmith, the *Thinkers50* #1 Executive Coach and *New York Times* bestselling author of *The Earned Life*, *Triggers*, and *What Got You Here Won't Get You There***

"Mautz brilliantly fills a hole in leadership writing with an insightful, pragmatic book, jammed with tools that help you develop the most important leadership skill of our time: mental strength."
    —**Brian Niccol, chairman and CEO, Chipotle**

"Need to push limits? Push through challenges? You'll need confidence, self-control, big thinking, focus. That is, you need to be mentally strong. Mautz provides a potent toolbox for it all."

—Scott Beal, CEO, Barr Brands International

"To achieve exceptional results, it often requires transformation, both professionally and personally. Mautz provides powerful insight into what it takes—mental strength—and provides the tools to get there."

—Noel Geoffroy, CEO, Helen of Troy

"Leadership is more than a title or position. It's a choice. As such, being a highly effective leader requires continual effort and the willingness to improve, often through adversity. This book is a training manual for leaders to boost their mental strength and lead in ways that can yield extraordinary results for their teams and organizations—and the world."

—Edgar Sandoval Sr., president and CEO, World Vision

"Who wouldn't want to be mentally stronger? It's the key to achievement for pressing past adversity at work and in life. In this book, you get a menu of tools to build your key mental muscles. You'll learn to regulate your emotions, thoughts, and behaviors in the right way, as habits, backed by habit-building science. A must read for all leaders out there."

—Taylor Montgomery, chief marketing officer, Taco Bell, North America

"In *The Mentally Strong Leader*, Scott Mautz guides readers through the process of developing habits to remain clear-eyed and focused in a world of never-ending change and uncertainty. A must-read for those looking to understand how to achieve success in leadership today!"

—**Tanveer Naseer, MSc, Inc 100 leadership speaker, award-winning leadership writer, host of the "Leadership Biz Cafe" podcast, and author of *Leadership Vertigo***

The

MENTALLY STRONG LEADER

The
MENTALLY
STRONG
LEADER

Build the **HABITS** to Productively
REGULATE Your **EMOTIONS**,
THOUGHTS, and **BEHAVIORS**

SCOTT MAUTZ

PEAKPOINT
— PRESS —

Peakpoint Press books may be purchased in bulk at special discounts for sales promotion, corporate gifts, fund-raising, or educational purposes. Special editions can also be created to specifications. For details, contact the Special Sales Department, Skyhorse Publishing, 307 West 36th Street, 11th Floor, New York, NY 10018 or info@skyhorsepublishing.com.

Peakpoint® and Peakpoint Press® are registered trademarks of Skyhorse Publishing, Inc.®, a Delaware corporation.

Visit our website at www.skyhorsepublishing.com.

10 9 8 7 6 5 4 3 2

Library of Congress Cataloging-in-Publication Data is available on file.

Cover design by David Ter-Avanesyan
Brain illustrations by Mike Borkowski

ISBN: 978-1-5107-8058-3
Ebook ISBN: 978-1-5107-8062-0

Printed in the United States of America

To all the experiences over the years that forged my mental strength.
To friends and family, who offer strength-building perspective.
To Deb and Emma, who are my strength.

Contents

Introduction

It's the contrast I'll never forget.

I sat in the meeting in a dull, poorly lit conference room, while my coworker, sitting next to me, struggled to adjust one of those office chairs gone wrong, the up and down lever broken, lumbar wildly loose, one wheel off-kilter.

Despite the drab, mind-numbing accommodations, one thing rose above all else. The leader running the meeting *sparkled*. I mean he wasn't just good, he was *really* good. An aura exuded from him that said, "Hitch your wagon to me, and together, we'll go places." We were smack in the middle of a wildly challenging time, and yet he was unfazed, calm, never overreacting or underreacting. He led with a measured steadiness, always in command of himself and the environment he operated in. In fact, adversity seemed to sharpen him.

This "inner control" he emitted (that's all I could think to call it at the time) manifested itself in all the ways his frazzled employees desperately needed it to. In the course of one meeting, I felt his supreme confidence creating suction in the room, in a way that fostered trust and drove all to simply *believe* despite the difficult circumstances we faced. I watched him deftly guide us toward a bold risk worth taking, with crisp decisions and a decisiveness that quickly cleared a path toward a stretching, compelling goal. I embraced his call for the resilience, perseverance, and focus it would take to see our way through the continued obstacles sure to come. I observed his intentional, patient approach to show that he was listening, even to overly conservative counterarguments, all while tempering any frustration, instead intermingling positivity with a call to action.

Again, while I didn't have the perfect term for what I was witnessing, for what made that leader stand out, I knew I'd seen it before, in all the very best leaders I'd worked for. I saw it consistently in times when I was astonished at what we were achieving despite the circumstances.

Now, I can put words to what I felt that day, equipped with the hindsight of having since seen many, many leaders over my thirty-plus years of organizational experience, and aided by the reams of research and data I've conducted, collected, and analyzed. It might not coalesce into a term you've heard before, but it's one vital to understand. I'm talking here about pinpointing what separates the very best leaders from people who happen to be in leadership positions. I'm talking about who it is that guides the way to something exceptional, through a barrage of difficulties, with a steady, reassuring hand. I'm talking about what I was witnessing that day, that I can now articulate.

A *mentally strong* leader.

The term "mental strength" is most often used interchangeably with mental toughness, resilience, or perseverance. In the context of leadership, it encapsulates all of this—and yet it's far more. It's not just reactive, it's proactive. It's not just surviving, it's thriving. It applies professionally and personally.

Mentally strong leaders are skilled at regulating how they emote, how they think, and how they act, all in service of pressing toward exceptional achievement, through a range of stressors and challenges, both external and internal.

This can be you, too.

As I think back to that day and how that leader stood out, and of all the leaders in my research and experience that did so, it leaves me with an inspired call to action for you.

Become a self-disciplined leader who gets your emotions, thoughts, and behaviors all working for you, not against you, paving the way to accomplishment, for your team and yourself. Become a leader who closed the gap to greatness—professionally and personally. Become a leader to be emulated, remembered, revered.

Become a mentally strong leader.

1 The Power of Being Mentally Strong

Would you rather be an Olympic gold medal winner, or silver medal winner?

Duh, right?

Hold on, though. Research from the University of Virginia[1] might make you second-guess your first-place dream. A study of 654 Olympic track and field athletes over a fifty-two-year period, involving both gold and silver medal winners from around the world, revealed something counterintuitive. The silver medal winners were ultimately more successful, made more money, had better jobs, and even lived longer.

Whaaat?

To make sense of this, consider the case of the 2014 Winter Olympic women's hockey final. Team USA led by two goals for 56.5 minutes, holding Team Canada scoreless; until disaster struck in the final three and a half minutes. Canada suddenly scored two quick goals, then went on to win in overtime, 3–2. The US team got the silver medal, and their dejected look on the medal stands became a viral meme, and a thing, known as "silver medal face."

Such is the circumstance of how many silver medals are won, with "if only" dampening the glow of success, with the lifelong goal of truly being "the best" left unrealized. But the study showed that it's this experience of a pivotal setback, forcing the athlete to learn from it, adapt, adjust, and bounce back, stronger, that leaves a life-altering imprint. It's the exposure to "failure" that moves them closer to sustained success. As Scott Baker, principal behavioral scientist at BetterUp, says, "Psychologists have found that these types of seismic restructuring events are incredibly important for growth—they shape us."[2]

Or they can knock us for a loop we never fully recover from.

Oh, and by the way, leaders face the potential for these kinds of setbacks not just once every four years, but *every single day*.

It's a concerning reality for leaders of any kind, but especially for those striving to achieve something exceptional, in whatever form. So, what's a leader to do? It's such a profoundly important question that I dug in to find an answer. I mean, I *really* dug in.

AN EYE-OPENING FINDING

I started the journey of this book over thirty years ago, carefully studying what made great leaders around me great. Why did the achievers achieve to such a meaningful extent, even in the face of daunting challenges? Much of this study took place during the quarter-century I spent in marketing at Procter & Gamble, a company broadly known as a leadership and talent engine (no company has produced more CEOs of other companies from their marketing function).[3] I've added vastly to this knowledge base in the years since I left corporate with intense academic research, feverishly working to discern the "success despite setbacks" superpower.

One set of studies I conducted, in particular, brought this book quickly into focus.[4] I asked three thousand employees one central question:

"Thinking of the highest-achieving organizations you've ever been a part of, that overcame the most obstacles, what attributes/behaviors did the key leader embody?"

When I started this research, I didn't know if anything would break, if any themes would emerge. My skepticism proved wrong. I thought if anything did stand out from the pack, it would be something "classic," like strategic thinking or innovation skills—typical step-change forces. Again, I was wrong. (Not that these things aren't important, of course.)

To my surprise, a whopping *91 percent of respondents* described the same dynamic, the same profile: a self-disciplined, even-keel leader difficult to rattle. They exuded control, an intentionality over their emotions, thoughts, and actions. Their sense of self-determination, of being in control, sent an encouraging message to their organization, as did their unswerving confidence. They drove forward with a boldness, decisiveness, and resoluteness, ever-focused on the goal. The respondents didn't know it, but they were describing *mentally strong leaders*—and the key ways they applied their mental strength.

Excited by my finding, I subsequently confirmed it in thousands more data points: in exchanges with learners who have taken my global runaway hit LinkedIn Learning Course Ten Habits of Mentally Strong People, in dialogue with post-keynote advice-seekers, and as part of workshops/classes I teach, across a multitude of organizations. I also did follow-up interviews with many of the mentally strong leaders described to me in my research, including those whose had completely transformed their business/organization, all in the face of brutally challenging conditions (an "acid test" of leadership, if you will). The same (this time, self-reported) strengths surfaced.

Over and over it was reinforced: the presence of this self-regulation skill—the presence of mental strength—is what most directly correlates with people who blaze a path to meaningful achievements—in many cases, directly in the face of considerable challenges.

DEFINITION OF A MENTALLY STRONG LEADER

Let's make sure we're all working from the same definition. A mentally strong leader is **one with the ability to regulate their emotions, thoughts, and behaviors to achieve exceptional outcomes, despite circumstances. They manage internally, so they can lead externally.**

They're a calm port in the storm, in control of themselves and their environment, somehow getting sharper when adversity arises, brandishing self-discipline and endurance as a beacon of light. And as I discovered in my research, they display their mental strength across the six essential "tests of leadership" that most directly link to exceptional achievement. More on this shortly.

In such an exhausting, chaotic work world, with so much instability, fear, and debilitating distraction, where inspiration can go missing at times, an important truth cuts through the smoke.

Mental strength is *the* leadership superpower of our times.

WHAT MENTAL STRENGTH ISN'T

A few clarifications. When I use the term "mental strength," or "mentally strong," I'm not talking about acting tough. I'm not talking solely about emotional intelligence, or EQ, although it's certainly part of it. Mental strength, especially in the context of leadership, goes beyond regulating emotions. It also involves managing attitude, thoughts, behaviors, and beliefs to help you/your organization, steadily, to something exceptional, through something challenging. Also note that when I say "mental strength," I'm not referring to mental health. Nor am I saying that the absence of mental strength equals mental illness. That's a separate umbrella, very worthy of separate discussion.

Finally, I'm not implying that the opposite of mental strength is mental weakness; one is not mentally strong or mentally weak. We all have a baseline of mental strength (and we all work through moments of weakness at times). In fact, psychotherapist and mental strength expert Amy Morin says, "Mental strength is something everyone possesses to a certain degree."[5] But however strong you are, there's always room to get stronger. And it's especially important to do so in the following ways.

THE SIX TESTS OF LEADERSHIP THAT REQUIRE MENTAL STRENGTH

Mentally strong leaders apply their skill set most effectively to six specific tests of leadership that most directly correlate with exceptional achievement (the six areas that demonstratively emerged in my research). Each test *necessitates self-regulation skills* to navigate them effectively (and can be thought of as the big, overall habits you're working toward with this book). The tests are: fortitude, confidence, boldness, messaging (sending the troops the right messages of positivity and intent), decision-making, and goal-focus. Let's look at what excellence in each of these areas accomplishes, and foreshadow the tools you'll get in this book to help you develop powerful self-regulating skills for each area.

1. Fortitude

Fortitude not only requires determination, it takes self-determination—intentionally managing your emotions, thoughts, and behaviors to help you persevere (rather than making it more difficult to do so). It's worth the effort, as developing fortitude gives you the courage to wade through tension, not wilt. Fortitude also:

- helps you reframe setbacks
- helps you handle the "daily grind"
- fuels a problem-solving mindset
- helps you thrive under pressure and perform in crisis

- helps you effectively handle, and plan for, adversity
- sparks a refusal to engage in victim mentality
- feeds healthy debate
- gives you the courage and wherewithal to have difficult conversations

You'll get tools to enable all of this in chapter 3.

2. Confidence

The link between confidence and achievement is undeniable. So, it stands to reason that self-critical emotions, thoughts, and behaviors can evaporate your confidence (and the advantage it gives you) in the blink of an eye. Building and maintaining your confidence steers you, and others, through insecurity, toward the most capable self. It also:

- gives you the self-assurance to embrace relevant criticism
- helps you push past fear of failure, manage self-doubt, and even embrace healthy doubt
- keeps you from making irrelevant comparisons and seeking approval
- helps you stop negative self-talk and prevail over imposter syndrome
- drives the belief you're "enough," while fueling a disciplined approach to learning/improving
- encourages your most optimistic self
- helps you exude executive presence, further increasing others' confidence in your leadership

You'll get tools to enable all of this in chapter 4.

3. Boldness

Boldness requires the right frame of mind, focused on empowering thoughts and beliefs versus limiting thoughts and beliefs. Developing boldness pays huge dividends as it fuels your fearlessness to push the team, and yourself, higher, harder, further, faster. It also:

- fuels big thinking
- helps you shake up unhelpful stories that teams fall into
- emboldens you to take smart risks
- pushes you past uncertainty and into embracing change
- gives you the conviction to lead change

You'll get tools to enable all of this in chapter 5.

4. Messaging

As a leader, employees constantly take cues from you. Your behaviors, thoughts, and what you emote have a direct impact on how they view themselves and their work; you can send helpful or unhelpful messages. This is disproportionately true regarding how much you resist contributing to negativity (feeding positivity instead), and the quality of your presence and intent. Growing in this area helps you fuel motivation, energy, and trust. More specifically, it:

- helps you navigate negative emotions in the moment
- prevents you from losing your temper, and helps you choose your words carefully
- helps you avoid negativity traps (like pessimistic complainers and debilitating emotions)
- sparks you to proactively fuel positivity

- helps you be an active listener, sending the message that coworkers are heard
- drives you to show up with transparency and integrity, enhancing trustworthiness
- helps you set a balanced tone; demanding yet empathetic, calm yet with urgency, etc.
- gives you the discipline to act consistent with your values, reinforcing your character

You'll get tools to enable all of this in chapter 6.

5. Decision-Making

Emotion, bias, and undisciplined thinking are all enemies of good decision-making. Self-regulation skills (mental strength) play a huge role here in giving you the courage and conviction to be decisive and the ability to make good decisions that propel you toward what you're trying to achieve. It also:

- raises awareness of your biases/bad habits, preventing them from negatively affecting decisions
- helps you develop a data-based, analytical approach to decision-making
- helps you set a clear decision-making process/structure, with crisp decision-making meetings
- helps you discern the who, what, how, when of decision-making
- encourages you to explore a better third option
- helps you develop better predictive ability and greater decision confidence

- feeds your willingness to make tough, unpopular calls, delaying gratification as needed

You'll get tools to enable all of this in chapter 7.

6. Goal-Focus

Wayward thoughts, emotions, and actions distract you from the goal at hand. Intentionally regulating each here helps keep you from being distracted, giving you the discipline to focus on the most important things that contribute to progress and goal achievement. It also:

- helps you set powerful goals and visualize what it will take to achieve them
- inspires you to establish a more thorough set of expectations
- helps you focus on what you can control, and focus and concentrate when you most need to
- helps you hold others (and yourself) accountable
- guides you to build goal-momentum on small victories
- helps you stop procrastination and perfectionism
- helps you adjust goals as needed along the way

You'll get tools to enable all of this in chapter 8.

Now, imagine excelling at all six of these leadership tests, fueled by your masterful self-regulation skills, muscled up by your mental strength. (If you already pass all these tests with flying colors, congratulations! The rest of this book will be one heck of a tune-up for you, then.) Think of the impact you'd have, the difference you'd make, the imprint you'd leave behind. Nothing returns a greater ROI than your commitment to becoming a mentally strong leader. Nothing amplifies your ability to produce exceptional results, even in the face of adversity, like mental strength.

MENTALLY STRONG LEADERSHIP IN ACTION

You're probably expecting high-profile stories of mental strength to be the driving inspiration for this book. Like the story of Kobe Bryant, a basketball icon who created an alter ego of self-discipline, the "Black Mamba," to help him summon courage at times the most was asked of him. Or Sarah Blakely, the founder of Spanx, who in 2012 became the youngest self-made billionaire, and who famously tells stories of how her mental strength was forged (at the dinner table, where her family would exchange stories about what they had failed at that week). Or Anthony Ray Hinton, a man wrongfully accused of a crime and given the death sentence, who watched fifty-four men walk past his cell on their way to execution and another twenty-two who committed suicide, bearing it all, stoically, for thirty years, as one of the longest-surviving death row prisoners in the state of Alabama.[6]

All dramatic stories of mental strength.

However, the real driving force behind this book is perhaps more relatable stories of everyday leaders turned everyday heroes through application of their mental strength. Sure, I've had my share of such stories throughout my life I could contribute (professional, personal, medical, and otherwise). Occasions that required me to draw upon my mental strength have further honed my expertise on the subject. I'll pepper that in here and there throughout this book. For now, I'll share a perspective beyond my own: a range of simple, relatable examples of mentally strong leadership that have inspired me. They're drawn from my years of research and experience, from instances where I personally witnessed mentally strong leaders in action, or from stories of such people shared with me.

Here are some of those stories, with mentally strong self-regulation skills on display. You just might see yourself in them—or aspire to.

A Story of Fortitude

Sharon, a business leader at a packaged goods company, refused to give in to the increasingly aggressive demands of a big retail customer. If she did, it would mean a short-term sales gain but a substantial decrease in profitability for her business. In a series of intense, heated meetings, the retailer threatened to pull distribution of one of the company's biggest-selling products if Sharon didn't concede. But, despite being under tremendous pressure to grow sales significantly, she didn't cave to emotion or short-term thinking/actions. She held strong and made a hard call. They would stop doing business with the unreasonable retailer (for fear of damaging the long-term overall business if she caved to the demands). This meant an instant, catastrophic 15 percent drop in sales.

Pressure poured in from her chain of command to reverse the decision, but still she held steady, refusing to play the victim. She reframed the sales loss as a huge opportunity to create next-level partnerships with other hungry, eager retailers. The shell-shocked, dejected sales force pushed back on Sharon at first, joining the chorus of people begging the leader to reverse her decision. Again, she held, productively addressing the debate head-on and having many tough conversations, while continually reframing the setback as an opportunity. At the same time, she embraced a problem-solving spirit, giving the sales force more flexibility and tools to meet the demands of the other, more strategic, retailer partners. Over the course of a very long eighteen months, business with the other retailers steadily began taking off, with never-seen-before double-digit monthly gains being posted. Within a year and a half, the company had more than made up the sales lost with the unreasonable retailer and had stronger partnerships with retailers that would secure profitable, long-term growth.

A Story of Confidence

The team needed to get this educational initiative right, and Maya knew it. As the manager of the biggest project the foundation had ever launched, she certainly felt the pressure. Funding at the nonprofit was tight, and a disproportionate amount of it was behind this effort. Maya had never led anything this big—self-doubt and a fear of failure were creeping in.

She committed to draw on her mental strength to embrace her doubt and get it to work for her, driving her to focus and work as efficiently as possible. She resisted the temptation to compare herself to a successful peer who had run a separate big project successfully, and refused to feel like an imposter. She reminded herself that she belonged here, in this moment, was fully qualified and appropriately skilled, and would succeed. She acknowledged when she was beating herself up, but quickly moved past it to a more confident mindset. She accepted criticism along the way as learning opportunities, and focused on learning and improving along the way as she orchestrated her team's launch efforts. In the end, the team got it right with the nonprofit's biggest-ever initiative, opening the gates for more successful endeavors like it to follow, and fueling Maya's confidence to even higher levels.

A Story of Boldness

Kurt, a school administrator, had a big idea to reshape how teachers and parents interacted to create the best possible learning environment for the students. They'd establish formal partnerships between the two, with aligned goals, specific agreements, and creative rewards. Nothing like it had ever been tried at Kurt's school. He faced huge skepticism every time he presented it in board meetings, parent meetings, and teacher meetings. People clung to an established narrative/belief that things like this "don't work in this district."

But Kurt carefully maintained the proper mindset, focusing on what was possible, not giving in to limiting thoughts and feelings of what wouldn't work. He kept working to ignite a risk-taking spirit, trying to inspire change. He pushed through to launch a small, experimental pilot program, which failed at first. But by applying lessons learned from the failure, each pilot program got better, and a willingness to experiment further emerged. Eventually, Kurt won everyone over with a crisp, clear vision for change and for how to roll out the teacher-parent initiative more broadly. He received broad acclaim for his efforts.

A Story of Messaging

Charlotte was sure that her recommendation to overhaul and transform the maternity benefits and leave policies at her company would be approved. She went into the meeting to ask for a signature as a formality, and was instead shocked when senior human resource leaders rejected her proposal (with a fair amount of negativity). Anger churned inside, but Charlotte knew she couldn't control their decision, only how she'd react to it. Her entire team was watching—aggravated emotions, thoughts, and reactions would be of no help. What kind of message would it send to her team, and the senior leaders, if she flew off the handle?

She took a deep breath, composed herself, and calmly sought to understand the leaders' reasoning behind the denial, actively listening along the way, exhibiting a core value of curiosity and desire to learn. While hearing the litany of reasons, she refused to get weighed down by all the pessimism, ignoring feelings of defeat and deflation. She instead emitted a positive vibe, energized by the fact that at least she was getting supreme clarity on what was wrong with her proposal, so she could address it. As she responded, she chose her words carefully, being certain not to let unhelpful emotion slip in, balancing the tone of her communication between acknowledging where they were right and respectfully, transparently expressing points of disagreement. She returned to the same group one month later with a revised proposal. This time, she was met with success and a volley of appreciation from her leaders and employees for how she handled it all. The right messages had been sent and received.

A Story of Decision-Making

Vijay had many decisions to make, quickly. A venture capital firm was taking over, and while he'd keep his role as the company's CEO/founder, they were asking him to change the business model. It was a highly emotional thing for Vijay, as he had built the business from the ground up, beginning in his garage. And he knew he was biased about many of the decisions that had to be made, given how close he was to it all.

But he also knew he'd have to shake off those biases, leave his personal feelings behind, and develop a disciplined, data-based, highly analytical approach to how to change the business model. As he did, he also clarified and brought structure to the decision-making process with the VC board (they wanted to be involved), all the way down to how decision-making meetings would be run, and even how they'd test their decisions before implementing them. Vijay led the way with a decisiveness that impressed the board. The business model evolution worked, and Vijay sits at the head of a now far more successful endeavor.

A Story of Goal-Focus

Javier, the sales leader, wasn't sure how they could do it. He and his team were given a huge, important sales target, a 25 percent increase—in a plodding, slow-growth category. The first quarter was soft, the goal already slipping away. But Javier knew giving in to feelings of frustration, negative thinking, and acts of desperation wouldn't help. So, he kept his team, and himself, focused on the target, his vision for achieving it, and a clear set of expectations for how they'd deliver it. The next sales quarter was better, but marginally so. Yet Javier still celebrated the small victory and built on it to spark momentum.

While pressure continued to mount, he held his team accountable, despite numerous distractions. The company was going through a reorganization, a major customer was in turmoil, and the economy was visibly starting to sputter. Still, Javier kept his team focused on the goal and what they could control, all while carefully discouraging both procrastination and perfectionism—forward progress was of paramount importance. Through a series of decisive sales pitches, smart moves with key customers, and relentless focus, the sales team stacked up increasingly strong months. Sales exploded in the last quarter, even as Javier and his group navigated still more distractions (a new boss and a new CEO). By year's end, against all odds, Javier and his team celebrated achievement of their ultimate goal.

BUILDING POWERFUL MENTAL HABITS TO SELF-REGULATE

So how exactly, then, do you develop your mental strength? How do you regulate your emotions, thoughts, and behaviors to achieve exceptional outcomes, despite circumstances, and do so across the six essential tests of leadership that most directly drive achievement (as outlined)?

With a word that's essentially a synonym for self-regulation. Habits.

The whole point of building habits is to create little systems of self-regulation, to bring discipline to your thoughts, feelings, and behaviors, so all three can serve you well. This is where the full power of this book comes in. You'll build *a specific set of powerful mental habits that make you mentally stronger and that train your brain to self-regulate across the six vital tests of leadership*. In fact, you'll find a menu of mental habits to choose from to improve your fortitude, confidence, boldness, messaging, decision-making, and goal-focus. There are over fifty tools to choose from in this book, all backed by research and all tested with real-world leaders and their organizations.

The expectation isn't that you adopt every supporting habit or use every tool in this book, but that you develop the areas that *you* most need to strengthen, for *your* situation, in ways most relevant and appealing to *you*. That's the point of the menu approach: to give you plenty of options to choose from, thus maximizing the likelihood that you'll find an appealing set of mental habits and tools to adopt for each area you want to improve.

GETTING OFF TO A STRONG START (WITH HABIT-BUILDING SCIENCE)

Research shows we get mentally stronger with age.[7] Makes sense, given the impact that experience or "been there done that" has on us all. But why wait for the passing years to develop this critical attribute? This book is about accelerating the learning curve and increasing your mental strength as a leader (and in general), *right now*. But, since time is undefeated, that means you can't just supplant all that experience easily. It takes incorporating the right habits into your routine. All of which you now have access to in this book.

Two things to help you get off to a fast start.

First, for every self-regulating habit to build, you'll see there's a supporting "Habit-Building Tool." Habit-building science shows that habits are formed through repetition, and getting your "reps" in is easier when you have a system or framework to follow, with clear cues to trigger that habit.[8] So that's how each tool is designed, as a system or framework that's easy to adopt (with other habit-building tricks built in as well). You'll also find plenty of examples to help illustrate each tool in use.

Furthermore, you'll encounter "Your First Small Step" and "In Moments of Weakness" sections. That's because habit-building science also indicates habits form with an initial small step, one that eventually evolves into a routine. And habits stick when you know how to overcome missteps, moments of weakness, as you're trying to form those habits.[9]

Also, know that in the next chapter, you'll take a Mental Strength Self-Assessment. This will help you set a baseline of how mentally strong you are right now, identify where your strengths and areas of opportunity are, and show you the habits and tools you need to train up each area. It will be your personalized mental strength-training program.

So, now you know what being mentally strong means (and doesn't mean), why it matters (it most directly correlates with achievement), and what it looks like in practice (it's applying disciplined regulation of your emotions, thoughts, and behaviors across the six tests of leadership that most directly link to achievement, through habits you build). You also know that the ability to adopt a customized set of supporting habits/tools lies ahead. Dive into chapter 2 now, and then we'll get to habit forming in the chapters thereafter.

NOTES

1. A. Leive. September 2018. "Dying to Win? Olympic Gold Medals and Longevity." *Journal of Health Economics* 61: 193–204.
2. S. Baker. May 2, 2021. "Build Resilience Like a (Silver Medal) Winner," betterup.com/blog.

3. K. Whitler. January 12, 2019. "Study Results: The Top Companies That Prepare Marketers to Become CEOs," *Forbes*.

4. A combination of quantitative and qualitive research conducted with employees in over one hundred companies, across a range of industries, from millions to billions in revenue, headquartered in multiple different countries.

5. A. Morin. February 5, 2020. "7 Reasons You Need Big Mental Muscles to Succeed," psychologytoday.com.

6. P. Pompliano. February 23, 2021. "7 Mentally Tough People on the Tactics They Use to Build Resilience," theprofile.com.

7. P. Clough, "The Mental Toughness Questionnaire: MTQ48," corporate-energising.com, 34.

8. J. Clear. "The Science of Developing Mental Toughness in Your Health, Work, and Life," jamesclear.com.

9. Ibid.

2   The Mental Strength Self-Assessment

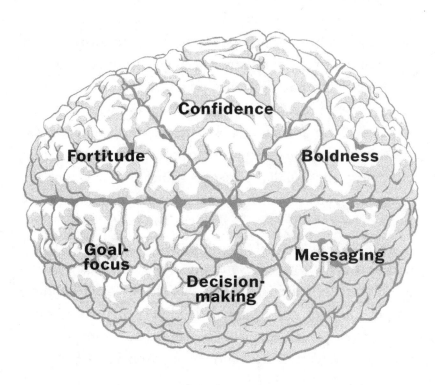

H ow mentally strong are you?

Being a mentally strong leader starts with awareness of where you currently stand on this front. That's the point of the Mental Strength Self-Assessment—it gives you a baseline measurement. It indicates your overall mental strength, and how you "rate" on each key area within (areas that most correlate with achievement, and that require self-regulation habits for success).

The assessment also provides a preview of the habits to build/supporting habit-building tools for each of these components of mental strength (all at your disposal in this book).

Answer each of the following 50 questions, *honestly*, across each of the six areas (fortitude, confidence, boldness, messaging, decision-making, and goal-focus). The entire self-assessment will take about 15–20 minutes. Don't overthink it—just go with your gut, first reaction to each question. Do pay attention to any emotions or feelings that are triggered as you answer each question; they might be pointing to something you need to work on, change, keep doing, or amplify, which you'll be able to address after you've completed the assessment. The remaining chapters in this book are focused on helping you build the mental habits that are right for you, which you'll do with the menu of habit-building tools also included.

After you've answered these questions, you'll be instructed on how to score your assessment, and what that score means for you. You'll also get guidance on what habits/habit-building tools in this book will help you "level up." By the way, note that you can print a template for the Mental Strength Self-Assessment at scottmautz.com/mentallystrong/templates.

Fortitude

1. Are you resilient in the face of setbacks?

1	2	3	4	5

Never   Sometimes   Always

2. How often are you able to stay motivated despite the "daily grind"?

1	2	3	4	5

Never   Sometimes   Always

3. How often are you able to successfully, efficiently solve problems?

1	2	3	4	5

Never   Sometimes   Always

4. Do you perform well under pressure?

1	2	3	4	5

Never   Sometimes   Always

5. Do you perform well in times of crisis?

1	2	3	4	5

Never   Sometimes   Always

6. Do you model helpful behavior in times of adversity?

1	2	3	4	5

Never   Sometimes   Always

7. Do you avoid victim mentality?

1	2	3	4	5

Never　　　　Sometimes　　　　Always

8. When involved in a debate, how often do you ensure it remains healthy and productive?

1	2	3	4	5

Never　　　　Sometimes　　　　Always

9. How often do you engage in difficult conversations (discussing something uncomfortable) as opposed to avoiding them?

1	2	3	4	5

Never　　　　Sometimes　　　　Always

10. When engaged in a difficult conversation, do you handle it well (navigate it to a productive outcome)?

1	2	3	4	5

Never　　　　Sometimes　　　　Always

Confidence

11. Do you handle criticism well?

1	2	3	4	5

Never　　　　Sometimes　　　　Always

12. Do you keep self-doubt from limiting you?

1	2	3	4	5

Never   Sometimes   Always

13. Do you avoid approval-seeking behavior?

1	2	3	4	5

Never   Sometimes   Always

14. Do you avoid comparing yourself to others?

1	2	3	4	5

Never   Sometimes   Always

15. Do you avoid beating yourself up with negative inner talk?

1	2	3	4	5

Never   Sometimes   Always

16. Do you feel like you're "enough"?

1	2	3	4	5

Never   Sometimes   Always

17. Do you avoid feeling like an imposter?

1	2	3	4	5

Never   Sometimes   Always

18. **How intentional are you about being optimistic?**

1	2	3	4	5

    Never   Sometimes   Always

19. **Do you believe you can figure things out as you go (without having all the answers)?**

1	2	3	4	5

    Never   Sometimes   Always

20. **How often would others, when asked, say you have executive presence (an aura that instills confidence in others to follow you)?**

1	2	3	4	5

    Never   Sometimes   Always

Boldness

21. **How frequently do you challenge the status quo?**

1	2	3	4	5

    Never   Sometimes   Always

22. **How often do you take calculated risks, operating outside your comfort zone?**

1	2	3	4	5

    Never   Sometimes   Always

23. How often do you think big, trying to stretch the limits of what seems possible at that time?

1	2	3	4	5

Never   Sometimes   Always

24. How often do you challenge unhelpful beliefs or perceptions that you/others are stuck in?

1	2	3	4	5

Never   Sometimes   Always

25. Are you comfortable leading change?

1	2	3	4	5

Never   Sometimes   Always

26. Do you model the positive mindset needed to be successful in times of change?

1	2	3	4	5

Never   Sometimes   Always

27. When leading change, do you have a clear vision for that change?

1	2	3	4	5

Never   Sometimes   Always

Messaging

28. **Are you able to manage your negative emotions effectively in the moment they arise?**

1	2	3	4	5

Never   Sometimes   Always

29. **How often are you able to keep your temper as a leader?**

1	2	3	4	5

Never   Sometimes   Always

30. **Do you avoid saying demotivating things to others?**

1	2	3	4	5

Never   Sometimes   Always

31. **Do you avoid letting complainers drag you down into a negative mindset?**

1	2	3	4	5

Never   Sometimes   Always

32. **How often do you proactively exhibit a positive mindset?**

1	2	3	4	5

Never   Sometimes   Always

33. How often would others, when asked, say you're a good listener?

1	2	3	4	5

Never   Sometimes   Always

34. How often are you transparent with others (when it's appropriate to be transparent)?

1	2	3	4	5

Never   Sometimes   Always

35. How often do you act with integrity?

1	2	3	4	5

Never   Sometimes   Always

36. How often do you act in a manner consistent with your values?

1	2	3	4	5

Never   Sometimes   Always

Decision-Making

37. Are you confident in decisions you make?

1	2	3	4	5

Never   Sometimes   Always

38. **Are you disciplined in how you make decisions (thoughtful, structured, principled, and intentional, versus deciding "on the fly")?**

1	2	3	4	5

Never   Sometimes   Always

39. **How often do you effectively collect/analyze data to inform a decision?**

1	2	3	4	5

Never   Sometimes   Always

40. **Do you make well-reasoned, effective decisions in times of adversity?**

1	2	3	4	5

Never   Sometimes   Always

41. **How often would you (or others) say you're decisive?**

1	2	3	4	5

Never   Sometimes   Always

Goal-Focus

42. **How often would others, when asked, say the goals you set are motivating?**

1	2	3	4	5

Never   Sometimes   Always

43. Do you break your goals down into achievable pieces?

1	2	3	4	5

Never   Sometimes   Always

44. How often would others, when asked, say they're clear on what you expect from them?

1	2	3	4	5

Never   Sometimes   Always

45. How often do you focus on what you can control (versus what you can't)?

1	2	3	4	5

Never   Sometimes   Always

46. How often do you hold others accountable?

1	2	3	4	5

Never   Sometimes   Always

47. How often do you hold yourself accountable?

1	2	3	4	5

Never   Sometimes   Always

48. Do you avoid procrastinating?

1	2	3	4	5

Never   Sometimes   Always

49. Do you avoid perfectionism?

1	2	3	4	5

Never   Sometimes   Always

50. How frequently are you able to focus on the task at hand (versus getting distracted)?

1	2	3	4	5

Never   Sometimes   Always

SCORING

First, know that the value of this assessment isn't just the score you get, but in carefully considering the questions you're answering. What emotions and thoughts were sparked by what questions? What did you learn about yourself or get reminded of? What actions are you inspired to take?

Note that you'll get an overall MSS (Mental Strength Score), and a score for each of the six areas (fortitude, confidence, boldness, messaging, decision-making, and goal-focus). Follow the guidance accordingly for each score. It's all intended to help you grow mentally stronger, to increase your ability to productively self-regulate your emotions, thoughts, and behaviors for exceptional achievement (despite circumstances).

Your Overall MSS (Mental Strength Score)

Let's start by assessing your overall MSS (Mental Strength Score). Add up the total number of points you have across all fifty questions. As you experienced, each question has a maximum score of 5 points, which means your maximum total score is 250 points.

Once you have your point total, see which tier of mental strength you land in below. Remember, this is mental strength within the context of leadership. And remember that everyone has a baseline of mental strength: the opposite of mentally strong is not mentally weak. So, you won't see a Strong-to-Weakling scale like at the "strongman" carnival game (the one with the big hammer and bell).

Here are the four tiers of mental strength, and next steps based on which tier you fall into.

Beacon (225–250 points)

You're a beacon of mental strength. You exude it, are a role model for it. People are drawn to your disciplined, mentally strong leadership. You have tremendous influence on others, always seeming to send the right message at the right time, inspiring them to aim high, motivating them to power through the host of challenges they face, and encouraging the expenditure of their discretionary energy. Your confidence rubs off on others, while your decisiveness and focus keep the organization constantly moving forward.

Next steps: Maintaining mental strength requires constantly practicing the right mental habits. So, even if you're "top-tier" mentally strong, it's important to keep at the underlying work. Draw on the variety of habits/tools in this book to stay sharp on this front. And if you scored lower than you'd have liked in any of the six areas of the assessment (i.e., not scoring enough 4s or 5s), or had a low score on one question in particular, focus your efforts there first. Know that each question in the Mental Strength Self-Assessment links to a corresponding habit to build/supporting tool that you can reference in a later chapter of the book.

For example, say that while you scored in this top tier, you still didn't score as you wanted on question 44, in the Goal-Focus section of the assessment: "How often would others, when asked, say they're clear on what you expect from them?" In chapter 8, "The Goal-Focus Habit," you'll learn to build a habit of setting expectations thoroughly, and find a supporting tool called the Expectation-Setting Spectrum that will help you build a habit to improve in this area. You'll also find a quick reference summary of all the habits/supporting tools in this book in chapter 9, "The MAP (Mental Action Plan)."

You can also refer to the "Your score by area" section that follows for further guidance.

Source (200–225 points)

You're a source of mental strength to others at times, and you often draw on your mental strength as a source to help you succeed (whether or not you realize it). You haven't quite reached "beacon" level yet, as there is opportunity to be more consistent and forceful with your mental strength. You can strengthen the signal you send. You can build off of your solid sense of discipline to more frequently push people (and yourself) to even greater heights, with greater resilience, while more consistently sending a message that sparks energy and trust.

Next Steps: Identify which of the six areas of the assessment you scored lower in than you'd have liked (i.e., not scoring enough 4s or 5s), and start your strengthening efforts there. Know that each question in the Mental Strength Self-Assessment links to a corresponding habit to build/supporting tool that you can reference in a later chapter of the book.

For example, say you weren't satisfied with your scores on questions 13–15 in the Confidence section of the assessment: "13. Do you avoid approval-seeking behavior?," "14. Do you avoid comparing yourself to others?," and "15. Do you avoid beating yourself up with negative inner-talk?" In chapter 4, "The Confidence Habit," you'll find a habit to build that helps you better monitor the relationship with yourself, and a supporting, comprehensive tool called the Self-Acceptance Scale that will help you build habits to improve in all three of these areas. You'll also find a quick reference summary of all the habits/supporting tools in this book in chapter 9, "The MAP (Mental Action Plan)," all so that you can "level up" your mental strength.

Finally, refer to the "Your score by area" section that follows for further guidance by area.

Determined (175–200 points)

You have a good foundation of discipline and resolve. While you might not yet be emitting mental strength consistently to others, there are strengths to build from. You have an opportunity to be more proactive and consistent in regulating your emotions, thoughts, and behaviors. There's room to push harder to get to even more meaningful improvement, to build a greater reserve of fortitude to guide you through the corresponding challenges more frequently. You can evolve from being determined to "get there," to inspiring others to do the same.

Next Steps: Discern which area of mental strength requires the most attention, and would have the greatest positive impact on yourself and others, and start there. Remember, this is about mental strength within the context of leadership, so you want yours to be a force multiplier. And remember, you're strong when all your muscles are strong (not just your legs, for example). So, balance your mental muscle-building efforts across all the areas that need it. Know that each question in the Mental Strength Self-Assessment links to a corresponding habit to build/supporting tool that you can reference in a later chapter of the book.

For example, say you were particularly dissatisfied with your score on question 41 in the Decision-Making section of the assessment: "How often would you (or others) say you're decisive?" In chapter 7, "The Decision-Making Habit," you'll find a habit to build that helps you default to being decisive, and a supporting tool called the Cornering Indecision visual that will help you build a powerful habit to improve in this area. You'll also find a quick reference summary of all the habits/supporting tools in this book in chapter 9, "The MAP (Mental Action Plan)"—all so that you can "level up" your mental strength. So, create a plan for building all of the necessary tools into your routine. And consider applying the "weight-adding" approach detailed in the final tier description that follows.

Lastly, refer to the "Your score by area" section that follows for further guidance.

Novice (175 or below)

You have a baseline of mental strength to build from, but you have a lot of work to put in to become mentally strong— and that's okay! (You're far from alone.) Think about it this way: you're in the early stages of weight training. Meaning, to become mentally strong, you need to add more weight in two ways:

- Give the concept of mental strength more weight (more importance), and along with it, a commitment to work on it.
- Add more weight as you go to get stronger. In other words, start building your mental strength with some of the easier, "low-hanging fruit" habits to establish, then build up from there, to more and more difficult habit-building challenges (adding more "weight" as you go).

Next Steps: Develop a plan for doing exactly this. Using this questionnaire and the MAP in chapter 9 as help, make a prioritized list of the mental strength areas you need to improve, along with the habits and habit-building tools to get there. Start with the areas that will be easiest for you to improve upon so you create some momentum.

For example, say you didn't like your score on question 23 in the Boldness section of the assessment, "How often do you think big, trying to stretch the limits of what seems possible at that time?" But you know that this is something you can easily and quickly improve, because you've just been given a project at work that's going to require you to think big. Now, the good news kicks in. Each question in the Mental Strength Self-Assessment links to a corresponding habit to build/supporting tool that you can reference in a later chapter of the book. So, you turn to the corresponding habits and tools regarding thinking big (in chapter 5, "The Boldness Habit"), and you're off and running. You create a plan where you're adding on other relatively easy "wins" and incorporating the corresponding habits/tools into your routine, one at a time, steadily increasing the difficulty as you go. You'll also find a quick reference summary of all the habits/supporting tools in this book in chapter 9, "The MAP (Mental Action Plan)," all so that you can "level up" your mental strength.

Finally, refer to the "Your score by area" section that follows for further guidance.

Your Score by Area

Now let's look at your scores by specific area and what it means for you, as well as a "mini-preview" of the habits/supporting habit-building tools you'll find in later chapters that will help you level up.

Fortitude Score

There are 50 possible Fortitude points in this assessment. Anything 40 points or below marks a priority opportunity for strengthening. Realize why fortitude is so essential for achievement (especially in the face of challenges) and why it's one of the six tests of leadership (that also necessitates mental strength/self-regulation skills). Fortitude is mandatory in a work world where adversity is becoming the norm more than ever, where the things that wear us down, professionally and personally, are in ever-increasing supply. So, a less-than-optimal score here means a weakened "defense system," unimpeded exposure to the energy-draining elements of the everyday. You'll find a host of fortitude-strengthening habits and supporting habit-building tools in chapter 3, "The

Fortitude Habit," each of which lines up with the questions in the Fortitude section of this assessment (plus some additional habits/tools outside of what the assessment directly measures). These include habits/supporting tools to help you reframe setbacks, solve problems with discipline, perform under pressure and in crisis, bravely conduct difficult conversations, and more.

Confidence Score

There are 50 possible Confidence points in this assessment. Anything 40 points or below marks a priority opportunity for strengthening. Realize why confidence is so critical for achievement (especially in the face of challenges) and why it's one of the six tests of leadership (that also necessitates mental strength/self-regulation skills). Confidence is nonnegotiable in an increasingly challenging work world where reasons to doubt yourself are around every corner, where self-belief (or lack thereof) becomes a self-fulfilling prophecy, and where, more than ever, organizations look to their leaders for belief and inspiration. So, a less-than-optimal score here means a weakened sense of self, making it nearly impossible for the best version of oneself to emerge, largely obstructing mental strength development (as confidence is a "feeder trait" to the other five tests of leadership). You'll find a menu of confidence-strengthening habits and supporting habit-building tools in chapter 4, "The Confidence Habit," each of which lines up with the questions in the Confidence section of this assessment (plus some additional habits/tools outside of what the assessment directly measures). These include habits/supporting tools to help you handle criticism effectively, monitor your relationship with doubt and with yourself, practice two types of optimism, exude executive presence, and more.

Boldness Score

There are 35 possible Boldness points in this assessment. Anything 30 points or below marks a priority opportunity for strengthening. Realize why boldness is so essential for achievement (especially in the face of challenges) and why it's one of the six tests of leadership (that also necessitates mental strength/self-regulation skills). Boldness is the antithesis of status quo, the courage elixir that pushes you past ordinary achievement to extraordinary achievement. It's what makes growth happen. So, a less-than-optimal score here means you start with more of the same, you ascribe to limited versus limitless, you hold yourself back with pragmatism instead of lifting yourself up with possibility. You'll find many boldness-strengthening habits and supporting habit-building tools in chapter 5, "The Boldness Habit," each of which lines up with the questions in the Boldness section of this assessment (plus some additional habits/tools outside of what the assessment directly measures). These include habits/supporting tools to help you think big, change a group's unhelpful set of beliefs/narratives, foster a risk-taking spirit, lead change with conviction (by setting an inspiring change vision), and more.

Messaging Score

There are 45 possible Messaging points in this assessment. A score of 35 points or below marks a priority opportunity for strengthening. Realize why messaging is so vital for achievement (especially in the face of challenges) and why it's one of the six tests of leadership (that also necessitates mental strength/self-regulation skills). Messaging is the signal you send to those around you, whether positive or negative, encouraging or toxic, that inspires people and adds to the workplace culture and spirit, or detracts from all of it. So, a less-than-optimal score here means opportunities to motivate missed and unwanted/unnecessary withdrawals from the trust and energy level of your workplace. You'll find a host of messaging-strengthening habits and supporting habit-building tools in chapter 6, "The Messaging Habit," each of which lines up with the questions in the Messaging section of this assessment (plus some additional habits/tools outside of what the assessment directly measures). These include habits/supporting tools to help you navigate negative emotions in the moment, avoid losing your temper and using demotivating language, avoid stealth negativity traps and proactively exude positivity instead, be an active listener, exhibit transparency and unyielding integrity, and more.

Decision-Making Score

There are 25 possible Decision-Making points in this assessment. A score of 20 points or below marks a priority opportunity for strengthening. Realize why decision-making is so central to achievement (especially in the face of challenges) and why it's one of the six tests of leadership (that also necessitates mental strength/self-regulation skills). Decision-making is at the epicenter of the leader's job, what they do all day, every day, the quality of which discerns high-potential leaders from just leaders (or managers), and is often the difference between success or failure. So, a less-than-optimal score here means a disadvantage from the get-go, too many incorrect paths chosen, too much momentum counteracted. You'll find a breadth of decision-making strengthening habits and supporting habit-building tools in chapter 7, "The Decision-Making Habit," each of which lines up with the questions in the Decision-Making section of this assessment (plus some additional habits/tools outside of what the assessment directly measures). These include habits/supporting tools to help you avoid decision-making biases, create discipline and structure to drive better decisions, maximize decision confidence and decisiveness, and more.

Goal-Focus Score

There are 45 possible Goal-Focus points in this assessment. A score of 35 points or below marks a priority opportunity for strengthening. Realize why goal-focus is such an imperative for achievement (especially in the face of challenges) and why it's one of the six tests of leadership (that also necessitates mental strength/self-regulation skills). It's as simple as this—if you stay focused on the thing you're trying to achieve, you're far more likely to achieve it. Let your focus stray, and associated achievement wanders away as well. You get what you measure; you achieve what you focus on. So, a less-than-optimal score here means effort that drifts to anything but what matters most for getting where you want to go. You'll find a variety of goal-focus-strengthening habits and supporting habit-building tools in chapter 8, "The Goal-Focus Habit," each of which lines up with the questions in the Goal-Focus section of this assessment (plus some additional habits/tools outside of what the assessment directly measures). These include habits/supporting tools to help you set intrinsically motivating goals, set thorough expectations, avoid distractions and focus on what you can control, stop procrastination and end perfectionism, and more.

Strength in Numbers

Congratulations! You know where you stand now on your mental strength and where to put in the work. That's the strength of this self-assessment: the data-based, research-backed, guiding numbers it provides.

But also know you can draw from strength in numbers; in knowing the truth that you're not alone. We all have some elements (or many elements) of mental strength that need some "leveling up." And remember, you're not either mentally strong or mentally weak; we all have a baseline of mental strength to build from.

The good news is, you've got everything you need in the chapters ahead to build a tailored approach that's right for you in your situation. So, get to learning how to productively regulate your emotions, thoughts, and behaviors and flex that mental strength by adopting the habits and habit-building tools that lie ahead. Before long, you'll be pushing *to* something exceptional, *through* something challenging. All while *feeling* something extraordinary.

Your mentally strongest.

3 The Fortitude Habit

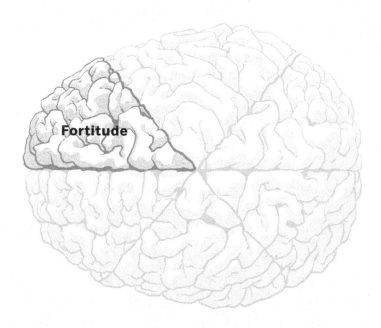

Fortitude

Is the environment you operate in becoming less and less challenging? Are you pushing through fewer and fewer setbacks? Of course not. Just the opposite. Which means the need for a mentally strong leader has never been greater. The imperative for the bellwether test of leadership that is fortitude (one of the six that most directly links to exceptional achievement), has never been in more demand. Just ask Sharon, the business leader from the chapter 1 "Story of Fortitude," who stopped selling to a huge customer, despite intense pressure, to secure long-term gains. That took resolve.

By the way, it's just really important to develop fortitude in general. Research shows fortitude/resilience positively influences work and life satisfaction and engagement because it not only makes you feel better in trying times, it's an essential resource for well-being in general.[1] Other studies show fortitude can even prevent burnout,[2] reduce depression,[3] and protect from physical illness.[4] And a study of arctic scientists showed mental toughness directly helped the scientists deal with environments of extreme physical demands.[5]

By definition, having the fortitude to push through challenges, onward to achievement, is no easy task. But the ability to do so comes from having the right mindset, skill set, and ability to reset. It requires smart self-regulation of emotions, thoughts, and behaviors that can either help or harm your sense of resolve. In this chapter, you'll get a toolbox of habits and supporting tools, many of which Sharon used, to help you reframe setbacks, increase stamina, problem-solve, deliver under pressure and in crisis, tackle tough conversations, engage in healthy debate, and more. All to build your fortitude mental muscle, prop you up, and push you through. As with every chapter, adopt the habits and supporting tools that speak most to you. It's those habits that will serve as powerful self-regulation mini-systems.

Fortitude Habit #1: Reframe Setbacks

When you're trying to press on through challenges, there are always letdowns along the way. But it's not the drops that define you; it's how you pick up. What follows is a "pick-me-up" for helping you pick up and persevere along the way, in the right way.

Habit-Building Tool #1: The Lenses of Resilience tool asks you to make a habit of reframing how you/your team think of setbacks—in four specific ways—as represented in Figure 3.1. The arrow in the center represents the resulting fortitude and way forward to success.

Fig. 3.1 The Lenses of Resilience

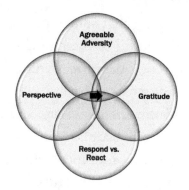

Think of this a "reframework." Let's look through each reframing lens.

The Agreeable Adversity Lens

While adversity is, by its very nature, challenging, and even painful, there's always a productive element to it—something "agreeable." This lens is about seeing adversity as an opportunity as opposed to a threat and pinpointing the good in hardship. To find the agreeable adversity, ask three questions:

1. *What possibilities does the setback present?*

It's easy to see all the difficulties as adversity unfolds and harder to see the possibilities. But the opportunities are there, if you're honest with yourself and keep an open mind. For example, when COVID-19 first struck, I had a client who feared having to close their retail store, given the lack of customers. They were having trouble finding any good in the difficult situation, until they realized they had an opportunity to sell more products online, via door-to-door delivery, and in other creative ways. They saw the chance to build stronger bonds with their surrounding community and forge a stronger brand. They persevered through hardship by seeing possibility in initial adversity.

It's also worth noting that sometimes adversity closes off options for you. It's painful in the moment, but then something amazing happens. As you're wading through the fog of "What now?" your senses sharpen in search of alternative opportunities. Suddenly, the fog clears, and a new opportunity, previously obscured because your attention was elsewhere, emerges and comes into focus. Real possibilities arise from being forced to look for alternatives.

2. *What can we learn from this setback?*

The tension that adversity brings forces you to experience things you haven't before, to rise to challenges, to test, and to learn something about yourself. In other words, it leads to self-discovery and growth. As an example, I'll share my own experience when COVID-19 first struck. At that time, my keynoting business took a big downturn, with live events getting put on hold or canceled. Fortunately, I saw a chance to grow my portfolio of offerings by building a home studio that

I could use to broadcast keynotes to a remote audience or to prerecord keynotes/trainings. I learned so much about technology applications along the way, and I'm better for it. I discovered that I really like creating content in front of a camera for people to consume at their own pace, and I learned a lot about my ability to adapt.

3. *Would a pivot be a better way forward?*

This one is related to the first question, but is worthy of its own discussion. People who are resilient pivot to whatever new approach/direction is needed, if adversity dictates it. They turn quickly and decisively, but not carelessly, toward what needs to happen next, without getting hung up on the past or clinging to the way things have always been done. I do plenty of things wrong in life, but I can count as a strength my ability to adapt and pivot to a new direction when something isn't working or doesn't go as expected. The key is to recognize that everything in life is a work in progress, and sometimes the path to success is not the one you started down. It takes a willingness to change and the discipline to stop plowing forward just because you've already put effort into something. Your past efforts are in the past, but they're not wasted. They *had* to happen to lead you toward what's next.

The Gratitude Lens

In the face of setbacks, you're instinctively drawn to what you've *lost*—like your forward momentum, your sense of comfort, your confidence, time, or resources, for example. Resist this natural temptation and instead focus on what you *still have* that's good. In fact, apply the Distance Principle, which says:

- Take the distance of how far you've come on something, and subtract how far back a misstep brought you.
- Note, however, that it's called a misstep, not a *misleap*, for a reason. So, don't get overly emotional and catastrophize the situation—you likely didn't go as far backward as you think.
- That remaining distance, that progress still made, is something to be proud of.

As an example, one client of mine was making great progress on development of an innovative new product. Suddenly, they hit what felt like a huge roadblock: the first consumer test of the product was not favorable. The team felt deflated. So the team leader got everyone together to introduce the Distance Principle, to objectively discuss how big of a setback the misstep really was, and to celebrate how far they'd come to date. He then had the principle printed on plaques and asked everyone to keep it at their desks to read at the start of their day. It was a reminder of progress made, despite adversity. Morale rebounded, they overcame issues uncovered in the consumer test, and the project moved forward. That's the power of the Distance Principle.

The Respond versus React Lens

Setbacks are triggers. They're an interruption you weren't expecting or were hoping to avoid, a wrinkle in your plan, which provokes something in you. The question is, what will it provoke? Will you *respond* or *react* to the setback? The two choices produce very different outcomes.

Reacting to adversity means attention goes to emoting; emotionally carrying yourself in a (most often) unhelpful manner. You put your energy into being exasperated, lamenting that you're exhausted, getting stuck in "it's not fair," feeling like a failure, or catastrophizing (exaggerating the negative impact of the setback).

Responding to adversity means focusing on taking action. It's minimizing your emotional reaction (we're not robots, after all), accepting where you are, knowing the pain is temporary, and putting your energy into "What should I do next? How can I move forward?" It means saying "not yet" instead of "I failed," and getting back to work on what it will take to get there.

For example, your plan was to impress your new boss right from the get-go, launching you into a good relationship. But your first big meeting did not go well. So, you ask yourself, "Will I spend my energy reacting or responding?" You can catastrophize how bad the meeting was and how hard it will be to recover, or you can get into action mode, meeting with your boss to learn from your mistakes and show your interest in improving.

Responding instead of reacting is a lens of self-awareness. The idea is to trigger action, not emotion.

The Perspective Lens

Resilience is strengthened by broadening your perspective on the setback you're facing, which you do through *relationships* and *remembering*.

Babson College research shows drawing on *relationships* and networks is essential to bolstering resilience. This is as opposed to conventional wisdom, which says resilience is all about internal fortitude, an inner grit you draw upon when needed. The key is to be self-aware of what your resilience-building needs tend to be and to cultivate a network you can lean on for help.[6]

For example, as the Babson researchers point out, maybe in the face of setbacks you need an empathetic ear to unload your emotions on (so you can get to responding instead of reacting more quickly). Maybe you need validation, encouragement, or a confidence boost. Maybe you need help finding a path forward. Or maybe you just need a good laugh. Understand what your resilience needs are and know who you'll turn to for that kind of help.[7]

Remembering past experiences with adversity also provides helpful perspective. Odds are, you ultimately survived the misfortune and gained something valuable from the experience that you can apply to your current situation. In fact, I'll bet some of your greatest accomplishments required learning and reapplying from prior adversity. As you consider past setbacks, it helps to think about assumptions you made that proved to be wrong (to avoid this time around), or behaviors you engaged in that either helped you through or held you back.

For example, a major publication I once wrote for had to reduce staff and laid me off. When, years later, I faced the threat of another similar opportunity evaporating, I thought back to my prior experience. I recalled the incorrect assumptions I was making at the time, like "Well, that's that, I'll never get another opportunity like this," which wasn't true. Seeing that I was wrong back then made me question my assumptions this time around and helped me persevere through the situation. Similarly, I remembered being stuck in "It's not fair" mode, feeling sorry for myself—until I got on with it and found other places I could create and share content. Thus, I was sure to skip "It's not fair" that second time around.

Your First Small Step: Because adversity can quickly pull you down into a distracting, prolonged cloud of negativity, your first step is a promise. A promise to yourself, that the very next time you encounter a setback, you won't default to a downward spiral; you'll instead look through the Lenses of Resilience.

In Moments of Weakness: Staying resilient is hard work. But remember that life shrinks or expands in proportion to your courage and perseverance. No doubt, there will be low points along the way where you'll struggle to keep pushing, where you'll feel like a failure. It happens to everyone. But know that mentally strong leaders, the leaders who separate themselves from others, don't succeed because they never fail. They succeed because they *do* fail and have the will to keep it in perspective and use it as a propellant. They succeed because they keep missteps from feeling like mis-leaps. You can too; just keep referring back to the Lenses of Resilience.

Fortitude Habit #2: Mind the Grind

Gratitude again comes into play in this habit and supporting tool, but in a different way. We'll apply it to a special fortitude problem—dealing with the grind of working through adversity, which can wear you down. Resilience erodes as the routine wears on and stressors and challenges keep piling on. It requires a reset, a step back to mindfully appreciate all that's good in the daily grind while you're toiling through the rest.

Habit-Building Tool #2: I call this practice grindfulness—a combination of gratitude and mindfulness.

Fig. 3.2 Grindfulness

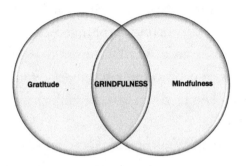

More specifically, it's:

Being present in daily life, noticing details in the grind of it all, and expressing appreciation and joy for those details in the moment.

It's a powerful habit for creating fortitude and resilience in the face of challenges, and for daily life in general. For example, say you were laid off from your job, so you immediately began pounding the pavement every day, interviewing, trying to find that next role. But it has been going on for a while now, and it's really starting to wear you down, affecting your mood and disposition, magnified by the "no" after "no" you're getting. In the midst of it all, you recognize that you've come to love and appreciate the quiet, reflective morning breakfasts you're able to have each day. That little spark tunes you in to more small things to appreciate about your current situation, helping your disposition. That's grindfulness.

Another example. Say you're heading home after a stressful day at work and stop to get groceries, a weekly chore you're really not in the mood for. But on the way along your regular route, this time, you notice how the leaves soothingly shimmer on the trees along the road, sparkling in the fading sunlight—so you mentally pause to marvel at it. It helps your outlook. That's grindfulness.

It's being mindful to notice and appreciate positive aspects of the details of whatever grind you find yourself in. It's not about passively journaling those moments (a typical mindfulness practice), it's about actively living those moments and building a daily habit of doing so. It helps you build resilience, because it fosters the ability to appreciate more, even when things aren't going so well.

And it's the combination of gratitude and mindfulness that makes it so powerful. Sometimes, we struggle to express gratitude, especially as adversity wears on. We might be too restrictive of what deserves our gratitude, or our sense of gratefulness gets overpowered by all the irritations and disappointments we encounter. Likewise, mindfulness (calmly focusing your awareness in the present moment) isn't enough on its own either; you have to act on your observations or actively shift your perception in some way that improves your outlook.

Enter grindfulness, which lowers the bar on what to be grateful for and mindful of, and raises the frequency of expressing appreciation and joy in those "moments of grind," all to improve your temperament.

Your First Small Step: This habit starts with appreciating the toll that the grind of adversity (and daily life) can take on you; how it can directly deteriorate your fortitude. Accordingly, the next time you start feeling that grind getting to you, it should alert you to kick into your grindfulness practice.

In Moments of Weakness: It's hard to keep up expression of gratitude when adversity keeps you down. But you have a crystal-clear cue for when to call on your grindfulness habit—anytime you start feeling worn down. If you miss an opportunity to express it, getting caught in a downturn instead, commit to find just one small detail in your daily grind to be thankful for. Then build on it, looking for other things to appreciate as your plow forward, until you've reignited this hat-tip habit.

Fortitude Habit #3: Solve Problems with Discipline

One of the most fundamental things you can do to push through challenges is to be really good at solving problems along the way. To do so requires discipline of your thoughts, actions, emotions, and more, all of which you can productively regulate, for yourself and your team, by adopting what follows.

Habit-Building Tool #3: The Problem-Solving Eye, shown in Figure 3.3, is a robust framework for solving problems efficiently and effectively. Most tools in this book aren't as sequential and "involved" as this one, but it's worth the time investment, given how central problem-solving is to building fortitude, and thus, mental strength.

Fig. 3.3 The Problem - Solving Eye

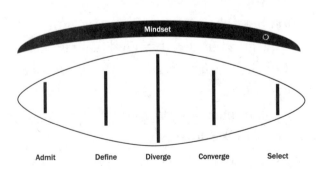

Mindset

Admit   Define   Diverge   Converge   Select

The framework is represented by the visual of an eye, with the overarching "eyebrow" encompassing the mindset required to be a great problem-solver, and the shape of the eye representing each of the steps along the way (which go from narrow in scope, to broad, then back to narrow). Let's go through the Eye, one element at a time.

Being a great problem-solver starts with a specific mindset.

Mindset

1. *Believe you can solve the problem.*
Never give in to a defeatist attitude, even when the solution is proving elusive. And don't just focus on the pressure you're under or the consequences of not solving the problem; focus on how rewarding it will feel when you have the solution— even if you have to compromise. When you experience setbacks, instead of saying, "We failed," say, "Not yet." In other words, just because you didn't solve the problem yet, doesn't mean you'll never solve it. Consider inventor James Dyson, who developed 5,127 prototypes before successfully creating the first bagless vacuum cleaner.[8] Undoubtedly, he had a fierce conviction that he could, indeed, solve the problem.

By the way, it also helps to recall problems you solved in the past, to further drive conviction that you will once again.

2. *Be ready to put in the work.*
How will you know when you/your team are ready to put in the work it will take to solve a problem? When you can answer "Yes" to the following questions:
- "Do I accept that I don't/won't know everything I'd like to know to solve this problem?"

- "Do I believe in my ability to figure things out along the way?"
- "Do I understand that I don't have to go it alone?"
- "Will I resist the temptation to accept easy answers, or to label opinions or biases as facts?"
- "Will I resist surface-level understanding, or applying quick-fix 'Band-Aid' solutions?"

Answer in the affirmative to all of the above, and you're ready to dig in, to do the hard work it takes to solve a problem at a deeper level. Said another way—solutions that work come when you're ready to work.

3. Be flexible.

When you approach problem-solving with a flexible mindset, it helps you adapt to the challenge at hand. Three types of flexibility are needed:

- *intellectual flexibility*—This means keeping an open mind, resisting typical thinking to consider creative solutions, being willing to challenge assumptions, and knowing when you need to dig deeper and learn more to be able to solve the problem.
- *emotional flexibility*—Meaning, not getting too emotionally attached to one potential solution, or overly emotional about the problem itself (in a way that negatively influences the solution, such as rushing to implement a fix or "overcorrecting" for the problem).
- *dispositional flexibility*—This means being inclined (having the disposition) to enjoy the process of problem-solving, being willing to improvise and experiment as needed, and being receptive to change that might be required to solve the problem.

4. *Attack the problem, not the person.*

You solve nothing, ever, when you blame and finger-point. Great problem-solvers address the problem rather than expose the person behind the problem. There'll always be time later to productively learn from who did or didn't do what. So, set the tone by getting into solution mode and bypassing slamming mode.

For example, say a salesperson on your team lost a key customer by not being responsive enough. First priority is to focus on winning that customer back. Later, you can diagnose what the salesperson did wrong and what can be learned from it.

With the proper overarching mindset in place, now look to the left corner of the Problem-Solving Eye, where you *admit* that you have a problem.

Admit

The first step to solving a problem is admitting you have one. Sounds simple, right? But one client of mine conducted a study that showed in their organization, for every ten problems the organization addressed, seven of them were initially ignored or rejected as an issue. In other words, 70 percent of the time, employees weren't admitting there was a problem, or at least not doing so fast enough. I don't know the exact situation in your organization, but I bet the percentage isn't too far off.

We can do better as leaders, and we must. All too often, I've personally witnessed the damaging impact of not admitting or ignoring issues, hoping they'll go away. For example, more than once, I've seen a leader deploy an organizational culture survey, get the responses, then explain away the bad results afterward (or worse yet, never share the results), rather than openly admitting issues exist and working to address them. Toxic.

That said, it's easy to fall into the Static Trap. It starts when we deny that a problem exists (*being static*, doing nothing about it), until it can no longer be ignored. Then, we *create static*, or distortion, around the problem—by making excuses about why the problem exists, downplaying its impact, or redirecting attention by finger-pointing. At the same time, while we've admitted the problem exists, we still haven't put our energy toward doing something about it; we *remain static* instead of taking action.

Avoid this trap by cutting it off at the start, by recognizing the signs of problem-denial and moving quickly into admission and action mode, instead. The signs to watch out for include:

- Refusing to talk, or even think, about the problem, or continually putting it off
- Minimizing the negative impact that's occurring to make it seem like less of a problem, like when you tell yourself you don't need to fire that abrasive employee you personally like, because they aren't really causing *that* much of an issue with the team
- Justifying *why* the problem is happening to make it seem like less of a problem
- Blaming and finger-pointing (denying any ownership of the problem)

Moving to the right in the Problem-Solving Eye, you properly *define* the problem.

Define

Albert Einstein said, "If I had an hour to solve a problem, I'd spend 55 minutes thinking about the problem, five minutes thinking about solutions."[9] Steve Jobs said, "If you define the problem correctly, you almost have the solution."[10] It's about habitually being disciplined enough to identify the *real* problem, so you're solving for the right thing, rather than rushing into solution mode. Not easy to do, as a study of over one hundred c-suite executives showed that 85 percent of them agreed their organization was poor at problem diagnosis, with 87 percent saying this flaw carried significant costs.[11]

To properly diagnose a problem, identify the problem's root cause, using the Five Whys analytical approach invented by Sakichi Toyoda and first used in the Toyota automobile production system.[12] The idea is to ask, five times in a row, why a problem occurred. The root cause of the problem will typically emerge by the fifth "why."

For example, say you're trying to solve the problem of an ineffective online marketing campaign. To get to the root cause of the problem, you ask "Why," repeatedly, like so:

- Why is the campaign ineffective? Because we're spending too much to get too little in return.
- Why is that? Because very few people are engaging with the ad.
- Why is that? Because the ads aren't persuasive or even relevant to the target audience.
- Why is that? Because we didn't understand the target audience's needs clearly enough.
- And why is that? Because we don't prioritize deep understanding of the consumer/customer.

And there's your root cause of the problem.

Pro tip: You can combine the Five-Whys analysis with the Pareto Principle, which, when applied to problem-solving, says that 80 percent of problems come from 20 percent of the causes of problems.[13] Meaning, start getting to the root cause of a problem by first considering the typical causes of your problems.

Because defining the problem is so important, here's another creative option altogether—Problem Reframing (popularized by author Thomas Wedell-Wedellsborg).[14] It's about finding a better problem to solve rather than identifying the root cause. For example, say you own a building, and the tenants are complaining about a slow elevator. Through root cause analysis, you determine you can (a) replace the elevator, (b) upgrade the motor, or (c) improve the algorithm that runs the elevator. Instead, your friend Lee, seeing a different problem, cleverly suggests that you add music to the elevator, install a hand-sanitizer dispenser, and add mirrors (so people can pass time by looking at themselves). Bingo, she just reframed the problem from "the elevator is too slow" to "the wait is annoying," and then solved *that* problem (by making it less annoying) in a much cheaper way. Notice, the original solutions could have worked too (replacing the elevator, etc.). But through a different understanding of the problem, you uncover better, easier solutions.

To engage in problem reframing, use these questions/ statements:

- Ask, "What's a different, better problem to solve that still accomplishes our end goal?"
- Start the problem-reframing session by using this fill-in-the-blank statement: "The problem is not that _____, it's that _____."

- Ask, "What category of problem are we facing?" (Is it a people problem? Incentive problem? Software problem? Lack-of-training problem?)
- Ask, "What was different at a time when this problem didn't exist?"

Note that bringing in outsiders (people not as close to the issue) to provide input on any of these questions can help.

With the problem clearly defined, you move now to the center of the Eye, its widest point (where scope and focus are the broadest), and you *diverge*.

Diverge

You diverge by brainstorming a host of possible solutions to the problem. I won't focus on any one brainstorming method over the other, because there are countless techniques. Choose the method you like best, but employ it with the three most important general principles for brainstorming and diverging kept in mind.

1. *Stop self-monitoring.*

It's critical when brainstorming and diverging to turn off your self-monitoring brain. Doing so maximizes creativity, as a study from the National Institutes of Health showed. In the study, freestyle rap artists were asked to perform both well-rehearsed and improvised numbers, while their brain activity was measured. While creatively improvising/riffing, the part of the artists' brain known to be the judging, self-monitoring part was virtually shut down.[15] In other words, for many daily activities, it's important to self-monitor, so you don't just blurt out everything you think. But when it comes to maximizing creativity, it's essential to let the ideas flow and not let the judging part of your inner dialogue get in the way. To help with this, here's a simple trick. If you catch yourself judging ideas while brainstorming, quickly say to yourself, "Flow, not no." It creates awareness of the self-monitoring autopilot that can switch on inside all of us, instead encouraging you to let the ideas flow.

2. *Optimize your open-mindedness.*

This is related to the above point but worthy of its own consideration. While you want everyone at a brainstorming session locked in and ready to fully participate, you don't want them locked in, or fixated, on one particular idea or area of ideas. It's critical to remain open-minded to invite in all the possibilities that could surface.

An interesting experiment from the University of Hertfordshire illustrates this point.[16] In the study, people were asked to count the number of pictures in a newspaper. Most completed the task within minutes and dutifully reported there were forty-three photos (which was correct). However, they were all so locked in on the task in front of them that no one noticed two key prompts. One was in large type on the second page that read, "Stop counting—there are 43 photographs in this newspaper." The other, even better, prompt read, "Stop counting, tell the experimenter you've seen this and win $250." Both instructions went unnoticed until after the researchers asked respondents to go back through the newspaper to see if they spotted anything unusual. The study showed that when we get tunnel vision and become too locked in on our objective, we can miss opportunities right in front of us.

3. *Honor everyone's input.*

Just as you want to resist judging your own ideas too quickly when brainstorming, resist criticizing others' ideas too, or at least resist offering criticism without respectfully, constructively building on their idea to improve it. For example, the animation company Pixar has a rule of "plussing it up." Meaning, criticism must always contain a new idea or suggestion for strengthening the original idea—it must contain a "plus."[17] This ensures a positive tone, maintains respect, and strengthens ideas.

Further honor everyone's brainstorming input by having a good method for capturing every idea, so people feel heard. If they don't, nothing shuts down ideation faster.

Moving further to the right in the Eye, it gets narrower because it's time to *converge*.

Converge

What's worse than having no choice in a matter?

Having too much choice.

That's why you now converge and narrow the number of solution options. To do so, invoke a classic creative problem-solving technique, which, at its core, requires balancing convergent and divergent thinking. A few key principles to keep in mind in this phase.

1. *Have criteria in cement.*

In advance of ideating potential solutions, have a firm set of evaluation criteria in place, so you can determine which ideas make the cut for final consideration. For example, you can evaluate a list of brainstormed ideas based on feasibility of execution, how fast the idea can be implemented, originality/innovativeness, most upside, scalability, profitability, or best fit with organizational goals. You might even have a more emotional evaluation criteria, such as "exciting enough to motivate us through the challenges it will present."

2. *Identify the evaluators.*

Who gets to vote on the ideas? Some groups use "power-dotting," where everyone gets to vote, which they do by placing a circular sticker next to their favorite ideas on a list of ideas. Ideas with the most votes win. Other groups gather all the ideas and have a smaller group (often consisting of key leaders) decide on which ideas will move forward. And there are plenty of iterations in between. The point is, know who gets the deciding vote(s). This prevents a chaotic end to a brainstorming session, where whoever is loudest or most passionate ends up dictating what ideas/solutions win. That just leaves participants feeling frustrated and played.

3. *Compare, contrast, combine.*

It's also helpful to compare and contrast the ideas on your list, looking for ways to combine or group them thematically for simplification. For example, say you notice several ideas center on a similar theme: improving the appeal of your company's core product line. It becomes a major theme you converge on. You might even choose to prototype the idea "finalists" to further narrow options down. Of course, at this point, you can/should discard entire groups of ideas (or single ideas) that simply aren't attractive enough.

Let's converge one step further, moving to the far right side of the Eye, where you *select* the best solution or take the best course of action.

Select

It's important here not to overthink it, constantly revisiting your options. It's easy to fall into this trap, because when you keep rehashing options over and over, it *feels* like you're problem-solving, doing something useful. But you're not—you're just spinning. Overthinking and problem-solving are not the same thing.

It's also important at this final stage of the framework to remember the Law of Commitment, which has two parts.

1. *Debate. Decide. Commit.*

Once you've debated and then selected a solution, everyone on the team should commit to its execution as if it were their own idea. This isn't as easy as it sounds. Here's an example I've seen happen about a hundred times. You're in a meeting where a solution to a problem is chosen, but not everyone agrees or speaks up. Afterward, some of those meeting participants engage in a "meeting after the meeting," where people share their true feelings about the solution chosen, and start fueling doubts about the call made. That leads to half-hearted execution of the solution, and ultimately, there's a good chance the solution chosen won't work. Not helpful.

So, it's critical to encourage open debate, from all the stakeholders, then make the call, and ask everyone to commit to the decision, with no second-guessing.

2. *Create commitment, not compliance.*

The idea here is to create and maintain momentum for the chosen solution, in a way that *encourages the expenditure of discretionary energy* to execute it well. You do this by ensuring stakeholders feel three specific things regarding a solution:

- Safe
- Involved
- Accountable

For instance, say you've decided to solve your organization's poor performance issue by instituting mandatory training. You could just announce it and then expect people to comply ("or suffer the consequences"). Or you could have a plan to create *commitment* to the solution, ensuring stakeholders feel safe, involved, and accountable, as follows:

You'll make them feel safe with the solution by continually touting the benefits they'll get from the training, the skills they'll build, and by continually reinforcing why this solution is the best one (and won't bring them harm). Ask yourself, "What will make people feel safe about this solution?"

You'll make stakeholders feel involved by enrolling them in the design of the training, getting their feedback, and acting on it. Ask yourself, "How can I get people maximally involved in implementing this solution?"

You'll make them feel accountable by putting clear measurements in place so everyone will know if the solution (mandatory training) is working or not. Ask yourself, "How can I ensure people feel accountable to deliver the solution successfully?"

Your First Small Step: Download and print out the Problem-Solving Eye diagram at scottmautz.com/mentallystrong/templates, familiarize your team with its use, and pick a problem to solve to try it on. Excellence in solving problems requires an intentional method for doing so, so committing to use of the Eye is a great first step.

In Moments of Weakness: Teams most often falter in problem-solving either by not being disciplined enough about defining the problem (rushing into solution mode instead), or by not generating enough creative solutions that are substantively better than status quo rather than incrementally better. Be aware of these two common stumbling blocks, and if you trip over one, acknowledge your error, fix it, and keep pressing forward.

Fortitude Habit #4: Perform under Pressure

Ever disarm a ticking bomb underwater? Unless you're an action movie star, probably not.

Or unless you're a US Navy bomb disposal expert, whose peformance under presure is clearly essential to their job. (Talk about the need to productively self-regulate emotions, thoughts, and behaviors!) They, along with US Navy SEALs (another group used to performing in high-stakes situations), inspired the tool that follows.

Habit-Building Tool #4: There's a saying: "pressure makes diamonds." Accordingly, remember the Diamond Directive, four points to follow so you shine (like a diamond) in high-pressure situations. See Figure 3.4.

Fig. 3.4 The Diamond Directive

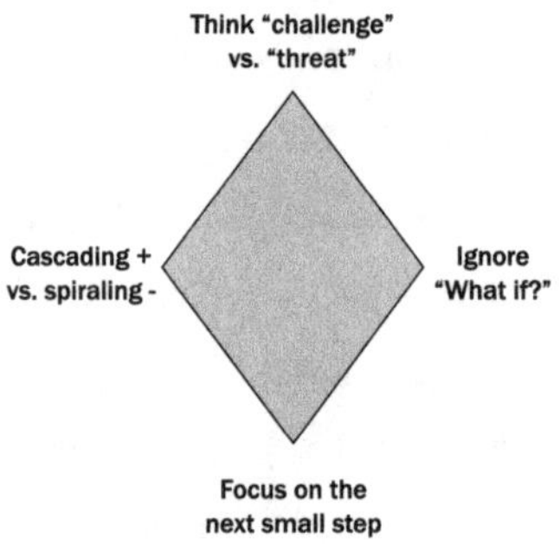

To form a habit of performing under pressure, take each point of the diamond, one at a time.

Think "challenge" versus "threat."

So much of your ability to thrive under pressure is based on your mindset and your initial response to the stress that's triggered. If you see something as a *threat*, your body responds in unhelpful ways, like a fast-beating heart, sweaty palms, a sick feeling in your stomach, and difficulty focusing. You're imagining everything that could go wrong. And feeling anxious makes you more anxious. It undermines your ability to perform.

But if you tell yourself, "I'm prepared for this *challenge*," you'll handle the stress better; your focus increases dramatically and your thoughts and emotions are more controlled. It enhances your ability to perform. It also helps to regulate your breathing in high-pressure situations. Take a few deep breaths, slowly inhale, and exhale through your nose while saying to yourself, "I've got this." It triggers a relaxation response and settles the mind to help it focus. This is why some martial arts instructors have their students train with a mouthful of water.

Ignore "What if?"

Repeatedly asking "What if?" when you're under pressure focuses you on all the things that could go wrong; it's an unhelpful rabbit hole to go down. I once heard famous race car driver Mario Andretti say, "The key to racing is to look ahead, not at the wall, because you steer where your eyes take you." In other words, concentrate on potential negatives of the situation around you, and you'll steer right into them. A self-fulfilling prophecy.

Anytime you feel a "What if" coming on, replace it with a "What will," as in, "What will now happen, is that I'm going to . . ." For example, say you're about to give a big presentation and you catch yourself thinking, "*What if* I freeze up during my talk?" You instantly recognize that's not productive, and switch to saying, "*What will* happen is that I'll relax and let all the rehearsal I've been doing kick in." It's about focusing on what needs to be done, not what might happen.

Focus on the next small step.

When the pressure's on, it's calming to just focus on the next small step in front of you instead of stressing over all the things that must (or could) happen. It's about focusing on the process, not the outcome. For example, when I give a keynote to an especially large audience, even as a seasoned pro, I still might feel a few butterflies beforehand. So, I focus on delivering the opening line of my keynote. Then the opening story. Then the first major insight, and so on, one step at a time.

After a few small steps, I've reached a state of flow, and any nervousness has vanished. Break that high-pressure situation into small steps and take them one at a time.

Cascading positivity versus spiraling negativity.

This one's related to the above, but merits its own discussion. One bomb disposal expert told of trying to defuse a mine while underwater. At one point, he realized he'd become trapped, unable to move his hands or feet.[18] Rather than let panic take over, he thought, "I'm still breathing, so that's good. Now what else do I have going for me?" Then he realized he could at least wiggle his fingers enough to untangle the line trapping him. Then he turned his focus to that next positive thing that would make his situation slightly better, and kept building from there. His point was to "have cascading positivity as opposed to spiraling negativity." He started with the good (while being realistic about the facts), which calmed him, helping him to focus on what else was good, what he could control, and what to do next. You can too.

Your First Small Step: Re-create the simple (but powerful) Diamond Directive visual. Anticipate the next time you'll be in a high-stakes situation. Imagine what could go wrong in that situation and being in that moment when it does. Then practice going through each point of the Diamond Directive in that imagined scenario. When the situation actually arrives, keep the visual handy to help you stay steady. Before long, performing under pressure will become a habit.

In Moments of Weakness: A moment of weakness here would be finding yourself panicking in the middle of a high-pressure situation. More than likely, your thoughts will be racing, and not many will be good. Stop, pause, and ask yourself,

"Are my thoughts helping me right now?" The idea is to break the distracting spiral of negativity and calm yourself long enough to come back to the Diamond Directive for help.

Fortitude Habit #5: Shine, Don't Shrink, in Crisis

Leaders do one of two things in crisis: shine or shrink. They shrink when they're paralyzed by uncertainty and don't act quickly enough (or at all). They shrink when they blame, point fingers, and dodge accountability, or when they overreact and lose their cool. In other words, leaders shrink in crisis when they don't serve the organization in the way the organization needs them to at a critical time.

But mentally strong leaders, with self-regulation-enhanced fortitude skills, shine in crisis. They know how to act, what to do, how to be. And they know that in times of crisis, true character arises. So, they use adversity as the chance to show their character, knowing that people always remember how you acted in such times (whether good or bad).

For example, ever had a boss or coworker who turned nasty when things got challenging, by blaming, pointing fingers, or dodging accountability? If so, I'm betting you haven't forgotten it. It's also likely that you remember times when leaders stepped up and brought out their best in adversity. The point is, there may be no more lasting, career-impacting impression you'll make than how you show up in times of crisis. So, make a habit of doing it well. Here's how.

Habit-Building Tool #5: When crisis strikes, follow the CALM Credo, a highly effective approach for shining in times of crisis. The credo asks you to first remember that in times of crisis, emotions run high—so don't throw gas on the fire by overreacting. Be the calmest person in the room at all times. Don't get overly emotional. Don't jump to conclusions or make uninformed assumptions. Always speak in a controlled tone and act with a steady, measured confidence. Know that people will take their cues on how to behave from you. Remember that staying calm keeps everyone focused on what must be done rather than on what might happen.

In addition to projecting calm, remember the acronym CALM, four things to exhibit in times of crisis that will help everyone involved push through it. Let's go through each letter.

Candor. Adversity creates doubt and fear. Honest communication creates certainty and eases fear, if done well. The key is to share information frequently, clearly, and truthfully. When you're certain about something, say so. When you're almost certain, say that. And when you're not sure about something, you're in the process of understanding it better (which will be often); say that. When acknowledging your uncertainty, acknowledge your audience's distress, with compassion, by saying something like: "How I wish I could give you a definite answer right now."

It's also important in crisis to communicate both reality and hope. Employees need the truth, but they also need to feel optimistic. For example, I've seen leaders focus solely on communicating the reality of a critical situation, thoroughly demotivating the audience in the process. And I've seen leaders sugarcoat reality and provide nothing but sunshine and hope, leaving the audience skeptical and confused. It's important to get the balance right.

Anchoring. In times of adversity, people need a steadying force, an anchor, to provide some sense of certainty, when so much else seems uncertain. Provide that by:

- highlighting what *isn't* changing (that people wouldn't want to change, like the company culture, for example)
- reminding them of resources they have at their disposal to help them weather the storm
- being visible and available to employees (and the chain of command) as you navigate the crisis
- sharing how you'll communicate with employees, how frequently, in what form (email, town hall, etc.)
- being clear on expectations, roles, and responsibilities resulting from the crisis, and what must be done next

This is about emphasizing what employees can count on during crisis and what they'll be counted on for.

Lighthousing. Serve as a lighthouse for your organization by giving them something to steer toward during the crisis—a guiding beacon. Provide, and repeatedly reinforce, a motivating, common goal everyone can rally around.

For example, Admiral Thad Allen of the US Coast Guard is one of the world's most practiced leaders in crisis response. He's managed responses to terrorist attacks, natural disasters, and devastating oil spills. The primary lesson Allen learned across all these experiences was the need to clearly define and frame the problem in a way that gets everyone on the same page and *unified in their efforts* to successfully navigate through the crisis. After Hurricane Katrina hit New Orleans in August 2005, Allen quickly saw it was no ordinary hurricane in terms of its impact, and so compared it to a weapon of mass destruction. This clearly defined and framed the scale of the problem, rallying and inspiring volunteers to give their best relief efforts. He unified everyone with a compelling, common goal: "Treat any storm victims you come across like they're your own family."[19] You can provide that kind of common, motivating goal in crisis too.

> Monitoring. I don't just mean monitor progress being made in getting through the crisis. I mean monitor *how people are feeling* along the way—check in on them periodically. (They won't forget that you did.) Ensure they're feeling supported, show caring and understanding, and remind them that they're not alone. Celebrate small victories along the way to further help keep energy and conviction up. In crisis, monitoring attitude and energy is essential if you ultimately want to work your way out of that crisis. You want to fuel belief that everyone is in it together, and that the crisis is not insurmountable; that they can, indeed, navigate their way through.

Your First Small Step: Start thinking of crises as an opportunity to showcase your mentally strong leadership. Recognize when you're next in crisis mode, and conduct a CALM Credo check as soon as possible. Ensure you're prepared to act in accordance with the credo to maximize your leadership effectiveness. (Write down the CALM acronym if it helps.)

In Moments of Weakness: It's easy to show up the wrong way in times of crisis, as pressure is intense, there's no time for delay, and everyone's watching. If you do make a mistake, acknowledge it quickly (authenticity is especially important in crisis), forgive yourself just as quickly, and revisit the CALM Credo to get back on track.

Fortitude Habit #6: Preplan Reaction to Adversity

When adversity strikes, great organizations, and their leaders, rise to the occasion. But it can also strike fast and throw people off their game, igniting unhelpful thoughts, feelings, and behaviors. For example, a manufacturing plant suffers a serious safety incident, and soon thereafter, as an act of self-preservation, finger-pointing and blaming begins. Or a team misses a critical deadline, causing the leader, under tremendous pressure, to lash out at the team, publicly and unprofessionally. Or an industry regulation unexpectedly changes, causing panic and total distraction on your team.

But what if you had a plan for regulating how you and your team will handle adversity when it arises? Think of how it would lessen the likelihood of unwanted "knee-jerk reaction" behavior, and how it would help the team more quickly and efficiently adapt to the adversity. The next tool is that plan.

Habit-Building Tool #6: Whenever I started a new leadership role, I would share an Adversity Manifesto. It's a simple, one-page document you give to your organization *before adversity strikes*. It outlines what you expect from the team when adversity arises, and what they can expect from you. Think of it as a code of conduct for when storms hit, or as a fortitude "cheat code." Here's an example of one such manifesto I used for many years, to great effect (as I shared in *Make It Matter*).[20]

> ### Adversity Manifesto
>
> - Be the eye of the storm. A calm, cool, collected leader is a beacon. Never forget how many take cues from you.
> - Realize that adversity reveals true character. Use it as a chance to show yours. It's one of the most lasting impressions you'll make.
> - Drive out fear. Job number one is to steer the ship back on course. There will be time later to constructively learn from who did/didn't do what. And remember, we really are all in this together. Our mortal enemy is ignorance of the fact that the enemy is external.
> - Assemble a small, nimble coalition of experts for problem-solving and quick action. Roll up your sleeves and flow to the work. Overcommunicate.
> - Pull on that chain of command to help. Chains exist to provide added strength in times of need. That's why it's not called a "thread of command."
> - Remember, this too shall pass. It always does.

Sharing this manifesto announced several things to the organization:

- There will most certainly be adversity in the future—expect it. It's life in the working world.
- This is how to act when the going gets tough. Expect me to model it. Hold me to it.
- I expect the same behaviors from you.

Your First Small Step: Think through what's needed from your organization when adversity hits. Think of past experiences with adversity and behaviors and actions that were helpful, and harmful. Start writing your own version of

an Adversity Manifesto by listing the three most important behaviors you expect to see, and that you'll commit to
role-modeling.

In Moments of Weakness: If you make a mistake that
violates what you committed to in the Adversity Manifesto,
openly acknowledge it with your team (referring back to
the manifesto), and hold yourself accountable to course-
correct. It's important to show vulnerability and to recom-
mit to the "code of conduct" you've asked everyone to
follow. By the way, remember that while you might make
mistakes in times of adversity, you can never make a mistake of motive. If you always have the organization's best
interest at heart, and you don't put yourself before others,
you'll be given more leeway if you do mess up in following
the Adversity Manifesto.

Fortitude Habit #7: Vanquish Victim Mentality

Why is feeling and acting like a victim so harmful? Because
the underlying assumption when you do is "I'm powerless,"
which, of course, you aren't. It's a form of learned helplessness
that erodes fortitude and helps no one. For example, when
you're playing the victim, you place blame elsewhere instead
of taking responsibility. You feel like people are "out to get
you," you take slights as major offenses, you're overly negative, and you waste tremendous time and energy stuck in a
mindset of "It's not fair." You wear people out, talking about
your thing, making it everything, even though we all have our
thing. Let's shut it down when it shows up by making a habit
of using the following.

Habit-Building Tool #7: The Victim to Victor Strategies are four ways to vanquish victim mentality. We'll go through each.

1. *Fight the false comfort.*

While the powerlessness that comes from victim mentality can be devastating, there's a twist to consider. It can also feel comforting, as you feel validated and free from having to take action—because you believe you're powerless, after all. So, you're lulled into the easy part, making the case for why you're a victim, instead of tackling the hard part, doing something about it. When you catch yourself doing this, ask either of these questions:

- *"Do I just want things to change, or do I want to change things?"* Just wanting things to change is victim mentality. Changing things is an action-oriented way of taking responsibility to create a better outcome. For example, say the culture at work is toxic, with backstabbing and credit grabbing the norm. You can be frustrated or angry that it continues, wishing it would change, while finding comfort by "unplugging" from the situation and doing nothing, because you're convinced it won't change. Or you can do something to change it, like call a team meeting to intervene.
- *"How might I move from 'Why me?' to 'Why not me?'"* Being the victim means asking, "Why me?" (often repeatedly), while waiting for others to remedy the situation. But switching to "Why not me?" sparks action. It challenges you to think, "Why can't I be the one who does something about this situation to make it better?" Then, you can do just that.

The idea with these questions is to shake you out of a false sense of comfort born from a manufactured helplessness.

2. *Pinpoint your part in it.*

Victim mentality, by definition, involves removing yourself from blame. It's not your fault; you're the victim. It feels personal, which makes it easy to lash out and play the blame game. The more you do, the further you distance yourself from the thought that you might have played a role in your circumstance (if even a small one). The idea here is to break that cycle by asking yourself, "What was my role in this? How might I have contributed?" It's about owning your part, as hard as that might be.

To illustrate, say you get into a big argument with a coworker about something you're certain wasn't your fault, and so you feel victimized by their "unjustified" outburst. You could avoid them thereafter, harboring resentment, or ask yourself what part (again, if even a small one) you played in the circumstance, and how you might move things forward.

3. *Remember this: "No one cares. Work harder."*

Feeling like a victim is also emotional. Something is being done to you, and it isn't right, or fair. That emotion can be hard to let go of, focusing you on the injustice, paralyzing you into inaction. Sometimes you need more than a gentle shake. You need a jolt to snap out of it and productively move forward.

That's where NFL quarterback Lamar Jackson comes in.

After a 2019 game, Jackson attended the postgame press conference wearing a provocative T-shirt. The athlete, who would go on to unanimously win the league MVP award, did so because, in large part, he exemplified what his shirt said: No one cares. Work harder. In other words, leaders must lead, with unswerving accountability, and there are no excuses. Even if there are, no one wants to hear them.

While it's a harsh, somewhat exaggerated sentiment, there's much truth to it. Let's break it down. First, the "No one cares" part. If you're playing the victim, again, you feel like something has happened to you. Well, guess what? Lots of things happen to lots of people, all the time. It's not personal, but no one cares about your thing, because they got their own thing to worry about. Of course, your family, friends, and some coworkers really do care, so the statement has to be taken with a grain of salt. But it's undeniably true that the vast majority of people will not react well to your victim mentality.

Now the second part: "Work harder." Think of the last time at work you pointed fingers, made excuses, or played the victim. If you're honest, there's a good chance that, when looking back, if you had put more effort in, or worked smarter or differently, you might have been able to alter the outcome you're feeling victimized by. It's not always true, but it is often enough. The point is not to make you feel guilty or bad about yourself, or make you "own your part in it" (we did that with the previous strategy). It's to use this statement to snap yourself out of feeling like a victim, to instead focus on something you can control (your level and quality of effort). Thus, you're moving forward, doing your part to minimize future unfavorable outcomes, and the likelihood of feeling victimized again.

4. Give your rescuers resolve.

Those trapped in victim mentality often have a core group of "rescuers" they turn to for sympathy. The well-meaning audience often feeds the victim mentality by showing pity and joining in on the negativity, in an attempt to make the "victim" feel better. Be aware of who you turn to in such times—it might be your partner or a few coworkers, for instance.

Then, tell those people you're working on not playing the victim. Ask them not to play into that mentality when you come looking for a sympathetic ear. This increases their resolve to not "help" in that understandable, but unhelpful, way. This can be a difficult thing to do because it requires brutal self-honesty and vulnerability from you. Do it anyway.

Your First Small Step: Avoiding victim mentality first requires recognizing when you're starting to feel it. Start paying attention to the telltale signs (like overreacting, asking "Why me?," feeling powerless or stuck in "It's not fair," etc.), then use the Victim to Victor Strategies in that moment.

In Moments of Weakness: The moment you catch yourself in victim mentality, remember it's a choice—one that can quickly be altered. Pay attention to the body language and subtle signals others are sending as you're playing the victim (other than your "rescuers," odds are, the signals aren't affirming). Choose in that moment to make a different choice; to lift yourself out of it and spark positive forward movement (aided by the Victim to Victor Strategies).

Fortitude Habit #8: Foster Healthy Debate

What's one of the least productive things a team can do when trying to ideate or solve difficult challenges?

Agree.

Or at least constantly agree with one another, or agree by default (by not speaking up). But you just don't get a group's best thinking if it's nothing but head-nodding. As General

George S. Patton said, "If everybody is thinking alike, then somebody isn't thinking."[21]

But the alternative, debate, takes courage. And fear of conflict gets in the way. Research shows people don't have the fortitude to engage in debate primarily because of the organizational culture; they believe they'll be punished in some way for disagreeing. Or they don't have the disposition for debate (too introverted or unsure of themselves).[22]

For certain, though, developing a bigger fortitude muscle and leaning into the discomfort of debate is essential. People want the chance to share their thoughts and ideas, especially in times of adversity, and discourse invites more of both. In fact, Berkeley researchers found teams that debate their ideas generate 25 percent more ideas altogether.[23]

Furthermore, debate strengthens the ideas generated. Netflix cofounder Marc Randolph goes so far as to say, "There's no such thing as a good idea."[24] That is, until debate molds it into one. And knowing you're putting the best ideas forward strengthens your sense of determination to execute them effectively—especially important when you're trying to press through challenges.

When employees (including leaders) are reluctant to engage in debate, or when leaders manage it poorly, fortitude dissolves, ideas weaken, and challenges go unsolved. The culture is damaged as tension builds across opposing sides, spiraling into an "us versus them" mentality. But mentally strong leaders are disciplined about bravely encouraging productive debate and discussion on their team. They leverage debate to turbocharge ideas and bolster fortitude instead of letting it splinter the group's spirit. You can, too, by making a habit of what follows.

Habit-Building Tool #8: Done poorly, debate can be wildly uncomfortable and even viewed as the sign of a bad meeting (and bad meetings are often feared more than bad results). Instead, cultivate productive debate by assigning five team members to a Healthy Debate Hub. The idea is simple. Each person assigned to the hub serves as a watchdog for one of the five core principles of healthy debate, making sure each principle is adhered to during team get-togethers. With this collective hub working to monitor discussion, debate comes together as productive conversation, not a heated argument. Here are the five principles for the five members to oversee in the Healthy Debate Hub.

Fig. 3.5 The Healthy Debate Hub

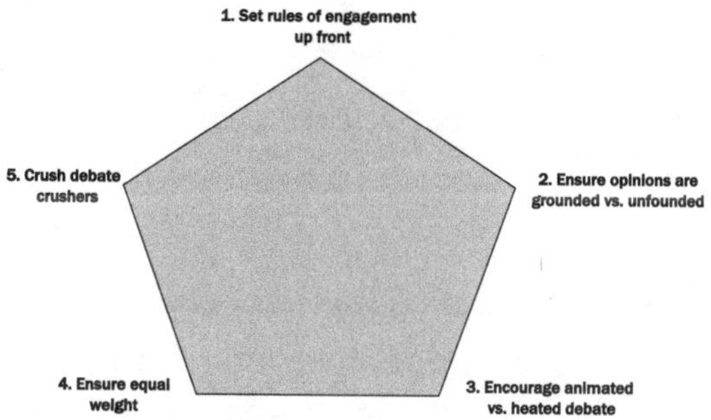

1. Set rules of engagement up front
2. Ensure opinions are grounded vs. unfounded
3. Encourage animated vs. heated debate
4. Ensure equal weight
5. Crush debate crushers

Let's go through each principle of the Healthy Debate Hub.

1. *Set rules of engagement up front.*

People are sure to shut down in a debate, or swerve into hot-blooded "protective" mode, if they feel their idea or identity is being attacked. So, for healthy debate to happen, you need two key environmental ingredients: safety and a sense of collaboration. You create both, up front, by sharing the rules of engagement for the discussion before it starts. For whoever owns this point on the hub, here's a script to use to achieve this end (inspired in part by teamwork expert Shane Snow)[25]:

- We're here as teammates, not adversaries.
- It's about what's right, not who's right (there's no debate "winner").
- Our common goal here is _____, and all ideas serving this goal are welcome.
- Commend, not condemn, opposing points of view. Acknowledge points well made.
- Be curious to learn more. Counterpoints should raise interest, not ire.
- Focus on the *con*tent (the ideas), not the *in*tent (assume everyone's intent is good).
- That said, there's no place for ego or personal agendas as we debate.
- Disagreement isn't personal.
- Nobody loses face for changing their mind.

2. *Ensure opinions are grounded rather than unfounded.* Debates can turn unproductive when unchecked opinion becomes the norm. Opinions, while important (of course), must be balanced with facts and supporting data. Otherwise people start tuning out, or discussion gets off track.

As an example, I've been in too many meetings where multiple opinions were flying around the room, none of them with underlying data-based support. As a result, the debate was "won" by whoever was the smoothest or loudest talker. Point being, facts and supporting data weren't driving the outcome.

When this kind of thing is happening, the hub assignee in charge of this point should respectfully say something like:

"I appreciate your perspective. What supporting facts/data do we need to understand, so we're fully and fairly evaluating your point of view?"

3. Encourage animated rather than heated debate.

Healthy debate can quickly spiral into *heal thyself* debate, where one or both parties feel hurt by words that sting. It's natural that emotion would emerge given that, again, debate can feel personal, and people don't like their ideas or identity being attacked. The key is to keep it as *animated debate* between people, driven by passion for a point of view, not *heated debate,* driven by emotion and personal attacks.

For example, your lead project manager is debating with your sales manager about the idea of purchasing new productivity software. The back-and-forth comments start feeling heated and personal, more emotional, less on topic. So, the hub assignee here intervenes to bring it back to debating merits of the idea. They say something like, "It's natural for emotions to come out. But disagreement doesn't mean division— we're on the same side. Passion is good. Getting personal is not. Let's try again."

4. Ensure equal weight.

Meaning, the person in charge of this point of the hub has the task of making sure everyone is heard and that equal weight is given to all input (not just the slickest or loudest communicators). They can do so by directly inviting each person to speak up, and by saying, after everyone has spoken, something like, "Great debate comes from equal weight. Let's remember to carefully consider what everyone has said."

Especially important here is to beware of the HiPPO—the highest paid person's opinion. If there is a clear HiPPO in the room, ask them to speak last. And when they do, if they're the ones that will be deciding which direction to take, ask them beforehand to thank everyone for the discussion, as it aided in their rumination (which helps reinforce that debate was very much needed).

5. *Crush debate crushers.*

Good, productive debates get brought to a screeching halt when debaters drone on or stray from the topic. People just disengage. The job of the hub assignee here is to keep things moving along by interjecting and saying something as simple as "Let's stay on track. Good debate is efficient debate."

Debate also shuts down when someone frequently interrupts, or when one side just doesn't bother to listen to the other. Step in here and say something like "If we all want to be heard, then we all must listen."

Lastly, a culture of "meetings after the meeting," as mentioned earlier in this chapter, also discourages good debate, as attendees figure they don't have to speak their mind, they can just wait to speak it afterward. For example, instead of speaking up during that big product design meeting about their concerns, several people huddle up afterward and bash the decision they didn't agree with. Not helpful (as also mentioned earlier). The hub assignee here should be on the lookout to squash this destructive behavior by saying something like, "Has everyone said their piece? If not, speak up now—no meetings after the meeting."

Your First Small Step: Assign five people to sit on the Healthy Debate Hub. Explain the concept (and the supporting principles), the specific role of each hub member, and use the Healthy Debate Hub for the next debate you anticipate having.

In Moments of Weakness: If a debate starts going off the rails, it's important to get back on track as quickly as possible, so you don't lose the gathered, collective intelligence. Healthy Debate Hub assignees should jump in and help one another to get things back on track (so it's helpful if each hub member knows the role of the others). After a wobbly debate session, pull hub members together to reinforce the importance of monitoring debate in the future to ensure it's productive, not poisonous.

Fortitude Habit #9: Bravely Conduct Difficult Conversations

Difficult conversations require a special kind of courage and fortitude, and are vital to opt into rather than out of (especially if you want to press past challenges on the way to achievement). The need for them is triggered by a variety of things. Just to name a few:

- You have to deliver bad news.
- You need to apologize for a mistake.
- You need to ask someone to change something about themselves or their behaviors/actions.
- You have to discuss something uncomfortable (perhaps also with someone intimidating).

And there are many reasons you might avoid them:

- You fear their emotions. (How will they act? Will they cry, get angry, shut down?)

- You fear *your* emotions. (How will *you* feel if they react emotionally?)
- You don't like conflict/resistance. (You feel you're not equipped to handle it well.)
- You think it's not worth the trouble. (You overestimate how painful the experience will be while underestimating how freeing it will be to have finally had that discussion.)

All understandable. However, mentally strong leaders know that not much good comes from putting off a difficult conversation, and that a surprising amount of good comes from actually having them. The key lies in knowing how to *prepare* for difficult conversations, and knowing how to *conduct* them. Let's get to developing this important element of Fortitude.

Habit-Building Tool #9: The Difficult Conversation Consideration tool helps you successfully navigate tough conversations by helping you methodically and intentionally prepare for and conduct them. Let's look first at the preparation phase.

Preparing for a Difficult Conversation

Tackling difficult conversations effectively begins with understanding what makes a conversation difficult in the first place. What's the source of tension? There are multiple potential sources, as you'll see momentarily. It's important to start here because *the source of tension impacts how you prepare for the conversation.* Take a look at the following table, which lists the common sources of what brings tension to a conversation ("Source of Tension"), and lists the corresponding "How to Prepare" partners.

Source of Tension	How to Prepare
Emotions	• Don't fear emotions (reframe as a growth opportunity) • Plan for emotions, envision a controlled response • Resist labeling them in advance
Power Structure (+, −, =)	• Commit to change *your* patterns
Relationship	• Focus on the predicament versus the personality • Go back to the "why"
Lack of Familiarity	• Are you confusing "difficult" with "different"? • Remind yourself that growth happens outside your comfort zone • Stop catastrophizing
Lack of Control	• Be okay with messy • Anticipate resistance

Let's examine each source of potential tension (that could make a conversation difficult), and accordingly, how to thus prepare for the conversation if that tension exists.

Emotions that arise during a discussion can quickly turn it into an uncomfortable undertaking. You don't have to fear the other person getting emotional. Think of an emotional response as an opportunity for you to grow your skills in handling conflict or resistance. And know that bringing your emotions to the table is natural (no matter how careful you are with your approach). The old idea of "checking your emotions at the door" just doesn't work in a difficult conversation. In fact, plan for emotions to arise—just be mindful to not let your emotions run away from you. Envision beforehand how you'll react to a variety of emotions from the other person, even highly escalated emotions—which should be with compassion, objectivity (you don't want to be overly swayed by their emotions, after all), and the amount of productive counter-emoting needed to make your point.

For example, you anticipate a difficult conversation will lead to outbursts of anger from the other. So, in your preparation, you imagine counter-emoting with a nonjudgmental, calm, but passionate tone that underscores your intent—that you're just trying to help.

Pro tip: You're more likely to react to an emotional response with unhelpful emotion of your own if you've labeled the person ahead of time. For example, if you're thinking, "I know this is going to be a tough conversation because this person is a crybaby." If that person does react with tears, they'll be playing into your preconceived label of them, adding to your frustration (as feelings of "Here we go again" flit through your mind). That won't help. Instead, if you catch yourself applying labels before going into a conversation, don't. Again, enter the discussion with as much objectivity and compassion as you can muster.

The *power structure* in play can dramatically affect the dynamics of a difficult conversation. Do you have more, less, or equal power to the person you're talking to? For example, in a conversation with a subordinate, you'd have more power, and might be worried you'll crush their spirit. In a discussion with a boss, you'd have less power and might feel intimidated. With a peer, you have equal power, but worry you won't get through to them because they don't report to you and don't have to listen to you.

The key here is to consider the power structure dynamic, and discern what unhelpful patterns *you* can change about yourself within that dynamic. The power structure is the power structure, you can't change that, but you can change the patterns of your behavior within that dynamic.

As an example, say you need to have a conversation with your boss about something he really needs to improve upon. But he's an intimidating personality, and you know you typically fall into a pattern of being very deferential to him. This time, in advance, you commit to breaking that pattern. If he pushes back, gets defensive, or tries to explain his behavior away, you commit to not deferring, that you'll stick to what you're trying to accomplish with the conversation.

Another example. Say you need to have a difficult conversation with a direct report that you really like. You know she has some tough personal issues going on, but that doesn't change the fact that she needs to improve dramatically on something. You know that you usually back off on any feedback with this person because they're already insecure, and since you're in the position of power, you fear deflating them even more. So, knowing this, in advance you commit to staying firm (yet compassionate), because the topic is just too critical.

The state of the *relationship* between you and the person you're having a difficult conversation with can impact the outcome. Primarily, either (a) the relationship is bad, so you fear preexisting tension will come into play, or (b) it's a relationship that really matters to you, and you're worried about damaging it.

Regarding (a): remember that difficult people, or people being difficult, rarely see themselves that way. There are almost always perfectly legitimate reasons for their behavior—such as differing reward systems, underlying insecurities, lack of training, personal issues, and so on. The key here is to focus on the predicament, not the personality.

Regarding (b): Go back to the "why." Why are you having this conversation in the first place? What's the benefit it will bring? Remind yourself of how freeing it will feel that you've finally had this conversation with someone you care about. Tell yourself in this scenario, "The pain is temporary, the positive is permanent."

The *lack of familiarity*, because of never having had a discussion like this with the person before, can certainly cause angst. But challenge yourself here. Ask, "Am I just confusing 'difficult' with 'different'?" Meaning, just because it's different from any discussion you've had (or just because the person is different than any other you deal with), it doesn't mean it has to be difficult. It's just a conversation you haven't had experience with before. To feel better about the unfamiliar situation, remind yourself that growth happens outside your comfort zone. Don't let discomfort with the unknown run off with your imagination. It'll be okay. You'll learn from the discussion and grow stronger for it.

For example, you're a new manager, with two people now reporting to you. One of them is severely underperforming, requiring a tough discussion. You've never had a hard conversation with an employee before, and the total lack of experience keeps you from seeking out the discussion. It doesn't help that the employee strikes you as a difficult employee, very dissimilar to who you are and how you think. But you remind yourself that "difficult" and "different" aren't the same thing, and then bravely initiate the conversation. It turns out not to be so bad after all (the employee totally understood where you were coming from), and you feel relieved after having the discussion. With some experience under your belt, you feel better about tackling the next tough conversation.

Will it always work out exactly this way? Certainly not. But the point is to not amp yourself up into believing it will automatically be a super-difficult conversation, when sometimes it turns out to just be a different conversation.

Having a *lack of control* over a conversation can easily make it feel difficult. The discussion could go off the rails, you worry, and you don't like knowingly entering a conversation you might not be able to control. Or you worry you won't have all the answers to any of their pushbacks. For instance, you need to have a difficult conversation with your employees, immediately, about a just-announced, company-wide salary freeze and head count–reduction effort. You know everyone is agitated, and that you don't have answers to a lot of questions they'll have. It doesn't feel good.

Plain and simple, learn to be okay with messy. You can't control what you don't have the answer for in that conversation, but you can control the amount of listening, learning, acknowledging, and question-asking you do. You can't control everything about the outcome. But you can remember that progress isn't always clean, on a straight and narrow path. People need the chance to process in real time, and as for the conversation you're having, it probably isn't an easy thing for them. Give them that space, and grace. Believe that messy is okay.

It also helps here to simply anticipate resistance. Know that resistance interrupts conversation flow; it's natural. But you don't need to control all the ebbs and flows of the conversation river. Just gently guide that river to the place where it opens up into an ocean of possibilities (like when people feel heard and understood, among many other potential productive outcomes).

Conducting a Difficult Conversation

You now understand how to prepare for difficult conversations. Let's turn our attention to how to actually carry them out. Unregulated emotions, thoughts, and behaviors here are like little land mines that can quickly throw the conversation off course. So, while engaged in a tough conversation, follow these four principles:

1. *Acknowledge your responsibility in the mess, and acknowledge your discomfort.*

Doing so helps defuse their emotion by acknowledging you have some underlying emotion, too, and that you're human. And it honors them, by showing them they're not alone in making mistakes. It creates a more level "playing field" and makes it easier for them to accept what you have to point out. Do all of this right up front.

For example, start a difficult conversation with something like, "I need to have a difficult conversation with you about _____. I want to acknowledge that I've contributed to this situation by _____, and I want you to know that having this discussion doesn't come easy to me because _____."

2. *Press REC (respect, empathy, curiosity).*

Imagine that you're being recorded in your difficult conversation. This is how you'd want to show up for the world to see—with respect, empathy, and curiosity. Here's a tell-tale test to determine if you're ready to do so (inspired by Brené Brown[26]):

You know you're ready for a difficult conversation when you're ready to sit next to the person to have it, rather than sitting across from them, when you're ready to put the issue *in front of* you rather than *between* you.

Think about it. Picture sitting *next* to someone to have a discussion rather than *across* from them. It forces you to have a different tone, with different body language. Sitting next to them instinctively brings out respect, empathy, and curiosity, showing that you genuinely want to understand and help. So, while engaged in that difficult conversation, even if you aren't physically sitting next to the person, imagine that you are.

Pro tip: If you sense that someone isn't sharing everything that's on their mind (they're giving one-word answers, they're largely silent, or they're giving body language signals that indicate they're withholding something), ask what Harvard communications expert Debbie Goldstein asks: "What are you thinking, but not saying?" It further demonstrates respect, empathy, and curiosity, showing them that you're paying attention, that you care what they think, and that you want to have a real conversation.[27]

3. *Focus on what you're hearing, rather than what you're saying.*

Don't waste hours over-rehearsing what you're going to say; it likely won't go the way you want it to anyway. Instead, focus on *really* listening and validating as much as you can.

For example, you script out everything you want to say to that coworker who has got to stop being so defensive, about everything. One minute into the conversation, you're "off script," as the coworker launches into a combination of ranting and heartfelt confession. Your plan is up in smoke, so you switch gears to do the best thing you can do, which is to *listen*, reflect, and respond in a validating manner, insofar as that is possible.

It might feel scary, but trust what happens when you focus on truly listening, rather than scripting what you'll say. You'll find the right words in the moment if you do—you'll know what response just feels right.

4.   *Outcome = your anchor.*

Meaning, you might go through a roller coaster of emotions in the conversation; just keep coming back to the outcome you're trying to achieve. Let that outcome be the anchoring point you tether yourself to, to hold you steady as you navigate the "gusts of wind" that come up during the conversation.

To illustrate, back to that conversation with the defensive coworker. During the more heated moments, you stay calm, remembering that this relationship is absolutely integral to your day-to-day job, and must improve. That thought is playing quietly in the back of your mind while you're coolly navigating the ups and downs of the discussion.

Your First Small Step: The first small step in having a difficult conversation is to lean into the discomfort and be willing to have it in the first place. It's actually a *big* first small step, as research shows that 70 percent of us regularly avoid having difficult conversations in the workplace.[28] So, schedule on your calendar a difficult conversation you've been putting off (thus forcing yourself to commit). Use the Difficult Conversation Consideration tool to start preparing for, and then conducting, the discussion. (You can find the template for the Difficult Conversation Consideration tool at scottmautz.com/mentallystrong/templates.) Also, here's a good first step right before the discussion begins, as you're feeling the nervousness. Pair that feeling up with a feeling of newness, as in, "Things will change because of this discussion." A new, better outcome will emerge. Focus on that sensation.

In Moments of Weakness: A common mistake you can make here is in not preparing for the difficult conversation well enough. This preparation is something you're likely not looking forward to, by the way. If the time is drawing near for that difficult conversation, and you're still not prepared, pair the prep work with thinking of things you *want* to discuss with that person, such as mentioning something they did well or that they deserve recognition for. Those topics might not be right for the difficult conversation, per se, but they can be shared later, while giving you something pleasant to prepare for at the same time. Also, if, in the middle of the difficult conversation, your heart is racing and you're thinking, "Wow, this isn't going well," it's okay. Remember, it's not supposed to be easy. The tension you feel is what tells you that you care about the other person, about handling the conversation well, about getting to a better place. The tension is what will make you stronger. So, take a pause if you need to, saying something like, "Let's pause for a moment so I can gather my thoughts. I really want to help here." Then get right back on track, leveraging what you've learned from the Difficult Conversation Consideration tool.

It might take a few tries before tough conversations get easier, and they might never feel "natural." In fact, so much can feel unnatural about them that it's natural to doubt yourself. Don't. Hard conversations can be hard. If you mess up, fess up (acknowledge your mistakes) and proudly get right back on that bucking bronco.

NOTES

1. Cohn, M. A., B. L. Fredrickson, S. L. Brown, J. A. Mikels, and A. M. Conway. June 2009. "Happiness unpacked: positive emotions increase life satisfaction by building resilience," *Emotion* 9(3): 361–68.

2. Gerber, M., A. K. Feldmeth, C. Lang, S. Brand, C. Elliot, E. Holsboer-Trachsler, and U. Pühse. December 1, 2015. "The Relationship between Mental Toughness, Stress, and Burnout among Adolescents: A Longitudinal Study with Swiss Vocational Students," *Psychological Reports* 117(3): 703–23.

3. Khazanov, G. K., and A. M. Ruscio. September 2016. "Is low positive emotionality a specific risk factor for depression? A meta-analysis of longitudinal studies," *Psychol Bull.* 142(9): 991–1015.

4. Yi, J. P., P. P. Vitaliano, R. E. Smith, J. C. Yi, and K. Weinger. May 2008. "The role of resilience on psychological adjustment and physical health in patients with diabetes," *Health Psychology* 13(2): 311–25.

5. Clough, P., D. Marchant, and K. Earle. 2010. *The Mental Toughness Questionnaire MTQ48*, page 31, corporate-energising.com, as found on scribd.com.

6. Cross, R., K. Dillon, and D. Greenberg. January 29, 2021. "The Secret to Building Resilience," *Harvard Business Review,* hbr.org.

7. Ibid.

8. "About Dyson." https://www.lb.dyson.com/en-LB/community/aboutdyson.aspx

9. Albert Einstein quotes, goodreads.com.

10. Steve Jobs quotes, goodreads.com.

11. Wedell-Wedellsborg, T. January–February 2017. "Are You Solving the Right Problems?" *Harvard Business Review*, hbr.org.

12. "Five Whys," en.wikipedia.org.

13. "Pareto principle," en.wikipedia.org.

14. Wedell-Wedellsborg.

15. Liu, S., H. Chow, and Y. Xu et al. 2012. "Neural Correlates of Lyrical Improvisation: An fMRI Study of Freestyle Rap," *Sci Rep* 2: 834.

16. Webber, R. May 1, 2010. "Make Your Own Luck," *Psychology Today*, psychologytoday.com.

17. Burkus, D. July 22, 2013. "How Criticism Creates Innovative Teams," *Harvard Business Review*, hbr.org.

18. Barker, E. February 2, 2017. "How to Be Calm Under Pressure: Three Secrets From a Bomb Disposal Expert," *Observer*, observer.com.

19. Berinato, S., and T. Allen. "Leading Through a Major Crisis," *Harvard Business Review—HBR IdeaCast*, episode 217.

20. Mautz, S. 2015. *Make It Matter*, HarperCollins Leadership, 195.

21. George S. Patton quotes, goodreads.com.

22. Kakkar, H., and S. Tangirala. November 6, 2018. "If Your Employees Aren't Speaking Up, Blame Company Culture," *Harvard Business Review*, hbr.org.

23. Nemeth, C. J., B. Personnaz, M. Personnaz, and J. A. Goncalo. July/August 2004. "The liberating role of conflict in group creativity: A study in two countries," *European Journal of Social Psychology* 34(4): 365–74.

24. Griffith, K., Fast Company Executive Board. May 28, 2021. "15 tips to encourage vigorous (but respectful) workplace debates," *Fast Company*, fastcompany.com.

25. Snow, S. January 17, 2019. "How to Debate Ideas Productively at Work," *Harvard Business Review*, hbr.org.

26. Brown, B. "Dare to Lead: The Engaged Feedback Checklist," brene-brown.com/resources.

27. Zetlin, M. November 9, 2023. "People Who Are Good at Dealing With Conflict Ask This 1 Question, Says a Harvard Communications Expert," inc.com.

28. "Understanding the conversation gap," *Bravely*, learn.workbravely.com. Accessed January 2, 2024.

4 The Confidence Habit

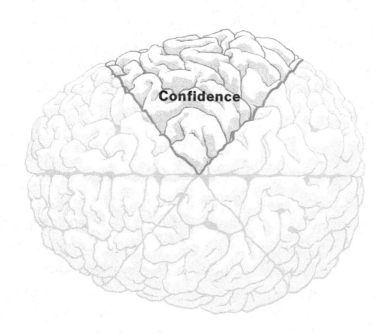

Building mental strength is a team sport. Meaning, not only can you not do it alone, but being mentally strong has an undeniable, positive ripple effect on your team. Especially when you ace the confidence test of leadership (another of the six that most directly links to exceptional achievement).

Steve Kerr, four-time champion coach of the Golden State Warriors basketball team, and a man who knows a thing or two about leadership, says one of the single most important things for leaders to understand is that "your team needs to see you as confident."[1] Anything less, and you're capping your group's potential. After all, a team is never more confident than its leader.

The shared benefits of your confidence are astonishing. Confidence lifts spirits, fuels resilience, puts its arm around perseverance, creates calm in crisis. Surprising research from Carnegie Mellon even shows that projecting confidence is more effective for establishing trust than *past performance*.[2] And all this before even mentioning what you already know: the personal benefits of being more confident are immeasurable.

Our friend Maya, from chapter 1, who successfully launched her nonprofit's biggest-ever educational initiative, learned a lot about confidence along the way. Namely, while confidence certainly is part of a team sport, it primarily requires self-regulation—of how you think and feel about yourself, with your actions underscoring both. Maya was one of many people who inspired the menu of confidence-building habits and habit-building tools in this chapter, including aids that help you manage criticism and self-doubt, help you stop comparing yourself to others, seeking approval, beating yourself up, feeling like an imposter, and more. All to steer yourself, and others, past doubt and into achievement.

Confidence Habit #1: Handle Criticism Effectively

Ever receive positive feedback, but blow it off, focusing only on the "negative" feedback you received? (I've been there, a lot.) This makes it even more important to get comfortable with negative feedback/criticism, remembering that making a difference, or putting a "dent in the universe," as Steve Jobs once called it,[3] means taking dents in your armor at times. Nobody said it was fair. One of life's great imbalances is the fact that what others risk by criticizing you is minuscule compared to what you risk by putting yourself out there.

But mentally strong leaders accept this and believe that criticism makes them stronger and actually increases their confidence rather than deflating it. Which it indeed does, as a multitude of research shows negative feedback (if properly processed) leads to faster learning than positive reinforcement.[4] It's about letting criticism feed your abilities, not your insecurities.

Habit-Building Tool #1: Build a habit of effectively handling negative feedback by following the Criticism Critical Path—a three-step routine that kicks in the moment you receive criticism.

STEP 1—Decide if the criticism is relevant. You decide who gets to criticize you. Not all criticism is created equal, not everyone gets a seat at the table. For example, your boss, some coworkers, your spouse, get a say. But Bob in accounting, who just doesn't like you, and your judgmental sister-in-law don't make the cut. Or maybe you just don't want to hear it from anyone who hasn't "walked a mile in your shoes." The point is, don't give unwarranted influence to those who shouldn't have it, especially when research shows we're *far* more likely to remember criticism than praise (it's known as the negativity bias).[5] I'm not saying limit those you'll accept criticism from so much that you deprive yourself of potentially valuable feedback. Just be intentional: set criteria for who qualifies, and mentally dismiss the rest. If you discern the person feeding you criticism in the moment isn't qualified to do so, you can still follow the next two steps (hoping to get some value out of it), or you can just politely listen until they're done.

STEP 2—Neutralize your first reaction, and just listen. It's human nature. That moment you're receiving criticism, your heart starts racing, and defensiveness kicks in. It hurts. In fact, psychology researchers have shown that the brain registers physical pain in the same region it does social rejection, so criticism can actually seem to sting.[6] As the criticism comes in, quietly take a deep, slow breath, and just . . . listen. Emotional reactions won't help.

Even if the criticism feels especially harsh and deflating, remember that while you can't change the words spoken to you, you can assign the meaning you give them. You can rise above any words. As Eleanor Roosevelt said, "No one can make you feel inferior without your consent."[7]

STEP 3—Find the nugget. Imagine holding a strainer through which criticism flows, sifting it to find the nugget of truth, which most criticism contains. After all, that's the intent of most criticism, to help you improve, even if it doesn't feel like it in the moment. It's a buried treasure, if you're self-confident and mentally strong enough to see it that way. For example, maybe in all that hard-to-hear feedback that you're a poor communicator lies a gem about how to get your ideas across more clearly. Sift through the emotion, find the elevation. To help find the nugget, simply ask yourself, "What are they right about?"

Your First Small Step: It's a step before the ones listed above. Start by reframing how you view criticism altogether. *Believe* that avoiding criticism is what makes you weaker, not the criticism itself. *Believe* that if you want to make an impact in life, you'll be criticized occasionally; anything worth doing attracts admiration AND criticism. *Believe* the philosophy of renowned theater critic Albert Williams, who explained why theater, art, and music critics do what they do.[8] It's not because they're mean-spirited or want to save you from wasting money on a bad performance. It's because they have a passion to create better art. Take the first small step of viewing any (relevant) critic as someone attempting to create better art—in the form of a better version of you.

In Moments of Weakness: If you catch yourself spiraling down from a critical comment in the moment, acknowledge that it's happening, and quickly switch laser-like focus to extracting whatever value from the criticism that you can. Afterward, if you catch yourself replaying the criticism repeatedly in your head, beating yourself up over it, force yourself to move forward by focusing on the adjustments you'll make and how you'll be better off for them. For example, popular stand-up comics practice their act dozens of times in comedy clubs before going on tour, taking criticism in the form of no laughter (or worse, booing). Then, instead of spiraling down from the criticism, they act on it to craft a better conclusion—a funnier show.

Confidence Habit #2: Monitor Your Relationship with Doubt

Confidence is not the absence of doubt. It's your ability to effectively *manage your relationship with doubt*, because we all experience doubt at times, no matter how confident we are. Mentally strong leaders push through to achievement, despite doubts they might have, because they manage that relationship well. That's the habit we'll work on forming next.

Habit-Building Tool #2: You maintain a healthy relationship with doubt (i.e., uncertainty about your ability to accomplish something) by regularly conducting doubt assessments. That is, by evaluating where you are on the Doubt Continuum:

Fig. 4.1 The Doubt Continuum

So, ask yourself, "Where am I on the Doubt Continuum? Am I overconfident, perfectly confident, embracing healthy doubt, or paralyzed by fear?" The idea is to ensure you're in neither danger zone (on the far ends of the continuum). The left-side danger zone is when you're overconfident. Meaning, you're not just supremely confident about the situation and your abilities, you're overconfident to the point of gross overestimation, assuming too much, operating in a vacuum, or blowing through "red light" warning signals. On the far-right-side danger zone, you're paralyzed by fear of failure, afraid to proceed—well past having useful healthy doubt or a little discomfort with a situation.

Now let's look at the areas in between. If you're *perfectly confident*, that means your confidence is well justified—you have enough data, practice, experience, skill, or whatever is required to feel confident about the situation, without being arrogant or dismissive. (There's nothing wrong with extending into "superconfident" as a leader, as long as it doesn't stretch into unwarranted, unhelpful overconfidence.)

If you're *embracing healthy doubt*, you feel a little uncertain about the outcome, maybe even skeptical, but at a level that's productive—it's not holding you back or causing paranoia. You're okay with not knowing everything and feel confident in your ability to learn and figure it out along the way. The doubt pushes you to work harder and smarter and focus more. Even venturing into some real discomfort is fine (that's where the most growth happens, actually). It's when that discomfort swells into dysfunction that trouble arises (and fear starts working against you).

Again, this is about ensuring that you're not in either danger zone: overconfident or paralyzed by fear of failure. Let's focus on what to do if you are.

Overconfidence: Overconfident leaders believe there's no doubt they're right, and won't let doubt into the picture, by *limiting* further input. Mentally strong leaders open up to the idea of being wrong by *seeking* further input (up to a point).

What input? Input that creates one thing in particular— friction, in the form of contradiction. Psychology research shows that inviting in contradiction is the key to overcoming overconfidence.[9] There is no friction or contradiction when you're operating in a vacuum, devoid of any resistance, with no one to check your assumptions, (over) estimations, and so on. So, seek out potentially opposing points of view. Then listen, be coachable, and act on what makes sense (whether that action is changing your mind, adjusting your approach, or acknowledging a blind spot of yours that surfaces).

For example, say you've spent several hours on your own preparing for a big presentation to recommend the launch of a new product. An overconfident leader might say, "Case closed—I'm ready to go!" A mentally strong leader might seek out other, likely differing, opinions on the presentation, like from the scientist who isn't fully on board with the new product's viability. Listening to that feedback might spark ideas to strengthen your case (or change your mind), and help you avoid a potentially troublesome blind spot you have—not understanding enough about the science behind the new product.

The point isn't to grind things to a halt through too much conflicting input, but to ultimately sharpen thinking and improve the output.

Paralyzed by fear of failure: To push past your fear of failure, *name and reframe*. Meaning, do two things. *Name* what you're actually afraid of. Ask yourself, out loud, "What am I really afraid of here?" Odds are it's not the failure itself you're afraid of; it's something associated with failure, like feeling shame, for example (which is quite often the case). So, name it, say it out loud. When you do, you go from a paralyzing, overarching fear, to something more concrete and finite in scope. You can then focus in on it and address it with specific plans to overcome it. It thus begins to lose its power, its hold, over you.

By the way, if you identify that what you're really afraid of is shame, please be extra cautious here, because shame is the most toxic of emotions.[10] Instead of making you feel bad about your actions or your efforts, shame makes you feel bad about *who you are*. It dupes you into forgetting that as humans we're all fallible and that failure shouldn't bring shame, but pride in the human struggle that helps you to grow.

Once you've named it, now reframe it. Understand that fear engages your brain in the wrong conversation. But you can change that conversation, for yourself, or anyone you're coaching through their fear of failure. For example, consider the following reframes:

- There are only three ways to actually fail: when you quit, don't improve, or never try.
- Failure is an event, never a person.
- Failure doesn't happen *to* you, it happens *for* you.
- You don't suffer when you fail, your ego does (and you/your ego aren't the same thing).
- Your fear of failure shouldn't scare you. It's there to tell you that something must be worth it—*or you'd be feeling nothing*.
- Failure is a key part of your life's portfolio—no successful person is without it in their set of experiences.

Your First Small Step: Internalize the knowledge that confidence doesn't come from an absence of doubt, but from how you manage your relationship with doubt. Start practicing self-assessments with the Doubt Continuum by pairing the assessments with times when a pending decision/action is particularly important (and can't be hampered by either overconfidence or fear of failure). This helps jump-start your appreciation for how helpful this tool can be. Thereafter, continue using the continuum in lower-stakes situations as well, until it becomes a habit altogether.

In Moments of Weakness: It's easy to slip into overconfidence or fear of failure, especially when big potential actions or decisions lie ahead, and distractions abound. That's true at the individual, and group, level. On the individual front, if you're in either danger zone, remember that these zones manufacture *limitations*, when you're looking for *limitless*. At the group level, enroll your team to the Doubt Continuum, and assign a "Continuum Controller," someone to help get you and your team back on track when you've unknowingly strayed into either danger zone.

Confidence Habit #3: Monitor Your Relationship with Yourself

Just as you can monitor your relationship with doubt (the extent to which you accept you can accomplish something), so can you monitor your relationship with yourself (the extent to which you *accept yourself*). After all, self-acceptance is one of the most fundamental forms of both self-regulation and confidence. So, let's make a habit of it.

Habit-Building Tool #3: You help maintain a healthy relationship with yourself by regularly conducting self-acceptance assessments. That is, by evaluating where you are on the Self-Acceptance Scale.

Fig. 4.2 The Self-Acceptance Scale

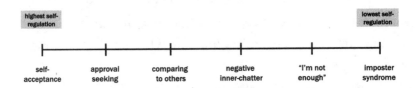

The idea is to stay on the left-hand side of the scale, in a place of self-acceptance and self-appreciation, rich with feelings of self-worth. And, essentially, to avoid anything to the right of this on the scale.

As you go from left to right on the scale, note how the level of self-acceptance gradually decreases, as does the amount of self-regulation involved. That's not a coincidence. The less you regulate your thoughts and emotions about yourself, the "darker" things get, going from the desired self-acceptance, to approval-seeking behavior, to comparing yourself to others, then beating yourself up with negative inner chatter, to believing "I'm not enough," all the way to where you believe you're an imposter (the lowest level of self-regulation).

Note that you can be on multiple points on the scale at any point in time. But, again, the idea is to self-regulate your way back to solely residing on the left side, in self-acceptance. Let's go through the scale now, from left to right. For anything other than self-acceptance, we'll address it, in depth, with "tools within the tool" to help you self-regulate your way back.

Self-Acceptance

Self-acceptance is key to overall psychological well-being. You can't really do a "work-around" to well-being if you're not in a place of self-acceptance. In fact, Harvard Medical School indicates that if you have low self-acceptance, the parts of the brain that help you regulate emotions and stress have less gray matter than someone with high self-acceptance—thus, these parts of the brain "actually have less tissue to work with."[11] In other words, it's hard to be mentally strong when you don't have enough self-acceptance gray matter as a foundation.

Self-acceptance starts with your awareness of (and belief in) the value of the unique you, continues with forgiveness of your flaws, and ends with self-regulating away from the thoughts, emotions, and behaviors that manifest themselves in the unwanted parts of this scale.

Approval Seeking

In this first, undesirable part of the Self-Acceptance Scale, you may or may not have reasonably good feelings about yourself, but you still need the approval of others to verify your thoughts and actions. This behavior is based on feelings of insecurity, which we believe we do a good job of covering up. But insecurity is unrelenting. In truth, people spot it a mile away and don't take well to it. As psychiatrist and author Marcia Sirota notes (edited for brevity): "Human beings are highly sensitive to power dynamics in relationships. We admire those who are confident; the 'Alpha.' And we're aware of those who are insecure and lacking in confidence; they come across as weak and needy—and we're inclined to react negatively toward them."[12]

And nothing screams "insecure" more than when you engage in approval-seeking behavior.

The thing is, the struggle for approval is an elusive, yet empty victory at best, and confidence-eroding or soul-crushing at worst. Approval is an insatiable beast; once you start chasing it, the pursuit is never-ending. Furthermore, seeking approval alters your behavior in unintended, unhealthy ways. In an attempt to gain acceptance in some form, you grow further and further from your authentic self. The gap between who you are and who you're acting like becomes a deep, dark one, into which your confidence plunges.

Here's how to overcome it. When you catch yourself in approval-seeking behavior, stop, and ask three questions.

1. *"Why am I seeking approval?"*
Is it because:
- you want to be liked
- you want to feel like you belong
- you're uncertain of your abilities
- you're unsure of getting the outcome you want
- you want to feel validated

Be honest with yourself. Pinpoint the reason, whatever it is. For example, you find yourself seeking approval from a "clique" of coworkers a level below you. You realize it's because you want to be liked and accepted by them, and you want to feel validated about the role you're in.

2. *"How is my need for approval holding me back?"*
Seeking approval is borrowing confidence, not building it. It creates a false, forced, temporary sense of comfort that disguises the damage it's doing. This question is about exposing the cost of your need for approval. To illustrate, back to that clique. After asking this question, you realize your need for approval from this group is causing you to act counter to your closely held value of kindness (because they act judgmental toward others).

3. *"What if I acted like I already have approval?"*
Imagine if you acted as if that group of coworkers already liked you; you wouldn't have to behave in violation of your values. Thus, they'd eventually come to appreciate the real you. Or, separately, if you acted like your boss already thought you were doing a good job, you wouldn't overanalyze every offhand comment they make, or keep asking for permission on everything.

You get the idea. If you act like you already have approval for whatever you're seeking approval for, odds are, you'll act much closer to your true, confident self, a confident self that others will see, and react to, in ways that will give you even more confidence.

Pro tip: To help spot when you're engaging in approval-seeking behavior, be tuned into feelings of *inauthenticity* (after all, you might be altering who you are in a bid to gain approval or acceptance from others). It's an emotional side effect often linked to approval-seeking behavior and should set off your alarm bells. Also, pay attention to when you're engaged in *people-pleasing* behavior (a form of approval-seeking). In that moment, say to yourself, "Think of the 'you-niverse' instead of the universe." It's a reminder to stop trying to be everything for everybody in a bid for approval. Take care of your needs first, so you stay balanced, energized, and better able to serve others in a more authentic way.

Another pro tip: When you catch yourself in approval-seeking mode (in a moment of weakness), recite this refrain: *"Chase authenticity, not approval."* It's meant to remind you of what's at stake; that when you're approval-seeking, you're moving away from who you are, depriving the world of the unique you. Then, engage in the above three questions immediately thereafter.

Comparing to Others

Moving further to the right on the scale, an encroaching lack of self-acceptance causes you to begin comparing to others. What does that most often yield?

Feeling small and inadequate.

Not surprising, considering that when you compare to others, you tend to compare your weaknesses to their strengths. You assume their success is due to their superiority, not favorable circumstances or a specific context they're operating in. It's an unwinnable war that devastates confidence, and it's a trap that's easy to fall into.

To overcome this unhelpful behavior, I offer an unusual "mini-habit." Whenever you catch yourself comparing yourself to others and experiencing a deflated feeling (like on social media, when you see an associate posting about their new job that's two levels above yours), picture the image of a giant dragon appearing before you. I call it the Comparison Dragon. Give it a name to help make it more personal—I've named mine "Vulgar." I even have clients who keep a dragon figurine on their desk to remind them of their unhelpful comparison tendencies.

Know that the more you compare to others, and thus feed the dragon, the bigger the dragon gets, the smaller you feel, the more dejected you become. Hold that image of the growing dragon in your mind. Then picture driving it away, which you do by stopping the comparison in that moment, and saying to yourself:

The bigger the dragon gets, the smaller I feel, the more dejected I become.

Then, say it again.

The bigger the dragon gets, the smaller I feel, the more dejected I become.

The truth is, the only comparison that matters is to who you were yesterday, and whether or not you're becoming a better version of yourself. The comparison dragon will flee, and self-confidence will return when you refuse to try and measure up to someone else's irrelevant circumstances.

For example, back to that social media post that has you feeling inadequate. You could choose to spiral down from there, lamenting how you're not as successful, or how much more talented they must be. Or you could recognize that the Comparison Dragon has reared its head again (curse you, Vulgar!) and drive it back by recognizing that you don't know the other person's circumstances. Luck, not talent, might have gotten them that job, or maybe they're not actually happy in the job (it came at too great a price). You conclude it doesn't matter anyway because your thing is a pretty darn good thing, and, after all, you're planning your own next, good thing.

Negative Inner-Chatter

As you move further to the right on the scale, self-acceptance continues to erode, replaced loudly by a quiet, negative inner chatter. Unfortunately, the daily challenges and tests of leadership provide a constant barrage of things that can go wrong, and an equal number of opportunities for you to beat yourself up when they do. But the more you beat yourself up, the more you start believing there's a limit to what you can achieve. And you don't want to lower others' expectations of you by doing it for them.

So, it's essential to cut the negative self-talk off, which you do by taking a Self-Compassion Break. It's a three-step routine to be kinder to yourself, and to maintain confidence accordingly.

Step 1—Stop beating yourself up for beating yourself up.

In that moment you're beating yourself up, acknowledge that you're doing it, without judgment (don't punish yourself for it). And avoid saying those negative thoughts out loud. Trevor Moawad, a mental conditioning coach for elite athletes, and named "the world's best brain-trainer" by *Sports Illustrated*, indicates it's *ten times* more damaging to your spirit of positivity if you verbalize a negative thought rather than just think it.[13] Instead, say something positive, or at least neutral, out loud, such as saying, with a smile, "I'm doing it again, aren't I?"

Step 2—Talk to yourself like a friend in need.

In fact, as you're changing your tone, channel empathy and compassion, specifically like you would when talking to a friend in need. After all, if a friend was telling you about a terrible meeting they had with their boss, clearly looking for compassion, would you say in response, "You're a complete loser!" No, of course you wouldn't talk to your friend that way.

So why would you talk to yourself that way?

Pro tip: When talking to yourself, use your name, versus "I." For example, if I were contemplating a mistake I made, I'd say something like, "Now Scott, we can get through this. Stay focused on what's been learned and how to do better next time." Using your name makes it feel like you're talking to someone else, which instinctively encourages you to be kinder to that "other" person.

Another pro tip: replace "should" with "could." So much of negative inner dialogue is about feeling sorry for yourself and replaying what you should have done or what should have happened. "I should have done this instead," "I should have never taken that risk," you tell yourself. But it's *so* much more empowering and productive to stop the shoulds and focus on coulds. "What could I do better next time?" "What could happen if I did this instead, next time?" "Could" versus "should" is a small difference in letters, but a big difference in confidence-building.

Step 3—Remember the 90:10 Rule.

So often when we beat ourselves up, it's at least in part because we fear what others will think of us and our shortcomings. That's why this last step is so important. The 90:10 Rule is a ratio, a formula, for how you should calculate your worth—which is to say it should be based 90 percent on self-worth, 10 percent on assigned worth. How you feel about yourself should flow dominantly (90 percent) from your own self-acceptance, self-appreciation, and self-love, 10 percent from assigned worth, what others feel about you.

Now, purists might not agree with allowing 10 percent for external validation, arguing that your self-worth should come only from you, never from what others think. But I'm a realist. Being completely indifferent to any signal that you're valued is unrealistic.

The problem arises when that 10 percent, occasional slice of external validation, rises to 50 percent, 70 percent, 100 percent, of how you value yourself. The problem arises when you focus on winning love rather than giving love.

Stay focused on the 90 percent, and treat the 10 percent for what it is, occasional validation.

As an example of the Self-Compassion Break in action, say you're beating yourself up over negative feedback you got from a client (and over the fact you're beating yourself up again). (Step 1) Having caught yourself in the act, you ease up. (Step 2) You switch gears and talk to yourself like a friend in need, saying "The feedback came from a place of wanting to help—it's not personal. There was a useful suggestion in it, and it's not as harsh as it seems." (Step 3) Then, you remember, "90 percent self-worth, 10 percent assigned worth." What others think is only marginally important anyway, relative to the value you know you bring to the world.

"I'm Not Enough."

One further click to the right on the scale brings us to this profoundly deflating sentiment. In *Find the Fire*, I shared the story of a hypnotherapist I interviewed who uncovered something astonishing.[14] Across the thousands of patients she treats, regardless of their ailment, regardless of the person, they all have the same exact root cause to their issue. One singularly debilitating, negative self-thought:

"I'm not enough."

Sound familiar? Oh, I've plunged these depths myself at times. But I'm here to tell you this:

You *are* enough. And you don't have to take on everything by yourself.

That's worth repeating.

You *are* enough. And you don't have to take on everything by yourself.

I'm not saying that being enough means it's okay to stop learning and growing. That would render this entire book useless. I'm saying this "not enoughness" epidemic so often stems from the fact that we feel our differences make us lesser than, when, in fact, they make us greater than. As the hypnotherapist told me, "You must believe you're meant to make unique contributions. You must believe you have the potential for your special kind of greatness, and that you're getting better every day."[15]

So, confidence is strengthened by getting in touch with "I am enough," and then strengthening your "enoughness" even further. Here's a simple way to do so. Create a two-column table with one column labeled "Eliminate" and the other "Elevate." In the "Eliminate" column, list all the triggers that make you feel bad about yourself, that make you feel like you're not enough (so you can later eliminate them). Ask yourself, "When do I feel like I'm not enough?"

Maybe it's toxic interactions with a specific person, like Maurice, a coworker who got promoted before you and doesn't let you forget it. Maybe it's a specific occasion, like when you're talking about your job with some more highly accomplished friends. Or maybe it's a combination of people and occasions, like when you get baited into deflating conversations with your in-laws during holiday visits. Write those triggers down, like so:

Eliminate	Elevate
Negative interactions with Maurice . . . Talking about my job with friends . . . Deflating talks with judgmental in-laws . . .	

The point is to be aware of what triggers your feelings of inadequacy, and then eliminate either (a) the occasion (like cutting toxic Maurice out of your life), or (b) the negative emotions you feel in those occasions (like refusing to feel inadequate when talking with in-laws).

The "Elevate" column is about taking inventory of what's lacking or missing that keeps you from feeling "enough" or from feeling successful, or that prevents you from moving toward something you want to achieve. With these things identified, you can then do something about it and "elevate" your skill in that area.

For example, maybe you need to elevate your skill at public speaking (so you can be more successful in general), or your experience level in sales (so you can get that dream job in your company), or your knowledge of how to get published (so you can finally write that book), or your ability to shine in big meetings (so you can get promoted to the level you aspire to). Here's what that looks like, added to the table:

Eliminate	Elevate
• Negative interactions with Maurice . . . • Talking about my job with friends . . . • Deflating talks with judgmental in-laws . . .	• My skill at public speaking . . . • My experience in sales . . . • My knowledge of how to get published . . . • My ability to shine in big meetings . . .

The point is to honestly assess what's missing in your repertoire and why. Then, take action. Ask for training/coaching/

help, whatever is needed, to start closing the gap between what's missing, and what would make you more confident (to elevate your sense of "enoughness").

Imposter Syndrome

Ever feel like you haven't earned what you've achieved, that you'll be discovered a fraud, or that everyone knows what they're doing but you?

It's called imposter syndrome, and it causes you to downplay your accomplishments and worth, doubt your intellect and skills, and discount your expertise and experience. Confidence, not surprisingly, evaporates in its presence at this far right side of the scale.

Before we get to the "fix" here, know that it might be something deeper than imposter syndrome at work. It might not be about you, but about the environment you work in that's triggering what you're feeling. It might be a workplace with deep biases, that doesn't value diversity, inclusion, and belongingness. Solutions for that lie in a different book. Here, we'll focus on what you can control: keeping imposter syndrome from imposing on your confidence. Do so by embracing any of the following five strategies.

1. *Own your accomplishments.*
Instead of feeling unworthy of where you're at, undeserving of praise or attention, ask yourself these questions:
- Where am I underestimating and underappreciating myself?
- What should I give myself more credit for?

- Where am I assigning too much credit to luck, or other external factors?
- What simply would not have happened, were it not for me?

It also helps here to pay attention to how you react when you're given a compliment. Don't dismiss, embrace. It helps build your skill for appreciating who you are, and what you've accomplished.

Pro tip: *Play defense attorney.* Imagine you're an attorney who must build a case to defend why you're in the role/position/standing that you are (i.e., the status you've achieved that you're doubtful of). What facts support that you belong there? Where is self-skepticism clouding the truth? For example, say you're starting a new job, and you feel unqualified or not ready, even though your résumé shows you're the perfect fit. Set your emotions aside and objectively build your "case" for why you belong. What qualifications and experiences stood out on your résumé? What strengths will serve you well in the new role? When have you "risen to the occasion" before to accomplish something that initially seemed like a stretch?

For some, focusing on your accomplishments will still produce a "Yeah but…" reaction. You might still focus on all the ways you're inadequate. Enter the next strategy.

2. *Be open to imposter discomfort, closed to imposter thoughts.*

Clinical psychologist Jill Stoddard stresses the importance of being able to sit with discomfort, to move forward with your life plan despite the nagging feelings of imposter syndrome.[16] It's known simply as "acceptance" in psychology circles. As

Stoddard says, "When you're willing to allow discomfort, you greatly broaden your options for choosing behaviors." In other words, yes, you might have doubts about whether or not you can really lead the team in your new role. But learning to be okay with it, to let that sit in the background, allows you to focus on deciding *how* to do it best, not *if* you can do it.

At the same time, try detaching yourself from your imposter thoughts. When they pop up, imagine them inside a cartoon bubble, floating above your head, completely detached from *you*.

You know these thoughts aren't trying to help you move toward the life you want to live, so why listen?

3.   *Think of your value(s) rather than your valuation.*
Yes, I'm referring here to both your value and your values. First, focus on the unique value you bring to the table, not your "valuation," what others might think you do, or don't, deserve. What skills, strengths, and perspective do you undeniably offer?

Think of your values, too—what you stand for, what represents your primary way of being (you'll get help in identifying your values in chapter 6). When imposter feelings make you cast doubt on yourself, keeping you from embracing the life you want to live, booing you from the cheap seats, your values are cheering you on from the front row. They're your reminder that what you're doing matters, that it supports what you stand for, no matter what anyone thinks.

For instance, yes, you may feel others are doubting that you can take on that teaching role at the local university. But you know that role is completely in line with your values of encouraging learning and helping others become the best versions of themselves. So, the imposter voice gets put on mute.

4. *Share your feelings and failures.*

Share your "imposter feelings" with people you trust. Odds are, they'll make you rethink your perceived shortcomings and rebuild your confidence. After all, they know you best, and can provide historical perspective on when you've doubted yourself before, and it turned out to be unwarranted. Share your failures, too, to get help putting them into perspective (as opposed to seeing them as disasters).

For example, say you're feeling like an imposter because you failed to hit your quarterly profit goal. When talking with a friend who has the same job you do, you learn that, she too, has missed her target on occasion, survived, learned from it, and grown stronger because of it.

5. *Know the struggle is real—for everyone.*

Imposter syndrome flares up when you feel you're the only one that's struggling. You think everyone else must be breezing right along. Not. True. Research shows an astonishing 82 percent of us experience imposter syndrome at times.[17] We're all just trying to figure things out as we go; even the person you can't stop comparing yourself to that seems to have everything worked out.

To illustrate, say you were promoted six months ago, but find yourself struggling and wondering if you even belong in the job. Several peers are thriving in that same role, making you feel even more like a fraud. But then you remember, sometimes you only see the elegant body of the duck gliding across the pond, not the legs churning furiously below the surface.

You remind yourself everyone struggles at times, and even confirm it when you share your imposter feelings with those peers (turns out their first six months were as tough as yours).

Pro tip: To help you spot the emergence of imposter syndrome, pay attention to when one, very specific feeling arises—*fraudulence*. It's an emotion uniquely triggered by imposter syndrome. Feeling it should trigger you to think, "Time to use my imposter syndrome strategies."

Another pro tip: The moment that, despite your best efforts, you feel imposter syndrome kicking in and your associated confidence starting to wane, try this. Say out loud, "WANE"—"We All Need Encouragement." Then practice your chosen strategy in that moment.

Your First Small Step: It's important to first discern how much self-regulation energy you'll need to expend on the self-acceptance front. Pinpoint where you tend to stray to the right on the Self-Acceptance Scale (download the template at scottmautz.com/mentallystrong/templates), and line up the "tools within the tool" above that you'll incorporate into your overall self-acceptance-building habit. Periodically schedule self-acceptance assessments, especially during times when you know you'll be engaged in challenging work (that might cause insecurity to creep back in).

In Moments of Weakness: It's impossible to stay on the left side of the Self-Acceptance Scale all the time. Drift happens. When you catch it happening, in any form, remember the key word involved here—*acceptance*. Acknowledge that you've slipped, and forgive yourself. Accepting that you're not perfect is a big part of this. Then, engage in the appropriate habit-building elements/tools you've adopted from the above.

Confidence Habit #4: Practice Two Types of Optimism

Optimism isn't a cure-all for anything, but it most certainly curates more confidence. But not all optimism is created equal. There are two forms, both of which you can regulate right into your outlook with the habit that follows.

Habit-Building Tool #4: Of course, you can't really schedule optimism, and it's not always easy to exhibit it. But you can make a routine of practicing a two-tiered optimism system. Start by practicing *direct optimism*, which means maintaining a positive outlook, no matter the circumstances. To do so, routinely refer to what I call the Attitude Anthem, a quote by Charles Swindoll: "Life is 10% what happens to me, 90% how I react to it."[18] It reminds you that attitude is a choice. And it really works.

Admittedly, it's quite difficult to choose optimism at times, especially in dire straits. That's where the second tier of optimism kicks in, called *dormant optimism*. Here, you actually give yourself permission to be pessimistic in the face of difficult circumstances that are likely to persist for a while. At the same time, you preserve some optimism, to be accessed later, as you know you can handle the adversity (you have before), and that you'll ultimately be better for it.

For example, as the COVID-19 pandemic wore on, many struggled to maintain direct optimism (a consistently sunny outlook), given the depth, breadth, and length of the negative impact the pandemic created. That included me, even though I'd consider myself quite mentally strong. When I felt my direct optimism straining, the second-tier dormant optimism kicked in. I embraced the reality of all the negative things happening (that would likely continue to happen for some time), and I allowed myself to feel some pessimism. At the same time, I drew on a belief that, based on experience, things would eventually get better and that I'd ultimately be better for it in some ways—dormant optimism.

Your First Small Step: Write the Attitude Anthem on anything you can keep handy. Refer to it frequently to begin building an overall optimistic outlook. Refer to it whenever you're feeling pessimistic.

In Moments of Weakness: When it's just too difficult to feel sunny in the moment, remember you always have that second-tier, dormant optimism, to lean on. And try this. When you find yourself giving in to feelings of pessimism, say to yourself, "I can keep myself down, or lift myself up." Then let either form of optimism enter.

Confidence Habit #5: Be Learning Agile

You *feel* confident when you know you've got it figured out. You *build* confidence when you know you can eventually figure it out, and then you do.

It's known as learning agility, and confidence soars as you develop it. More specifically, learning agility is *knowing what to do when you don't know what to do*. It's having a belief that you'll figure it out, and a talent for doing so. It's far better than letting your emotions, thoughts, and behaviors spiral into frustration (and a corresponding decline in confidence) at not being able to figure things out. In fact, the benefits go well beyond confidence building. Research from Korn Ferry shows those with high learning agility are an astonishing *eighteen times more likely* to be identified as high-potential employees, and twice as likely to be promoted.[19] So, this is a habit worth figuring out.

Habit-Building Tool #5: The Figure-It-Out Figure Eight is a habit-forming framework for figuring things out using learning agility, while simultaneously developing your learning agility (for future application). To demonstrate, we'll use one example throughout. Say you/your team have been tasked with marketing a new product strictly online, with a small budget. You realize that what you learned on those huge-budget launches doesn't apply, and recognize you don't know enough about this approach to execute it successfully. Enter the need for learning agility, and the Figure-It-Out Figure Eight.

Fig. 4.3 The Figure-It-Out Figure Eight

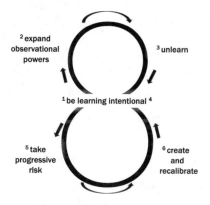

You start at the center, with being **learning intentional**, which is simply recognizing *when* you need to learn and committing to do so. Don't underestimate the power of this first step. Leaders most often don't engage in enough informative learning because they believe they don't have the time for it, and so don't make time for it. It's about stopping and saying, "I don't know enough to know enough." It means committing to do the hard work of learning, rather than "winging it" as you try to figure things out.

To illustrate, using our example, you've identifed the need for learning since you've admitted you don't know much about low budget, online-only marketing campaigns. So, you're ready to be learning intentional.

Next, you **expand your observational powers**. This is about constructing a learning plan to do two specific things: (a) identify varied sources of learning and (b) increase your ability to analyze the observations, data, patterns, and discrepancies those sources provide. It's about expanding your worldview, and sharpening the clarity of that view. It's how you learn.

To illustrate, back to the online-only marketing plan. As part of your learning plan, you identify several sources of learning to draw from: other successful and unsuccessful online-only launches, perspective from key customers, and industry trend data on online marketing. You also draw from your "knowledge network," preestablished sources of information you can quickly access. In this case, it's your advertising agency, who happens to have successfully executed a digital campaign for another customer. The idea is to use the variety of sources to expand your thinking, to keep seeking new options, solutions, or inspiration, to keep asking, "What else? What other approaches should I consider?"

On the analysis side, you increase your analytical ability by assigning a data researcher to the project and by asking the team to block out time to attend focus groups and do a quality debrief afterward. (Note, we'll get deeper into analyzing data critically in chapter 7, "The Decision-Making Habit".)

And just like that, your observational powers are magnified.

Pro tip: Build "low-hanging fruit" opportunities for learning into the learning plan. The idea is to make it as easy as possible to just get the learning cycle started, and to get everyone's appetite whetted to learn more. For example, you identify one of your sources of learning as attending a local digital marketing conference—an easy way to get the learning burning.

Now, it's time to **unlearn**. As you're analyzing all the data you've gathered from the variety of sources and considering all the approaches you could take, it's important to:

- let go of preconceived notions and biases
- ditch perspectives and ideas no longer relevant
- identify and challenge assumptions
- drop bad habits getting in the way of moving forward
- discuss opinions different from yours
- listen for understanding (not for convincing others)

This is about opening yourself up as much as possible to new thinking, maximizing your flexibility (it is called learning "agility" after all), all while remaining at ease in the face of the associated ambiguity and uncertainty. To learn, you have to unlearn some things and adapt to all that comes with it.

In the case of the online-only marketing plan, you consciously let go of your belief that only big marketing budgets work, and you challenge your assumption that you can't efficiently reach your target through online-only efforts.

You've been gathering and considering a lot of input, so now you return to the center of the Figure Eight, to being **learning intentional** once again. Whereas initially it was about recognizing *when you need to learn*, this time it's about recognizing *when you need to move forward*, to avoid getting stuck in analysis paralysis, or paralyzed by uncertainty. It's here that you ask, "Have we learned enough to choose a path?" If not, identify those few other learning plan elements. If your learning is sufficient, move to the next phase. Revisiting being learning intentional at this point is essential, because for too many leaders/organizations, this is where learning agility screeches to a grinding halt and paralysis takes over. So, reflect, fortify (only where needed), and move forward.

Going back to our example, you and your team take a pause to reflect on all you've learned so far, and feel confident it's time to move to the next phase.

So, it's time to **take progressive risk**. Research indicates that learning agile leaders take progressive risk: not risk for the sake of it or for thrill seeking, but risk that leads to opportunities and real possibilites.[20] It's about taking all that you've learned, assimilating it, and then moving forward with an approach/solution that stretches you outside your comfort zone (as this is where learning happens, as established in the Doubt Continuum earlier in this chapter). A mindset of stretching feeds a continuous cycle of learning and confidence building. And, by the way, you didn't put all that hard work into learning just to settle for incrementalism, right?

In our example, you decide on a robust online-only marketing approach that breaks new ground, even choosing to cut costs in other parts of your budget to further fuel the exciting new plan.

Then, it's time to **create and recalibrate**. Meaning, channel your learning into a tangible approach or solution that you can put out into the world and keep learning from. A big part of figuring things out is giving the world something to react to, to see if you've truly got it figured out yet. As I read on a building wall on the Facebook campus, *"Don't talk about building it, build it."* Whether it's a new approach, a prototype, a test market, a design, a proposal shared with upper management, or whatever, the point is to convert all the learning into action, and to get feedback on that action. You then learn from the feedback (while showing patience and empathy for the learning process and mistakes made), reflect, recalibrate, make adjustments and improvements, learn some more, and so on (until you really do have it figured out).

Pro tip: Think of mistakes you make along the way as science experiments. See miscues as part of scientific trial and error; part of the process for getting the formula right. In this way, you'll more easily accept mistakes and see failures as learning opportunities. When something goes wrong, you can detach from it (rather than getting overly emotional), seeing the experience like a scientific observer, there to record it in your notebook, certain not to repeat it, curious about what you'll discover in the next experiment. After all, experiments are practice runs in open-mindedness.

One last time to our example. Your online-only plan is really working, but it's not perfect. You keep learning and adjusting along the way, until you have a successful, sustainable, marketing model.

Note that the Figure Eight framework works in a continual, virtuous loop. You start by being intentional, fueling your learning through expanded observational powers, while being careful to unlearn as needed. You return to being intentional to reflect and discern if you've learned enough and if it's time to move forward. You then take progressive risk (which fosters more learning experiences), and move to creating a solution and recalibrating, until it's truly figured out. Then, you return again to being intentional about learning when it comes to the next thing you have to figure out. You've thus applied learning agility to figure something out while developing your learning agility along the way to be even better at figuring things out in the future.

Your First Small Step: Increasing your learning agility is a multistep process that takes particular intention to build. So, download the Figure-It-Out Figure Eight diagram at scott-mautz.com/mentallystrong/templates, and start by getting good at identifying when learning agility will be needed (like at times when you clearly need to learn more to inform the right course of action). You can also assign a "chief learning officer" responsbile for leveraging the Figure Eight to help your team be more intentional about learning.

In Moments of Weakness: The most common breakdown here is skipping the learning cycle altogether because "there isn't time." When you find yourself about to take an uninformed decision/action without making time for the Figure Eight, at least engage in a small part of it. Some learning, and some part of the Figure Eight, is better than none. Then commit to engage in the full Figure-It-Out Figure Eight next time around.

Confidence Habit #6: Engage in Deliberate Practice.

Practice is practice. You either do it, or you don't, right?

Wrong.

Confidence is maximized when you engage in deliberate practice, a special kind of practice that differs from your run-of-the-mill, mindless replication. Specifically, it's practicing with purposeful repetition, focused on incremental improvement, that builds mental muscle memory. It breeds confidence because you know you're improving (you can see/feel it) and because when it's time to actually perform what you're practicing, you don't have to think about it so much; you know your mental muscle memory will kick in. It's a way to put self-regulation on autopilot.

Habit-Building Tool #6: I'll illustrate the Deliberate Drill, the three-step system for engaging in deliberate practice, by walking you through how I practice for one of my keynotes. You can picture yourself doing the same for a big presentation at work, for example, but the system works for anything you want to deliberately practice.

STEP 1: Create a "scaled" routine for reps. You build mental muscle memory through repetition, so it's important to schedule occasions where you can get your reps in and stick to it. It's also important to break down the process you're practicing into smaller parts, deciding when you'll focus on the smaller part, or the whole (i.e., determine the "scale" of each practice session).

For example, my routine is to start practicing my keynote (no matter how many times I've given it) four days in advance of the event. On startup day, I ease into rehearsal by practicing key parts of the talk (like the opening and closing). Three days before, I run through the entire keynote once and also practice key transition points (like when moving from one key slide to the next). Two days before, I go through the entire keynote, twice. One day before, I run through it once, then on the morning of the actual event, I run through an outline of the talk, and drill down only on parts I want extra practice on. After this flow of scheduled, varied-in-scale reps, when it's "go time," the keynote flows from my consciousness without mental strain, freeing me up to focus on nuances in my performance (like dramatic pauses or specific movements on stage).

STEP 2: Catch and cure. This step occurs in the midst of your practice, when you catch your mistakes and try new approaches/

strategies to fix them for incremental improvement. This is as opposed to mindless repetition where you repeatedly rehearse while ignoring your mistakes. If I make an error while practicing my keynote, I either stop and fix it right in the moment, and then continue, or I make a mental note to go back to and address it when I'm done running through the entire thing.

It also helps to have a measurement system in place to know if you're making mistakes as you practice. You can do this in many ways, including having a coach give you feedback during your practice sessions. I measure how I'm doing by the amount of "verbal stumbles" I have to correct, and by timing my rehearsals to ensure I'm finishing on time.

STEP 3: Incorporate improvements. Finally, take the incremental improvements you've made on each individual part you've been practicing and build them into your overall process. The morning of my keynote event, as I'm running through an outline of the entire talk and practicing just key parts, I also make sure to integrate the adjustments I've been making the prior four days.

Your First Small Step: When it's time to practice something important, commit to engaging in deliberate practice, even scheduling such sessions on your calendar (with the words "deliberate practice" written as a mindset reminder). The point is, you're trying to avoid just jumping into mindless, repetition-type practice, which is all too easy to do.

In Moments of Weakness: Practicing stinks. But it's essential for building a habit. When you find yourself being undisciplined in your practice, go back to why you're practicing to begin with. Picture the identity you're trying to build (a polished keynote speaker) or what it would feel like to master the thing you're trying to excel at. Use that inspiration to get back to what it takes to achieve it—a deliberate approach.

Confidence Habit #7: Exude Executive Presence

The more others believe in your leadership, the more your confidence continues to grow, which means they'll believe in you even more, which further feeds your confidence, and so on. Nothing fuels this virtuous cycle like exuding executive presence—the ability to instill confidence in subordinates that you're someone they want to follow, in peers that you're a highly capable, reliable leader, and in senior executives that you have the potential for achieving great things. It's about personal power, not position power. Here's how to make a habit of it.

Habit-Building Tool #7: You'll exude executive presence by following the Integrated Aura model. It's a framework encapsulating the mind, body, heart, and voice elements of your presence, each of which you carefully regulate, all of which interact and interweave to form one cohesive, powerful aura, if tended to properly.

Fig. 4.4 The Integrated Aura model

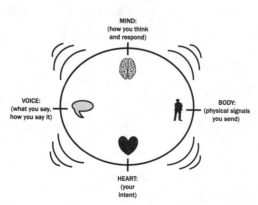

MIND:
(how you think
and respond)

VOICE:
(what you say,
how you say it)

BODY:
(physical signals
you send)

HEART:
(your
intent)

Note that while it's important to regulate each element, executive presence starts with being authentic. This isn't about trying to mindlessly replicate a model of some other person, but starting from a solid core of who you really are, and then being intentional about signals of leadership competency that you send. Let's go through each element, and how to use them in unison to elevate executive presence.

Mind

This is about *how you think* and *respond* when trying to project executive presence. Regarding *how you think*, are you:

- providing context of the "bigger picture"?
- providing long-term perspective?
- considering all stakeholders (and being inclusive)?

The idea is to show up like you're the CEO of your topic. I don't mean veer off into talking about the company vision all the time. I just mean, ask yourself, "What would a CEO's scope of thinking/commentary be on this subject matter?" Mimic that by providing as broad a perspective as you can, when you can.

For example, say you're giving management an update on your project. While relaying the necessary detailed facts about your progress, you also provide a broader viewpoint—how the project is showing promise for supporting the company's overall strategies, how it will help the profit pressure other divisions are under, and how it can inspire future innovation efforts across the company. With this more expansive outlook, you come across as the CEO of your project, able to articulate the necessary details, while providing helpful context, framing, and perspective.

The "mind" element is also about how you *respond* to comments or circumstances. Do you maintain your composure? Are you:

- cool, calm, collected, and respectful, no matter what?
- neither overreacting or underreacting (detaching)?
- staying on track rather than getting thrown off-track?

UCLA Anderson School of Management professor John Ullmen offers smart advice for maintaining your poise in the face of any stressors or pressure you encounter in the moment.[21] That is, *be emotionally proactive.* Meaning, enter your meeting or event with the emotional state in mind that's associated with you at your best.

For example, maybe you feel ready to tackle the world when you feel optimistic. Start off with that emotion, keep it running in the back of your mind, then return to it as quickly as you can when stressors hit and create different, unhelpful emotions. To bridge the gap as you're working your way back to your "helpful emotion," default to calm, cool, and collected until you get there.

It's important to reinforce here that no one said you can't be emotional. It's about (a) proactively using emotions to set a mental tone associated with the best version of you, and (b) not getting emotionally hijacked, instead working your way, calmly, back to helpful emotions.

To illustrate further, back to that project update you're giving. Someone interrupts with a blunt, anger-tinged question about an unfavorable article written about your project (which has nothing to do with your progress update). But you resist firing back with anger, and despite being momentarily thrown off, you default instead to calmly responding. All the while, you're working your way back to optimism, your "at my best" emotion you entered the meeting with.

Body

This is about *physical signals* you send. Are you:
- standing/sitting up straight, shoulders back, head up?
- keeping eye contact?
- uncrossing your arms and removing your hands from your pockets?
- staying still, while using fluid gestures/movements at the right times to emphasize points?
- avoiding exaggerated facial expressions (that make you look juvenile or goofy)?
- eliminating physical barriers between you and the audience, like a laptop or lectern?
- looking professional (rather than unkempt)?
- nodding and tilting your head to show you're listening?

Heart

This is about *your intent*. Are you:
- focused on having a positive impact (doing good rather than looking good)?
- looking after everyone's best interest (rather than yours alone)?
- enthusiastic/energetic about your ability to contribute to the topic, but eager/curious to keep learning?

If you're committed to having a positive impact, as broadly as possible, while focusing on *what's right* as opposed to *being right*, that's executive presence.

If you're pure of intent and others-oriented, you'll be more likely to say the right things, about the right things, in the right way. (Your *int*ent affects your *cont*ent.) That's executive presence.

If you're letting your passion come through regarding the topic at hand, while coming across as humble, curious, and open to being challenged and learning more, that's executive presence.

One last time back to your project update, to illustrate. You energetically talk about substantive problems the project is facing, and the potential solutions on the horizon, all while rewarding and recognizing contributions made by various teammates along the way. You eagerly answer questions, and ask them, to take advantage of the collective knowledge in the room.

Voice

This is about *what you say*, and *how you say it*. Are you:
- speaking firmly, with volume and assuredness, like you're in command?
- speaking clearly, concisely, with good pacing?
- staying on topic?
- answering questions/challenges directly (without being evasive)?
- supporting what you say with facts, data, and well-grounded opinion?

To round out the model, here are the three most commonly asked questions I get about executive presence.

1. *"What if I'm an introvert?"*

Executive presence is not one-size-fits all. It's about showing tailored charisma. Meaning, it's important to show enthusiasm, interest, and optimism—but in a way authentic to you. For example, extroverts can exude charisma with their outgoingness and high energy. Great. But introverts can be charismatic too, by being genuinely interested in others, listening well, asking good questions, and expressing passion for their ideas while being super articulate about why it's a good idea. One of the most "charismatic" leaders I ever worked for had a quiet, calm confidence and energy about her that made you want to run through a brick wall in support. (By the way, if you're soft-spoken, work on projecting your voice just 20 percent louder; it can make a big difference.) The point is, mentally strong leaders exude executive presence, but in ways authentic to who they are.

2. *"What if I don't have all the answers?"*

Executive presence doesn't require omnipotence. In fact, it's enhanced when you're open about what you don't know (and when you unequivocally admit mistakes). For example, think about two leaders: one who stands in front of the organization assuring everyone that she has all the answers, just follow her. The other says there are some things she's still figuring out, and while mistakes have been made along the way, she has learned a lot and it has informed a smart way forward. Which one is more credible? Which are you drawn to? No contest. (The vulnerable one.)

The key is that, even when you're communicating uncertainties, do so with confidence. Wharton research indicates leaders can honestly confess uncertainties without undermining their own credibility.[22]

3. *"How do I show executive presence remotely?"*

Executive presence is more challenging in a remote work world, for certain, but you can still project it by being intentional. Of course, all of the Integrated Aura model in Figure 4.4 still applies. However, pay extra attention to how you're sitting and speaking. Be sure to look at the camera, have a professional-looking backdrop with sufficient lighting, ensure your sound is crisp and clear, and use great visuals for any slides (not just a list of bullet points).

Pro tip: Tape a small picture of a group of people next to your camera lens to remind you to look into the camera (and to remind you to speak with a presence as if you were with them in person). Also, place the camera so you're seen from the waist up. This allows you to use the power of your body gestures to emphasize points (as opposed to people seeing only a "talking head.")

Your First Small Step: Prepare for your next several group meetings by reviewing and practicing the Integrated Aura model. Work your way up to applying it to higher-stakes opportunities for exuding executive presence, like at annual meetings, town hall addresses, or times of crisis, for example.

In Moments of Weakness: Here's the good news. Executive presence is about your presence (duh), which is an ongoing thing. Which means, when you fall off the horse and come across as anything but an in-control exec worth following, you can jump right back on and focus on getting it right the next time. Presence is an accumulation of impressions, not a one-time thing, and anyone can have an "off day." Keep picturing the identity you're striving for—someone others feel confident following/working with/investing in—and focus on that net impression, rather than perfection.

NOTES

1. V. Lipman. May 9, 2017. "Why Confidence is Always a Leader's Best Friend," *Forbes.*
2. P. Aldhous. June 3, 2009. "Humans Prefer Cockiness to Expertise," *New Scientist.*
3. Steve Jobs quotes, goodreads.com.
4. Vaish, A., T. Grossmann, and A. Woodward. 2008. "Not all emotions are created equal: The negativity bias in social-emotional development," *Psychological Bulletin* 134(3): 383–403.
5. Carretié, L., F. Mercado, M. Tapia, and J. A. Hinojosa. 2001. "Emotion, attention, and the 'negativity bias,' studied through event-related potentials," *International Journal of Psychophysiology* 41(1): 75–85.
6. Kross, E., M. G. Berman, W. Mischel, E. E. Smith, and T. D. Wager. March 28, 2011. "Social rejection shares somatosensory representations with physical pain," *PNAS* 108(15).
7. Eleanor Roosevelt quotes, brainyquote.com.
8. Williams, A. "What Make a Critic Tick?" July 4, 2002. www.chicagoreader.com.
9. Koriat, A., S. Lichtenstein, and B. Fischhoff. 1980. "Reasons for confidence," *Journal of Experimental Psychology: Human Learning and Memory* 6(2): 107–18.
10. Brown, B. 2012. *Listening to Shame,* ted.com.

11. Pillay, S. May 16, 2016. "Greater self-acceptance improves emotional well-being," *Harvard Health Blog*, health.harvard.edu.

12. Sirota, M. November 11, 2015. "People-Pleasing Always Backfires," huffpost.com.

13. Moawad, T. February 4, 2020. "It Takes What It Takes," HarperOne.

14. Mautz, S. March 2018. *Find the Fire*, 107–8, AMACOM.

15. Ibid.

16. Stoddard, J. November 1, 2023. "How to Thrive Amid Imposter Syndrome," *Psyche*, psyche.co.

17. McWilliams, A. E. February 25, 2019. "Closing the Confidence Gap: The Importance of Mentors," *Psychology Today*, psychologytoday.com.

18. Charles Swindoll quotes, goodreads.com.

19. Dai, G. 2014 "Fast rising talent: Highly learning agile people get promoted at double speed," kornferry.com.

20. Flaum, J. P., and B. Winkler. June 8, 2015. "Improve Your Ability to Learn," *Harvard Business Review*, hbr.org.

21. Ullmen, J. August 7, 2019. "Developing Executive Presence," *LinkedIn Learning*.

22. Gaertig, C., and J. P. Simmons. April 2018. "Do People Inherently Dislike Uncertain Advice?" *Psychological Science* 29/4: 504–20.

5 The Boldness Habit

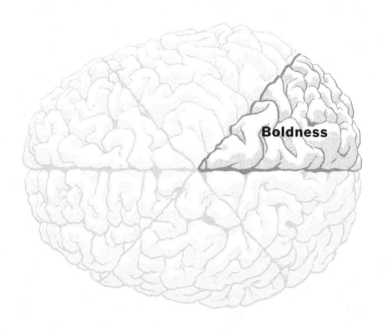

Boldness

I'm guessing you're reading this book for one primary reason. You want to grow. Personally. Professionally. Profoundly, perhaps. You want to grow yourself, your skills, your career, your business, your organization. Your mental strength (of course).

You want to develop something that will eventually lead to something, better.

How about we short-circuit things then, and jump on the fast track in this chapter? You will, because of this truth:

Boldness paves a direct pathway to growth.

It forces you to push your thinking, get out of grooves, press past discomfort. It sparks innovation, requires risk taking, and necessitates change. All of which blazes a path leading straight to growth. It's why it's one of the six tests of leadership that most directly links to remarkable achievement (as my research has shown), and necessitates the ability to regulate your emotions, thoughts, and behaviors. After all, you don't push limits, get unstuck, and blow by unease easily. It takes self-discipline and courage, like Kurt, the school administrator from chapter 1, who sparked change in parent-teacher relationships, had in abundance. Kurt did what you'll be able to do after accessing the tools in this chapter. Think big, shake up unhelpful old narratives, embolden smart risks, and embrace and lead change, with passionate conviction.

So, let's fortify your mental strength in a way that helps you push people, organizations, and yourself beyond normal limits, to something worthwhile. To outstanding accomplishment.

Boldness Habit #1: Think Big

Boldness and pushing limits require bigness. Of belief. Of intention. Of action. Of thought.

That last one is a common refrain. How many times have you heard, "We've got to think bigger!" Of course, who wouldn't like to aim higher, imagine on a grander scale, challenge convention, push limits, and achieve more? But there's one tiny little problem. Or, more accurately, a big problem.

How *exactly* do you think big?

That's what you're about to learn/practice.

An important clarification first. Thinking big does not require you to have an absolutely brilliant idea or a massive IQ. It's not an unobtainable skill reserved only for the brainiest, boldest entrepreneurs. It's more about having the right frame of mind, and habits, in place, and your skill for self-regulating emotions, thoughts, behaviors (and beliefs), raring to go. Nor is thinking big about being delusional (not grounded in reality). It *is* about stretching the limits of what you think is possible relative to your current beliefs. It *is* about inviting big, meaningful things into your professional (and personal) life and taking active control.

And it *is* about following the science-backed, seven-step process for thinking big that follows. Big things await!

Habit-Building Tool #1: This is the most multistep tool in this book, but with practice, it will become second nature (i.e., a habit). Here's the Think Big Blueprint, a seven-step process for habitually thinking big.

Step 1: Give yourself permission to dream big. One of the most common frustrations I hear from leaders is that there's no time to step back and think about strategy—they're too busy trying to keep up with execution and the day-to-day. It's the same thing when it comes to dreaming big, and thinking big. "Who's got the time, especially with all I have on my plate right now?" we tell ourselves. And it's made worse by another complication. We slip into feeling we don't have the right to dream big and think big. We reason, "Big things happen for other people, not people like me. Realistically . . ." So, you never chase that big thought down.

But if you want to dream big and think big, you've first got to *give yourself permission* to do so. You must believe that it's worth your time to think big, that you're qualified to do so, and that it will lead to an expanded world of possibilities for you. There's simply no other place to start.

I humbly offer this. I was blessed to have successfully run four of Procter & Gamble's biggest multibillion-dollar businesses. The common denominator across all four for me was my willingness to self-regulate away from limiting thoughts and beliefs—to dream, and think, big. From pushing the Gain laundry detergent brand past a billion in sales for the first time, to bringing the largest-selling prescription drug on the planet (at the time) over the counter (Prilosec), to achieving share gains no one thought possible on the Dawn and Cascade dish detergent brands, to achieving astounding things on two of the cornerstone brands of the company (Pampers and Charmin)—permission made it possible. The permission I gave myself, and my team, to dream, and think, big.

Now, no one said you should create completely unrealistic visions of grandeur. Think about thinking big on a continuum, the Big Thinking Continuum, which has four zones, as you can see in Figure 5.1.

Fig. 5.1 The Big Thinking Continuum

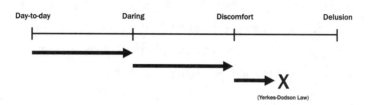

(Yerkes-Dodson Law)

I'll explain. It's about finding the sweet spot across these four zones. Thinking big means pushing past your day-to-day routine thinking, to be daring, and even stretching your-self beyond daring into unfamiliar territory, all the way to the point of discomfort, and a bit beyond. But not all the way to delusion. It's in this ideal spot, marked by the "X" in Figure 5.1, that big thinking, and big things, happen. In fact, this spot is the manifestation of what's known as the Yerkes-Dodson Law. The rule, a seminal psychology finding, says that peak performance happens in a specific circumstance: when you're in a state of optimal anxiety and discomfort.

So, if you're thinking "small" and thus engaging in endeavors not challenging enough, your stress level is too low, your full abilities aren't stimulated, and performance suffers. Think unreasonably "big" and engage in absurdly difficult endeavors, your stress level is too high, which becomes debilitating, and again, performance suffers.[1]

The good news is, your body will tell you when you're in the ideal state. For example, you might feel a pit in your stomach right before you try something that makes you nervous. But remember, that sensation isn't there to scare you; it's there to tell you that something must be worth it, *or you'd be feeling nothing.* Discomfort is a sign that you're accessing exciting possibilities and potential outcomes that you haven't accessed yet.

So how do you know, though, when you've strayed into debilitating, delusional territory? When the goals you're setting are ignoring basic truths, or when they require overcoming a realistically insurmountable number of barriers.

For example, I can think big all I want about my dream of becoming a professional baseball player, but with my lack of talent and athleticism, and my lack of training, at my age, it's not going to happen (and did I mention my lack of athleticism?). I'd frustrate myself to the point of having a breakdown. The point is not to discourage big thoughts, it's to put helpful boundaries on them, so your time spent thinking big is productive, creates *real* possibilities, and ultimately leads to peak performance.

So, give yourself permission to dream and think big, while putting a few helpful guardrails in place.

Step 2: Uncover the beliefs holding you back. Everyone has beliefs—but you might not realize how deeply they can influence you. We use beliefs to help us relate to the world around us. Beliefs (which aren't facts, per se) are often assumptions based on past experiences or convictions that something is true. Over time, these assumptions and convictions alter our behaviors, for better or worse.

If they're limiting beliefs, it's for the worse. And if they're limiting beliefs, they're often ingrained within you, so it's important to bring them to the surface to be dealt with. Here's how.

Think about a stretching goal you'd really like to achieve, but you've hesitated to take that first step toward. Let's use a more personal example this time—after all, mental strength applies to self-leadership, as well as leadership of others. Say you want to write a book and get it published, but you don't feel like you can actually pull it off. When you start feeling uncertainty and discomfort in thinking about that goal, that's your limiting beliefs emerging. To fully expose them, ask yourself these four questions:

1. *What resistance am I feeling inside while thinking about achieving this goal? Why do I think it's too difficult?* Regarding writing a book, you might say, "It's hard, a few friends tried, then gave up," or "I've seen the statistics on how many people actually get published." Keep in mind, you don't have to overcome any of this yet; we're just identifying limiting beliefs at this point.

2. *What assumptions am I making? Am I making global assumptions: "I am . . .", "Life is . . .", "People are . . .", "Things like this . . ."* Maybe you're assuming no one wants to read what you'd have to write, or you're assuming, "Things like this, getting published, just don't happen for people like me."

3. *What stories am I telling myself?* We can get caught up in our own unhelpful narratives that pull us off course from accomplishing something we'd love to accomplish. In our example, maybe your story is "I can see myself working so hard to write a manuscript, but then getting rejected by publisher after publisher." Not a helpful narrative if you're trying to think big and achieve big.

4. *What labels am I applying to myself that are holding me back?* Even beyond unhelpful stories you tell yourself, you can label yourself in a way that feels definitive and unfairly categorizes you. You tell yourself, "I'm a loser, nothing big I shoot for ever works out. Why should

I bother trying to write a book?" A label that needs to be torn off.

When you've finished answering these questions, step back and pause for a moment. You've just brought your underlying limiting beliefs to light. By the way, make sure you *name* those underlying beliefs. When you name them, and say them out loud, they begin to lose their power over you. For example, with our getting published example, you name, and say out loud, the underlying limiting belief that you're just not talented enough to write a book.

As you'll see in the next step, it's time to trade those limiting beliefs for empowering beliefs.

Step 3: Replace the beliefs holding you back. Limiting beliefs are toxic. But you hold on to them because they serve a purpose. They protect you from experiencing pain—the pain of rejection, disappointment, humiliation, etc.

This step is about exchanging your limiting beliefs for higher value, empowering beliefs.

To do so, you must accept that your limiting belief is not valid, or at least that its value is far outweighed by the new, empowering belief.

And to do that, question each of your limiting beliefs. Specifically, ask these four questions:

1. *How did I form this limiting belief?* Does it trace back to your childhood, to unhelpful advice you got, or to a domineering authority figure? Once you've identified the source, challenge its validity. For example, say you have a limiting belief that you're just not smart enough to figure out how to achieve a big goal that interests

you. Upon reflection, you trace it back to a toxic boss who never felt anything was good enough and who always made you feel small. In this new light and context, you decide his opinion doesn't matter and that it will no longer hold you back.

2. *Would people who know me question the validity of my limiting belief? Would superachievers question it?* (Like famous entrepreneurs, professional athletes, or Academy Award–winning actors.) Super-successful people likely wouldn't buy the limitation you've placed on yourself, because they wouldn't be where they are if they had similar beliefs. Friends would likely tell you, "You're selling yourself short, again."

3. *Was there a time when I didn't believe this? Why?* Limiting beliefs can quietly take over and distort the truth, before you realize it. For example, you might be revisiting a limiting belief that you're not good at making friends, when you suddenly remember how you were surrounded by them in college or university.

4. *What are the consequences of sticking with this limiting belief?* You can't let your limiting beliefs carry on unchecked. You must consider what those beliefs are costing you and what could be true if you'd let them go. To illustrate, you come to realize that if you continue believing that you'll never get published, you'll never have a book as the centerpiece of a business that could bring you financial independence.

Okay, so you've considered these four questions and see that the validity of your limiting beliefs doesn't hold up, and that the cost of holding on to them is too high.

This is a breakthrough moment.

It's time to leave what limits you behind and name a replacement empowering belief for each of your limiting beliefs. It's time to conduct a Belief Exchange.

On an index card, write in one column your old, limiting beliefs, and next to it, the empowering beliefs you're exchanging them for. Here's an example:

Fig. 5.2 Belief Exchange

LIMITING BELIEF	EMPOWERING BELIEF
"I'm not good enough."	"I have all the ability I need to succeed."
"Great things don't happen to people like me."	"Great things happen to people who put in the work."

1. How will this new belief help me reach my goals?
2. How will it help me in the short/long-term?
3. What about this new belief energizes me?

You write down your limiting belief of "I'm not good enough," and, having overturned its validity, you replace it with something empowering: "I have all the ability I need to succeed."

You write down your limiting belief of "Great things don't happen to people like me," and, having overturned its validity as well, you replace it with, "Great things happen to people who put in the work."

Confirm the value of your replacement empowering beliefs by asking yourself:

1. *How will this new belief help me reach my goals?*
2. *How will this new belief help me in the short and long term?*
3. *What about this new belief energizes me?*

Rework the language of your empowering beliefs as needed, until the answers to these three questions feel good to you. Then, keep the card you've created handy, continually reviewing it until your new empowering beliefs become ingrained. Along the way, recognize when you're not honoring the exchange and you're slipping back into an old, limiting belief.

Bottom line with this step, replace *limiting* with *empowering*, and the sky's the limit!

Step 4: Uncover the behaviors holding you back. We all engage in limiting behaviors—quite often without realizing we're doing it and most often without recognizing the negative impact it has.

Expose *your* limiting behaviors by answering the Six to Fix—six questions that uncover the most common self-manufactured behaviors that limit your perception and potential.[2]

1. *What excuses am I making that are holding me back?*
   Excuses become a source of comfort and justification; they keep you from taking the action you must take to accomplish something you want to achieve. For example, you want to apply for that exciting new role at work, but you convince yourself that you just don't have the time to prepare for interviews. An excuse that's holding you back from big thinking, big actions, and big potential.

2. *What negativity am I projecting that's holding me back?*
   The fuel of big thinking is positivity and possibility. Engaging in negativity is like throwing a big, wet blanket on all of that.

3. *What standards am I setting too low that are holding me back?* Michelangelo said, "The greater danger for most of us lies not in setting our aim too high and falling short, but in setting our aim too low, and achieving our mark."[3] I had a friend who set a goal of just keeping her job—even though she didn't like it. She was interested in a different job in a different part of the company, but never applied for it because she figured she was lucky to still have a job, and that was good enough. Sometimes, good enough is not good enough.

4. *Am I engaging in procrastination or perfectionism that's holding me back?* These are the silent killers of big thinking. We put off doing the hard work of big thinking, telling ourselves that we'll get to it later, or that the conditions aren't exactly right for it. With every delay, big thinking quietly, incrementally, drifts further and further away, pulling you deeper and deeper under a comforting blanket of mediocrity. (You'll get more help with procrastination and perfectionism in chapter 8, "The Goal-Focus Habit.")

5. *Am I letting fear hold me back?* Meaning, fear of failure, fear of criticism, or fear of change. Regarding fear of failure and/or criticism, remember from chapter 4 that there's only three ways to actually fail: when you quit, don't improve, or never try, and that anything worth doing attracts admiration *and* criticism. Regarding change, as we'll dive into later in this chapter, know that you simply can't get to what you yearn to be by remaining what you are.

6. *What other bad habits are limiting my perception or potential?* Do you have any bad habits that are directly

interfering with your ability to think big or make big things happen? For example, common bad habits here include overthinking everything so you rarely take worthy risks, comparing yourself to others so you feel small and unworthy of big things, or not listening to others so you have only your own perspective to work from.

When you've finished writing your answers down, step back and reflect on them, then circle all the limiting behaviors you're engaging in. Be sure to name them and say them out loud, so you can begin to break the hold they have over you.

And then you're ready for another exchange, in the next step, where we replace limiting with limitless.

Step 5: Replace the behaviors holding you back. Okay, so you've identified your limiting behaviors. Feels good to call them out, right? Well, now we're going to put them out, of service. Time to conduct a Behavior Exchange.

On an index card, or anything you can keep handy, write in one column your old, limiting behaviors, and next to them, the empowering behavior you're exchanging it for. For example:

Fig. 5.3 Behavior Exchange

LIMITING BEHAVIOR	EMPOWERING BEHAVIOR
Comparing to others and feeling deflated	"I'll compare only to who I was yesterday and if I'm improving or not."
Using the excuse that I'm not ready yet	"I'll put my best foot forward, learn, and adapt."

1. How will this new behavior help me reach my goals?
2. How will it help me in the short/long-term?
3. What about this new behavior energizes me?

Let's say you write down your limiting behavior of "Comparing to others and feeling deflated," and replace it with an empowering alternative: "I'll compare only to who I was yesterday and if I'm improving or not."

You write down your limiting behavior of "Using the excuse that I'm not ready yet," and replace it with a promising "I'll put my best foot forward, learn, and adapt."

Now, confirm the value of your replacement empowering behaviors by asking yourself:

1. *How will this new behavior help me reach my goals?*
2. *How will it help me in the short and long term?*
3. *What about this new behavior energizes me?*

Excitement should be building now for your new set of uplifting actions. Keep the index card accessible and keep practicing these new empowering behaviors, repeatedly. Recognize when you slip back into an old limiting behavior, and just exchange it for the new one. Repeat this pattern until your empowering behaviors become an energizing habit.

Step 6: Spark big thinking with big thoughts. You now have a foundation of empowering beliefs and behaviors that will fuel a big thinking mindset. Now it's time to get specific on how to spark big thinking. You do so by using the Smart Star. It illuminates five ways to spark big, bright thinking, and thus big impact.

Fig. 5.4 The Smart Star

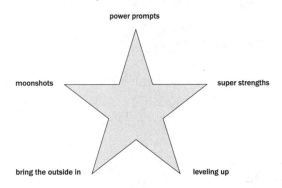

power prompts

moonshots   super strengths

bring the outside in   leveling up

Let's go through each point of the star.

Power prompts. These are empowering questions to ask, designed to spark big thinking. For example:

What's a big problem worth solving? Big problems equal big opportunities.

What would competitors be afraid we'd do? This can expose big ideas that take advantage of a competitor's weakness.

How can we reimagine the category we compete in? I'll explain. Tide laundry detergent, a huge US brand, decided they're not in the laundry detergent business. They're in the clothing care business, a much broader category.[4] This freed them to create a chain of Tide Dry Cleaner stores, and to launch products that didn't just wash your clothes; they preserved and enhanced them. It's about asking, what's the business you *really* compete in? How might you reimagine the category you're in to open up more opportunity?

All these prompts are intended to stimulate out-of-the-box thinking, focused on what's possible. Here's a complete set of power prompts you can use with your team, or on your own, to get the big thinking cranking.

(Note: for any of these prompts, you can use "I" or "we")

- How can we do this better than anyone else?
- How can we think more creatively about this?
- How can we take this to another level?
- What can only I lead?
- How can I work *on* a system rather than *in* a system?
- How can I be the champion for change sorely needed?
- How can I remove a barrier (or help solve a circumstance)?
- How can I fill an unmet need or do a deed that needs doing?
- What's a big problem worth solving?
- How can we reimagine the category we compete in?
- What legacy could I leave?
- How can I fulfill my purpose?
- If I knew I wouldn't fail, what would I try?
- What would take the business/organization to another level?
- What would I be proud to tell others I lead?
- What would competitors be afraid we'd do?
- What could I put in place that will outlast me?
- What if?

Super strengths. What are you really good at? A strength you can strengthen to accomplish things worth accomplishing?

For example, say your team is really good at generating new product ideas. Now imagine if you leveraged this strength and created a never-been-done-in-your-company, fast-track process to turn more of those ideas into real marketplace products, quickly.

The beauty of building from your super strengths is that it's a low-resistance form of big thinking. You face fewer barriers to making "big" happen, because you're operating from a place of strength.

Leveling up. This simply means taking the time to study next-level success stories: people or organizations succeeding at what you're trying to succeed at (or something similar), at a level well above where you're at. This can spur big thinking, or at least inspire you to set lofty targets you know are achievable, because someone else is already doing what you aspire to do. As an example, one college university client of mine had six staff members spend an entire month studying the top twenty MBA programs in the country, looking for themes and best practices they could learn from to inspire the redesign of their own MBA program.

Bring the outside in. Meaning, bring in people outside your group to offer fresh perspective, to challenge convention, and to question your way of doing things. A little healthy tension here can get you outside of your norm and stimulate big thoughts that you couldn't have generated otherwise.

Moonshots. Inspired by a visionary innovation group at Google called the "X" Company (not to be confused with the company formerly known as Twitter), a moonshot is the idea of aiming for a tenfold increase in something, versus a 10 percent increase.[5] In other words, it's about challenging incrementalism. One of the biggest barriers to thinking big is that we tend to brainstorm ideas that are just slight evolutions of ideas that already exist; tweaking something to get that small, incremental, 10 percent more.

A moonshot idea, named after president John F. Kennedy's push to land a man on the moon,[6] is meant to inspire big thinking by setting an audacious goal. Note, I'm not suggesting to set seemingly impossible goals that teeter into delusional (as is the true, admirable spirit of how the "X" Company thinks of moonshots). I'm talking about snapping out of incrementalism by setting a truly ambitious goal that, while daunting, seems possible, and that knowing, even if you get only halfway there, would still be game-changing progress.

So, you've got the Smart Star to spark big thinking. Now let's convert big thinking into big outcomes.

Step 7: Make big happen. Equipped now with a great process for thinking big, it's time to make big happen. Here are four tips to help convert all that big thinking into big outcomes.

1. **Develop the attributes of big thinkers.** If you study big thinkers over history, and I have, many exhibit a specific, finite set of characteristics: passion, courage, curiosity, optimism, and persistence. Ask yourself, "How can I make these a habit?" The head of innovation at a huge company I keynoted for had these five attributes printed on a poster and plastered everywhere in their labs. The goal was to encourage her team to see their big, innovative, lab-created ideas all the way through to the actual marketplace.

2. **Ask, "What must be true to succeed?"** This helps you isolate all the key challenges and tensions you'll need to solve if you want to make that big idea a big success. For example, say your team has the idea of launching the first ever green widget. As you ask, "What must be true to succeed?" you pinpoint that you must have access to green paint, which is currently hard to come by. Put that in the problem list to overcome. You get the idea; asking this helps you gain understanding of all the hills to climb, which allows you to organize and deploy your efforts and resources accordingly.

3. **Run fast at all the hardest parts.** The idea here is simple—make quick progress on the biggest parts of the biggest challenges that you're facing.[7] The work of converting big ideas into reality often collapses when the team takes on the biggest barriers too late. By then, resources might be depleted, energy might be lower, or it's too late in the development cycle. Better to make some early progress on tearing down those biggest barriers, which also builds up confidence that you can, indeed, make that big idea happen. To illustrate, a client company of mine in the insurance industry had a big idea for an innovative offering to an underserved population, and wanted to get it to market before competitors recognized the opportunity. They quickly identified the hardest parts: getting regulatory approval, and getting all their agents convinced the offering was a priority. They ran hard at those parts first, identifying and overcoming a number of substantial barriers that would have sunk the project if they were uncovered later in the development life cycle.

4. **Remember, everything starts small.** Microsoft, Amazon, Google, and Apple all started in garages. Rome wasn't built in a day, as the saying goes. It started as a few small hillside villages and took a long time thereafter to reach its full glory. The point is, thinking big doesn't mean that big things happen overnight. It takes time, attention, patience, and discipline. So many big things never come to fruition because they fall victim to a short-term approach. As Microsoft founder Bill Gates said, "Most people overestimate what they can do in one year, and underestimate what they can do in

ten."[8] I'm not saying you can't accomplish wonders in a year, just that it usually takes a longer-term view of things to get to the big thing you've envisioned. Just remember, from small beginnings come great things.

Now, let's look at what *not* to do to make big things happen. Here are three key things to avoid.

1. **Don't be unshakable in your beliefs and behaviors.** Wait, didn't we just talk earlier in this chapter about the importance of leaving behind limiting beliefs and behaviors and exchanging them for empowering ones—and then sticking to them? We did. And you should indeed make a habit of those new, motivating practices. But at the same time, you have to be a bit bendable; willing to adjust your approach based on new information and realities that emerge along the way.

For example, say you've exchanged your limiting behavior of being too negative for empowering behaviors of optimism and positivity. You're applying this new practice at work in pursuit of a big vision to be the first to launch an innovative new product. But along the way, you discover several problems with the product itself, and that the target audience isn't as big as believed. I'm not saying go negative again and abandon your big vision, but it requires tempering your optimism, addressing the issues, and adjusting expectations.

The ability to adjust on the fly and think realistically and flexibly about what you're aiming for, and how to achieve it, is critical to succeed at thinking big and making big happen.

2. **Don't confuse big thinking with wishful thinking.** This can happen in a few ways. You have a big idea, and then jump into executing it too soon, without thinking through all the barriers to overcome, what has to be true to make that big idea work, or without being ready to put in the work it will take. That's wishful thinking—to be avoided.

As it is when, in your desire to be persistent in making big happen, you blow by red lights signaling that something isn't working, and keep repeating what you're doing, hoping it leads to a different outcome. Also, wishful thinking.

That said, be careful of this last one, too.

3. **Don't move too slow.** In an attempt to be careful so you can improve the probability of achieving that big goal, there is such a thing as going too slow. Quite often, making big things happen requires working at the speed of a startup. Generate an idea, create a prototype for it, get it in the "marketplace" (whatever that is in your situation), then keep, cure, or kill the idea. Good big ideas can't wait. Bad big ideas can't wait to be killed.

Now, I'm not saying every big thought must be progressed at the speed of light; you'll know which ones require time, and for which ones the timing is as soon as possible. I'm just encouraging you to be intentional about setting the pace required to make *your* big happen.

There you have it: the Think Big Blueprint, a seven-step process for increasing your mental strength by knowing how to think bigger, and produce bigger outcomes. Put in the work to put it to work for you.

Your First Small Step: This is an involved habit to build, so start by reviewing and internalizing what each of the seven steps are. To make it easier to conduct the belief and behavior exchanges (Steps 2–5), download the corresponding blank templates at scottmautz.com/mentallystrong/templates. Also, think about the possibilities of going through this seven-step process with your entire team. Schedule time to do just that. Pair it with the time of year when you start thinking about next year's goals/plans, or any time it's time to make big things happen.

In Moments of Weakness: There are plenty of places to break down along the way in the process of thinking big, and that's okay. The key is to recognize when you're struggling a bit, keep returning to a "push limits spirit," and keep moving forward through each of the seven steps. You don't have to be flawless in executing each step to get tremendous benefit out of the process.

Boldness Habit #2: Change the Group Narrative

Think of your organization as a field of shimmering wheat. Imagine you're in a helicopter looking down on it, and from a distance, you see a swath, a path, cut through a portion of the field: ugly, dark, oft-traveled. That well-worn track represents something quietly insidious, a shortcut to status quo.

I'm referring to worn-out narratives, old tapes. Stories entire groups cling to that become a form of learned helplessness. It's a particularly nasty version of limiting beliefs and behaviors because it's shared and reinforced collectively, through conjecture, taking on a life of its own. The opposite of boldness, it's blandness.

> *"We've tried before, it won't work."*
> *"We don't have enough resources."*
> *"We'll never get approval."*
> *"We've never gotten past this barrier."*
> *"We can't do it because . . ."*
> *"This is just how it is."*

Old narratives exist because they serve a purpose, to protect people from potential failure, and free them from blame. And they become bigger than life when nobody challenges them. The stories get adopted as attitudes, which lead to beliefs, which become convictions, which create behaviors, which form habits. And few things are more difficult than breaking a bad habit, especially one that entire groups of people have subscribed to. Here's what to do.

Habit-Building Tool #2: This tool is a cousin of the Think Big Blueprint previously detailed, meant for a specific scenario: when a group is being held back by unhelpful old narratives/tapes, and you need them to quickly change course. It's meant to help you flip the script; to get everyone off of the old, unhelpful story, and write a new, more promising one. To get some boldness back in play.

To flip the script, use the Flip the COIN exercise. COIN is an acronym that stands for the following:

Challenge assumptions
Open minds to introspection
Introduce new information/perspective

Navigate underlying emotion (i.e., the *real* reason they're clinging to the old story)

To illustrate, here's an example of how one mentally strong leader in the industrial chemicals industry (we'll call her Michelle) used this exercise to great effect, letter by letter.

Challenge assumptions: Michelle entered her new sales director job greeted by a sales group that kept playing the old tape, *"We'll never crack that market you're asking about. Our competitor is too entrenched, and has been for years."* She asked the group to list all the reasons they believed this to be true, so they could collectively, objectively, discern hard fact from assumption. She then challenged each assumption.

Open minds to introspection: At the same time, Michelle asked each person to introspectively consider *what their role has been in perpetuating the assumption.* This is critical, as you can't change a story until the storytellers acknowledge the supporting storylines they've been writing. Said another way, you'll stay stuck until everyone ditches individual biases that collectively contribute to being stuck in the first place. The point is not to blame, but to unbind. In this case, one sales manager realized he had been inadvertently scaring away eager new hires from pursuing the potential market, just by constantly talking of it as "uncrackable." So, he stopped. Michelle also asked, "What must be true for the opposite of this assumption to be true?" thus opening up further introspection.

Introduce new information/perspective: She then brought in a customer team from a different industry to share an inspiring story; they had a 30 percent share in a market that, just two years prior, was completely monopolized by the industry's "eight-hundred-pound gorilla." Their story opened up minds to alternative approaches, and sparked energy for a bold, new narrative, and a plan to deliver it.

Navigate underlying emotion: All the while, Michelle paid attention to emotional undercurrents—the *real* reason the team was holding so tightly to the old story. It turns out the group had tried before to crack the market in question, several times, and had been severely rebuffed, by two other sales directors, each time they failed. So they were, understandably, reluctant. Understanding this, she created assurances (with substance to them) that this time would be different. They ultimately did crack the market, garnering impressive market share. It was a COIN flip that had everyone heads-over-tails about the results.

Your First Small Step: As you begin working to flip the script, remember that the old, unproductive narrative is likely deeply ingrained. Thus, begin your efforts entrenched in empathy (especially when challenging assumptions). And be ready to articulate up front exactly why the old story is so damaging if it persists.

In Moments of Weakness: People stumble here most often when asked to be truly introspective about why the old story still persists; when asked to identify their part in it, and how they might change it for the better. If this happens, be encouraging, letting them know they won't be judged, that it's okay to be vulnerable, that you're only interested in getting unstuck. Reinforce why status quo is a problem, and all the good that will come from flipping the script. Otherwise the old way will never go away.

Boldness Habit #3: Foster a Risk-Taking Spirit

Fueling a risk-taking spirit, as opposed to getting by without rocking the boat, is how limits get pushed, and possibilities push through. It's how you thrive rather than survive. It's how you achieve. Mentally strong leaders know this and, using discipline and savvy, create a culture of courage rather than caution. Now you can too.

Habit-Building Tool #3: Having studied hundreds of leaders who successfully created a risk-taking culture, where people truly believed risk taking was welcome, celebrated, and even expected, I can share with you an important insight. You foster a risk-taking spirit when you do two things in particular: send the right signals, and impede the wrong impulses.[9] It's so critical, it's illustrated in Figure 5.5:

Fig. 5.5 Fostering a Risk-Taking Spirit

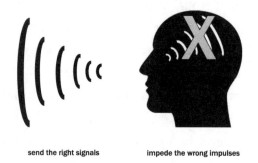

send the right signals   impede the wrong impulses

It's all too easy to send the wrong signals on the risk-taking front; you see it all the time. The manager talks a good game about the need to take risks, but when you do, and it doesn't work out, a lack of tolerance for failure arises, finger-pointing starts, and blame becomes the focus. The words don't match the pictures. In fact, when Harvard researcher Amy Edmondson asked executives how many failures in their organization were truly blameworthy, they answered between 2 to 5 percent. When asked how many failures were *treated* as blameworthy, the range shot up to 70 to 90 percent.[10] Blame then turns into other forms of punishment, none of which send the right signal about risk taking.

At the same time, internal forces within ourselves poison our risk-taking temperament. Natural impulses kick in, dating back to cavepeople times, when risks equaled a threat to our survival. Impulses that overcorrect, not just keeping you from doing really dumb, potentially life-threatening things, but that also keep you from taking smart risks that push limits in good ways.

Follow three strategies each for *sending the right signals* and *impeding the wrong impulses*, and you'll be a bold, mentally strong leader fostering a strong risk-taking culture.

SEND THE RIGHT SIGNALS

1. **Establish the rules of risk taking.** One client of mine in the casino industry described an interesting problem. They were having a throughput issue with one game in particular. Meaning, the ratio of people standing around watching the game, clogging up floor traffic, not spending any money, to people actually stepping up to put their money down and play the

game was way out of whack. Thus, a throughput problem. Which game?

Craps. If you've seen a craps table, you know it's intimidating because it looks complicated—the rules of the game aren't obvious. So, people are reluctant to step up and "roll the dice." Literally. If you don't understand the rules, why take the risk?

Meanwhile, back at work, people don't take risks either. Why?

Because they don't understand the rules—of risk taking.

So, to send a clear signal that risk taking is wanted, *establish the rules of risk taking.* The casino established the rules of risk taking by instituting craps training sessions. You could sign up with a group of friends to play craps for free, with fake casino money (at a table off the main traffic pattern). You'd learn the rules of the game, and thus the rules in play as you risk your money, without actually risking anything.

For you, back at work, establishing the rules of risk taking means fostering conversations about risk taking—asking, and/or answering, questions that would help define the rules. There's no risk to that, and it's the most direct way to get clear on the rules. What follows is a list of twenty questions to do just that: twenty questions you should be able to answer, if asked, that will help define the rules of risk taking. (You could also ask your boss these questions, if you're unclear on the rules.) It's about increasing boldness by decreasing degrees of uncertainty.

- What constitutes a good risk?
- What constitutes a bad risk?
- What happens if I take a risk and fail?
- What happens if I take a risk and succeed?
- What assumptions need to be true to make the risk one worth taking?
- What resources must be in place to help me succeed with the risk?
- Who needs to be comfortable with a risk I want to take?
- What information is needed to create comfort with taking this risk?
- What information is needed to demonstrate the risk is worth taking? (i.e., what's needed to "make the case" for taking that risk)
- What's the worst thing that could happen with this risk, and is it acceptable?
- What's the best thing that could happen with this risk, and is it exciting enough?
- What's the most likely thing to happen with this risk, and is it worth the effort?
- What precedent exists that informs this risk, and/or is precedent necessary to take it?
- What happens if you don't take this risk, and is it compelling enough to warrant taking it?
- What communication loops are needed to keep the manager up to speed as the risk is undertaken? (Relatedly, what other processes need to be in place to increase comfort level for taking the risk?)
- What are the milestones for success the manager would need to see along the way once the risk is taken? (i.e., what are the leading indicators that the risk is going to pan out)
- What depth of backup plan is required if the risk doesn't pan out?
- What type of personal growth would you/the team gain in taking this risk?

> - Would our competitors take this risk?
> - Would our competitors fear the successful outcome for us from having taken this risk?

Even in a truly risk-averse environment, this discussion can open up degrees of freedom. For example, if you asked a risk averse manager, "What are the rules of risk taking?" they wouldn't say: "Well, the rules of risk taking are, just don't take any. Ever." Who would say that? No one. It's about getting to a place where it's mutually understood and accepted what needs to be true to take risks.

2. **Ask for steps and leaps.** Acknowledge what you don't know, then bridge that knowledge gap with both steps and leaps. Meaning, fill in what you don't know by committing to learning, experimenting, adapting, and adjusting, one *step* at a time, along the way. At the same time, place a few bets, a few calculated *leaps* right into the face of the unknown, all in the name of "advancing the cause." Continually using the language of expecting steps and leaps sends a clear signal that smart risk taking is expected.

To illustrate, say you want to substantially advance the mission of your nonprofit, so that it's directly, meaningfully, impacting three times the number of constituents that it does today. You ask your team to take steps and leaps. The steps being, do basic research on what the targeted population needs most, and identify the biggest barriers to providing it for them. You also ask for a leap, a big bet, where you coordinate a donation drive to fund a new community center that will dramatically improve outreach.

3. **Celebrate "failed" risks.** Nothing sends a clearer signal about the behavior you want than celebrating the behavior you want. I've seen numerous clients hold "failure parties," where they got together to celebrate what was learned; what was positive about a risk that fell short. It doesn't have to be grandiose gestures; just the inversion of seeing failure heralded rather than punished makes quite an imprint. Note, I'm not talking here about easing up on high standards for performance. It's about reframing the definition of performance. Yes, success is ultimately about a successful end result, but it requires different kinds of "micro-successes" (i.e., learning birthed from failures) along the way.

IMPEDE THE WRONG IMPULSES

1. **Identify and challenge irrational risk-avoiding behaviors.** The instinct to resist risks can lead to irrational, risk-averse behaviors over time. For example, maybe you have an excessive need for certainty, an outsized fear of failure, or an unreasonable need to play it safe. You might avoid risks because you're overly concerned about looking foolish, have an overwhelming need for control, or have unrealistic expectations of what a successful risk looks like. Identify your insecurities and irrational, risk-avoiding behaviors, and commit to overcome them, so that you can be a role-model risk-taker for your organization. Or work with

your team to expose and overcome their irrational, risk-avoiding behaviors.

Pro tip: As I shared in *Leading from the Middle*, here's an effective rallying cry, or mantra, to help you resist this unhelpful impulse. Believe that one of your primary responsibilities as a (mentally strong) leader is to *assist success versus avoid failure.*[11] Write it down on top of every meeting agenda if it helps. If you act like you're assisting success, you're the embodiment of boldness, support, and empowerment. If you act like you're avoiding failure, you micromanage, you're indecisive, you aren't proactive and forward thinking, you're too conservative, unwilling to take risks.

2. **Resist the "systemic no."** Robert Goldberg, former managing director of the pioneer incubator Idealab, noted that in large organizations, just one of fifty managers could resist an idea, and in doing so, kill it.[12] To protect against this phenomenon, Amazon (in its earlier days) practiced the "institutional yes." If an employee presented a new idea to a manager, they had to default to "yes," or robustly articulate (often in writing) why they shouldn't do it.[13] You don't have to go this far—the point is to create tension to avoid defaulting to "no." Indeed, the biggest risk to accomplishing your big goal is often to *not* take smart, calculated risks.

It also helps here to get the math right. Meaning, as research from the University of Georgia shows, we consistently overestimate the negative consequences of taking a risk, while discounting the cost of doing nothing.[14] That's why one of my clients onboards new employees with an exercise where they assess potential negative consequences of a risk, *and* the cost of status quo. It establishes that smart risk taking is key for advancement in the company. Which brings us to the final strategy.

3. **Establish risk taking as a necessary skill to build, rather than a potential career-killer.** Many people default to not taking risks because they worry about the implication to their career if things go wrong. But imagine the power of turning this impulse on its head, and communicating that smart risk taking is a skill people are expected to build and will be evaluated on. One mentally strong leader I worked for (who I referred to in the introduction of this book) set the tone for risk taking by often saying, "I expect you to take risks. All I ask is that you be right 51 percent of the time."

Your First Small Step: Internalize the insight that successfully fostering a risk-taking spirit comes down to sending the right signals and impeding the wrong impulses. It's an essential organizing framework to understand that will shape your efforts on this front.

In Moments of Weakness: If you find yourself wrapped up in risk-averse behavior (whether it's you or your organization), step back and ask, "What unhelpful signals are being sent? What counterproductive impulses are we giving into?" Course-correct and rearticulate the cost of *not* taking risks.

Boldness Habit #4: Inspire the Right Change Choice

Pushing limits often requires change. And people don't like change. So, if you want to push limits, you have to be mentally strong enough, bold enough, to embrace change yourself, and to help your organization do the same.

Do so by introducing the one choice anyone must make as they face change, what I call the Change Choice, which is:

"Will you see change as happening *to* you, or *for* you?"

Of course, as a leader, you're most often choosing to have change happen *by* you. But I'm referring here to the recipients of change, those whom you must lead through the change. Will you deftly influence them to see change, not as happening *to* them, but *for* them? Eighty percent of whether or not you're successful with change comes down to this. If people see change as happening *to* them, it automatically frames change as a series of negative outcomes in their mind. If they see change as happening *for* them, it completely alters their attitude for the better. Change becomes an avenue toward positive things, fuel for pushing limits.

Here's how to keep the Change Choice front and center in your organization, while making a habit of inspiring the right choice.

Habit-Building Tool #4: Our reactions to change are deeply ingrained; we're often not aware of how we're reacting, we just react. It goes back to our wiring; we're wired for survival, and change represents a threat to that survival. As a leader, you can create awareness of the choices to be made in the face of change—and challenge, or support, those choices as needed. It comes down to sharing the TO and FOR Behavior Brief. It outlines what unwanted, TO behaviors, look like in times of change, and what the desired FOR behaviors look like. It provides a clear framework for how to act in change (and how not to).

Here's what TO Behaviors look like (behaviors you want to steer your organization away from):

"TO" BEHAVIORS

- You get frustrated, angry, and stuck in "It's not fair."
- You catastrophize what might happen to you because of change. For instance, you worry that the new computer program you have to learn at work will make you look dumb and feel inadequate.
- You play the victim, believing and acting as if you're powerless.
- You obsess over what you'll lose that's associated with change. For example, there's a reorganization at work, and you panic that you'll lose your status, identity, confidence, income, support network, or even your job. Your fear of loss causes logic to fly out the window.
- You assume change will mean nothing but more work for you.
- You never commit to the change, bury your head in the sand, and just wait for it to go away.
- You actively resist change, seeking out others who think like you in an effort to form an anti-change support group.
- You yearn for the status quo because it's safer.

Mentally strong people, who nail the boldness test of leadership, choose FOR Behaviors. These are behaviors to model, and for your organization to adopt.

"FOR" BEHAVIORS

- You know the only thing constant is change, and that adaptability is a critical skill.
- You simply observe uncertainty—without overreacting. You acknowledge its presence and move from thinking "beware" to thinking "benefit"—as in, the benefits that uncertainty unlocks, like creativity, resilience, and agility.
- You think of change like a personal software upgrade, a way to download a better version of you (You 2.0, if you will).
- You spend less time fighting change, more time forming it to fit a desired goal. For example, you get involved with the change, ask questions, voice your concerns, get clear on the case for change, explore how the change will make life better.
- You accept that change comes with some discomfort, as does growth.
- You understand that you cannot get to what you yearn to be by remaining what you are—change is the catalyst.
- You believe that you have the competence for change. You've been through it before and more than survived, and will again. For example, think of when you took on a new role or started working with a new technology. Perhaps you were apprehensive at first, but soon enough, with a little training, practice, and trial and error, you adapted just fine. We tend to forget these little victories and instead imagine defeat.
- You give change structure, breaking it into manageable pieces and developing supporting routines to quickly reestablish the familiar.

This tool is about helping your organization identify, and choose, FOR behaviors, while overtly avoiding TO behaviors. Think of it as a mindset manifesto for thriving in change.

Your First Small Step: Download the TO and FOR Behavior Brief at scottmautz.com/mentallystrong/templates. Print it out and share it with your organization, highlighting the FOR behaviors that will help everyone succeed in change. In this first step, you're just trying to get the organization aware of the dichotomy of behaviors that can happen in the face of change. You're trying to increase awareness of the right choice to make, the right path to take. Over time, repeatedly referring to the brief will help forge the desired habits.

In Moments of Weakness: Because our reaction to change so often happens instinctively, it's important to disrupt that "automatic mode" when needed. Your cue is anytime you spot a weak moment, where an unwanted "TO" behavior has popped up. Drive acknowledgement of it happening, and encourage an alternative FOR behavior. Keeping the TO and FOR Behavior Brief handy and visible, especially in times when your organization is going through a lot of change, can make a big difference in driving self-awareness, and thus self-selection, of the right group of behaviors.

Boldness Habit #5: Lead Change with Conviction

Mentally strong leaders, the most successful in boldly pushing limits, aren't just okay with change and the uncertainty it brings. They *crave it*, because they know they need it to disrupt, innovate, and push boundaries. They know uncertainty unlocks creativity, agility, and adaptability, among other boldness boosters.

And so they *create* uncertainty, by *leading* change, rather than allowing unhelpful emotions, thoughts, and behaviors to paralyze them into stasis. You can too, brilliantly, with the tool that follows.

Habit-Building Tool #5: Want to make sure your employees *never* feel inspired to be bold? Keep sticking to the status quo, never setting a vision for change when the organization clearly needs change to get to a better place. Of course, nobody wants that reputation. And it won't fall on you, if you use the Vision-Building Building, a framework for setting a clear, compelling change vision for your organization. I'll walk you through the framework, bringing it to life along the way with a case study of a company we'll call ABC Books—a regional chain of bookstores in the United States.

Here's what a completed Vision-Building Building looks like, using ABC Books as an example.

Fig. 5.6 The Vision-Building Building

(ABC Books)

State of the Union	Change Vision
What must change? Why?	Purposeful, exciting, different vs.
What's danger of not changing?	status quo, attainable
(online retailers are winning)	("create a warm, magical store experience")

1. Exactly what's changing?	2. By when?	3. What won't change?
- level of customer service - whimsy and hidden delight - build in-store cafes - in-store and community events	phase 1: 12 months phase 2: 36 months phase 3: 60 months	putting employees first in everything we do

4. How does it link to ABC's purpose/goals/strategies?	5. What's the + and - impact to individuals?	6. How will the organization be supported/trained?
delivers goal of #1 selling regional bookstore chain	+ better employee experience - intense expectations on service	comprehensive training seminar

Let's start with the roof, then we'll define each of the six building blocks that support it.

First, define the State of the Union. What must change? Why? What's the danger of *not* changing? In other words, make your case for change. For ABC Books, online book retailers were winning. People saw little reason to come into their stores anymore.

The State of the Union should inspire your Change Vision. A change vision is a mind-expanding, compelling future state. It should feel purposeful, exciting, different from the status quo, and attainable. It should answer the questions, "What do we dare to accomplish?" and "Who do we intend to be?" It should encourage the expenditure of discretionary energy. It should create commitment, not just compliance.

Boil it down to a single sentence, if possible. ABC's Change Vision was: "Create a warm, magical store experience that goes beyond books on shelves." Inspiring.

Now, the building blocks underneath the roof are six questions you ask to put more detail into, and to sharpen, your Change Vision.

1. **Exactly what's changing?** Leaders often make the mistake of painting too broad a vision that doesn't mean much to anyone. It's here you get clear on precisely what will change or needs to change about the organization's culture, strategy, goals, policies, processes, and systems. For ABC Books, they needed to change (dramatically increase) their level of customer service and the amount of whimsy and hidden delight in their stores, build in-store cafés to strengthen the experience, and create a calendar of in-store and community events.

2. **By when?** People need dates to aim for. And, by the way, break the change into pieces, or phases, if possible.

It's hard for organizations to swallow too much change at once. ABC broke their change vision into three phases: Phase one: twelve months, Phase two: thirty-six months, Phase three: sixty months.

3. **What won't change?** When so much else is changing, employees need an anchor, something they can count on that *won't* change. This familiarity helps them through the more difficult parts of change. ABC wouldn't change their culture of putting employees first in everything they do.

4. **How does the vision link to the broader organization's purpose, goals, and strategies?** The clearer the link, the more employees will be "sold" on the vision. ABC's link was clear—their change vision would deliver their goal to be the number one regional bookstore chain in terms of sales.

5. **What's the positive, and negative, impact to individuals?** This is about spelling out, for all recipients of the change, "What's in it for me?" People can't engage on what you need them to do in times of change until they understand how they'll be personally impacted. Being honest about the potential downsides of the change gives you more credibility when you tout the benefits. For ABC, there'd be a more positive employee experience working there. On the potential negative side, expectations for providing great customer service were going to be dramatically higher.

6. **How will the organization's people be supported and get the skill-building training they'll need to succeed?** It's not the change itself that people dread per se, it's the *transition*. For example, who wouldn't

mind losing ten pounds? That would be a nice change. But then think of the transition to that new, lighter state: all the exercise, food choices, and discipline it takes. It's the transition that tends to pose the problem. You help people through the transition of change when you show them how they'll be supported along the way, what training and resources they'll get, and so on. ABC Books committed to providing a comprehensive training and skill-building seminar to help employees succeed.

Pro tip: Don't forget to get early input on the Change Vision from key stakeholders, and to establish your Change Coalition, your team of people who will visibly help lead the change. And spend time anticipating barriers to implementing change that could arise.

Now you're ready to consistently craft a compelling vision for change, and change the trajectory of your organization.

Your First Small Step: Go to scottmautz.com/mentallystrong/templates to download a blank Vision-Building Building template. Identify something sorely in need of change at your organization, enroll your team, and get to work creating, and implementing, your change vision.

In Moments of Weakness: Creating a compelling vision for change, and seeing it through, is hard. When you're facing resistance, return to each element of the Vision-Building Building to determine what you need to strengthen, starting with the "Why" (your case for change). Change is an emotional journey that takes time—just keep returning to the Vision-Building Building to find areas where you can improve your approach.

NOTES

1. Yerkes-Dodson Law, *Wikipedia*, en.wikipedia.org.

2. Based on quantitative and qualitative research among three thousand executives.

3. "Michelangelo Buonarroti: Quotes," goodreads.com/author/quotes.

4. Based on my personal experience working in P&G's laundry category.

5. "Moonshot Thinking." x.company/moonshot.

6. Ibid.

7. Ibid.

8. "Bill Gates: Quotes," goodreads.com/quotes.

9. Based on drivers' analysis of what made successful risk-taking leaders/cultures so successful

10. Edmondson, A. C. April 2011. "Strategies for Learning from Failure," *Harvard Business Review*, hbr.org.

11. Mautz, S. May 2021. *Leading from the Middle: A Playbook for Managers to Influence Up, Down, and Across the Organization.* Wiley, 36.

12. Ismail, S. October 16, 2004. "3 Ways Companies Can Encourage Smart Risk Taking," CNBC, cnbc.com.

13. Confirmed with multiple Amazon employees.

14. Grable, J., A. G. Rabbani. January 2014. "Risk Tolerance Across Life Domains: Evidence from a Sample of Older Adults," *Journal of Financial Counseling and Planning*, 25(2): 174–83.

Hi all! It's the author, Scott. Being mentally strong includes a willingness to ask for help, which I'll model here. Would you consider leaving a review of this book on your favorite bookseller's website? I've put years of work into it, and need your help ensuring it finds its audience. The social proof a review creates makes a huge difference. Thanks for even considering.

And if you'd like help asking for help, download the Helping HANDS bonus tool at scottmautz.com/mentallystrong/templates. It's five principles to remember when asking for help. While asking for help is a sign of strength, not weakness, might as well do it right.

6 The Messaging Habit

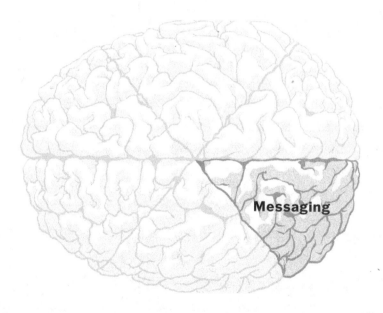

Messaging

The ability to regulate your emotions, thoughts, and behaviors, all to produce beneficial outcomes, means you're exerting control over the messages you send to yourself. They need to be supportive of what you're trying to accomplish, not counter to it. But being mentally strong also means consciously minding the messages you send to *others* through your emotions, thoughts, and behaviors. After all, as a leader, you live in a fishbowl, with eyes watching you from all angles, constantly taking cues from how you show up. You can either make people feel better about themselves, their work, and work environment, or worse. You can either help, or hinder, the collective goals being pursued with the nature of the "energy" you're sending out. And intention is one of the greatest aids you have for molding the kind of messages you want to send (as you saw in chapter 4, when sending a deliberate message via your executive presence).

Messaging might not be the first of the six tests of leadership that you'd predict ties so directly to achievement, but its impact couldn't have been more evident in my research. The amount of motivation and trust that is added, or drained, from an organization is inextricably linked to the extent to which you mindfully monitor (or not) the messages you send to your organization. And the messages you send in three areas, in particular, have a disproportionate ripple impact (whether positive or negative). Your:

- Reaction/contribution to negativity
- Proactive positivity
- Quality of presence/intent

How you navigate negativity (how you respond to it and resist adding to it), the extent to which you promote positivity, and the impression you leave through your quality of presence and purity of intent all matter, disproportionately. All three of these things have an outsized impact on the vibe of the place. And so, this chapter is organized around these three areas.

Charlotte, from chapter 1, who handled an unexpected rejection of her proposal in a way that sent all the right messages, used the habit-building tools in this chapter to help her along the way. Now, you'll have the same know-how at your disposal, including the ability to navigate unhelpful emotions in the moment, avoiding use of demotivating language and a toxic loss of temper, dodging stealth negativity traps, being proactively positive and a truly active listener, defaulting to integrity and transparency, role-modeling authenticity by living your values, and more.

Let's dig into one message-sending section at a time.

REACTION/CONTRIBUTION TO NEGATIVITY

Messaging Habit #1: Navigate Negative Emotions in the Moment

When emotions take over in a negative situation, it rarely helps. Mentally strong leaders simply don't give negative emotions the driver's seat in those moments (or ever). They're able to, for the most part, regulate their thoughts and feelings on the spot (we're not robots, after all, as previously acknowledged) and guide themselves toward a productive outcome. The tool that follows will help you do just that.

Habit-Building Tool #1: Any tool that would help here must be simple, repeatable, and able to be used almost reflexively, as it would be employed most often in emotionally charged moments. That's what makes the Redirect Rhythm so powerful. See the straightforward construct in Figure 6.1, then I'll walk you through it.

Fig. 6.1 The Redirect Rhythm

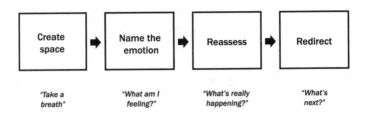

The idea here is to make a habit of quickly getting into a specific rhythm the moment that emotions start cropping up in a charged situation, to redirect you away from an unhelpful outcome to a productive one. There are four simple steps, and an accompanying "trigger phrase" to use along the way. Remember the steps, or the trigger phrases, or both (whichever works best), when your emotions start taking over. The steps are meant to happen progressively, fairly quickly.

> **Step 1: Create space.** You first have to create some distance from the intensity of the emotion. It's about breaking the gravitational pull of the emotion that's dragging you somewhere you don't want to be.

For example, say you're in a meeting with upper management where you're recommending a certain course of action, and it's not going well. Your heart is racing, your brow is sweating, panic is entering around the edges, and you're starting to berate yourself for screwing this up. Time to detach and say to yourself the first trigger phrase, *"Take a breath."* That's it. Stop. Pause. Breathe. Take a few beats to collect yourself.

Step 2: Name the emotion. Actually naming the emotion is a clever way to force you to become aware of your emotions (gaining awareness of your emotions being a classic self-regulation tactic). To trigger this, you ask, *"What am I feeling?"* This serves as a fill-in-the-blank prompt, of sorts. Putting it in the form of a question demands an answer ("I'm feeling _____."), which you then discern.

In our example, you name the emotions you're feeling as embarrassment and incompetence. And once you name the emotions, they begin to lose their hold over you (as we learned in chapter 4). That's no small feat, as research shows emotions associated with negative situations are stronger than those associated with positive situations and create more intense, unhelpful reactions than positive emotions create positive reactions.[1]

By the way, it's important to note that emotions can serve you well, too, of course, and you should embrace them when they do. Like when a friend is telling you about a personal tragedy, so feelings of compassion flood in, guiding you to act in caring ways. You'll sense in the moment if your emotions are serving you well or not.

Step 3: Reassess. This is where the great equalizer enters—logic. Emotions can cloud logic and reason, creating alternate truths. But logically reassessing the situation forces you to challenge the story you're telling yourself, reframing it in a way that defuses its emotional impact. The effectiveness of this is broadly supported in research, and is known as cognitive reappraisal.[2] You trigger a reappraisal by asking, *"What's really happening?"* It forces a realistic assessment of the situation rather than an exaggerated distortion. This forces you to focus on the underlying thoughts you're having rather than the emotion you're feeling. In other words, this is where you (rationally) think, before you act.

Back to our example. So, you face a choice. You could keep focusing on the embarrassment and sense of incompetence that you feel, playing into your story that this is an unmitigated train wreck, which will fluster you further and compel you to act tim-idly. Or, you can calmly focus on rational, underlying thoughts, "This isn't going well. I'm not expressing myself clearly, and they're skeptical of my recommendation." Not exactly pleasant, but more helpful, right? It's a more useful appraisal of what's actually going on. The factual nature of this line of thinking helps defuse the emotion, so that you can move to the final step.

> **Step 4: Redirect.** Something isn't working, so it's time for a new tack, to engage in a more productive behavior. You trigger that by simply asking, *"What's next?"* What can you do now that would produce a more beneficial outcome?

To finish our example, you quickly craft a plan; you'll ask for the opportunity to re-explain, and then focus on reinforcing your supporting data and what happens if the recommenda-tion isn't adopted.

You've now managed your emotions, focused on construc-tive thoughts, and identified productive behaviors to engage in next. It's a major step forward in passing the Messaging test of leadership.

Your First Small Step: As I said in an earlier chapter, avoidance starts with awareness. So, if you want to avoid unwittingly contributing to negativity (and sending an unhelpful cultural signal), practice spotting when your emotions are spiraling in a negative circumstance. Begin familiarizing yourself with the Redirect Rhythm, so you can call upon it quickly, in the moment you need it. (Write the steps or trigger phrases down if it helps.)

In Moments of Weakness: Negative emotions are a derailing force—it can be quite difficult in the moment to not let them pull you off course. If you feel that happening, let the flood of unhelpful emotion be your cue to change your rhythm, and flow into the Redirect Rhythm.

Messaging Habit #2: Avoid Losing Your Temper

Have you ever lost your temper? Of course you have.

Ever felt good about yourself afterward? Of course you haven't.

Losing your temper either instantly creates a negative environment or escalates one you're already in. Mentally strong leaders don't lose their temper, and you don't have to, either.

Note that the Redirect Rhythm tool we just covered helps you regulate a range of emotions, and it can certainly be used to navigate anger-charged moments. But losing your temper is a "specialty" emotion that can have devastating consequences, including sending a toxic message—so it warrants another option for you to choose from.

Habit-Building Tool #2: Temper your temper with the PALMS Up exercise. Here's how it works. Think of a bunched-up fist as a symbol of anger and losing your temper.

Think of an outstretched hand, palm up, as a symbol of peace. In the moment you feel your anger spiking, hold one palm out, facing up, and remember the acronym PALMS. Imagine it spelled out, one letter on each fingertip, like so:

Fig. 6.2 The PALMS Up exercise

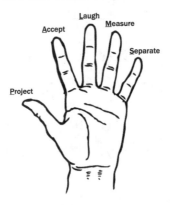

<u>P</u>roject
<u>A</u>ccept
<u>L</u>augh
<u>M</u>easure
<u>S</u>eparate

These are trigger words to help you calmly detach yourself from an overheated moment. Let's look at each.

<u>P</u>roject.

Ask, "What image am I about to project by losing my cool?" It's *never* a good one. Heated words are often regretted. The Mayo Clinic's top recommendation for avoiding angry outbursts is to think before you speak.[3] While you're thinking, picture how you're about to come across or the damage your words are about to do—it forces you to proceed carefully.

Pro tip: Picture a camera in the corner of the room, recording and sharing your reaction with the world. Will you be proud of what the world's about to see? It's a surprisingly powerful tactic. Harvard psychology research showed that the brain can't distinguish between past memories and imagined future states.[4] So imagining that camera sitting in the corner, recording your outburst and causing tremendous embarrassment, will register in your brain as if it were an actual past memory. You might even subconsciously wince a little bit, and thus be more likely to resist the anger you were about to put on display. So, visualize that video camera.

Accept.

Ask yourself, "Am I really just not accepting a different point of view?" Tempers can flare in the face of perspectives different from our own (it's human nature), but there are alternative responses. For example, in the heat of the moment, remind yourself to commend, not condemn, the opposing point of view. If you're opinionated or a bit closed-minded at times, "accept" is *the* keyword trigger for you.

Laugh.

Finding humor in the moment defuses anger; after all, laughter is the exact opposite reaction to an angry outburst. For example, I'd frequently crack jokes in tense team moments. It lightened the air in the room; kept me, or anyone else, from responding angrily; and kept us focused on the task at hand.

My teammates knew exactly what I was trying to do, and, thankfully, told me they appreciated it.

Measure.

Quickly measure the reaction you're about to give by pausing to ask, "Will my reaction be proportional to the offense at hand?" Likely not; it'll probably be overblown, if you're honest. Know that the tone someone is taking with you often creates overreactions (flaring your anger, for example). So, focus on their intent instead. For instance, instead of lashing out, ask yourself, "What are they really trying to say? What point are they making that's getting overrun by their tone?"

Separate.

Separate the person from the point. Conflict often arises from tension in an underlying relationship, not from the point at hand. For example, when you're interacting with someone who pushes your buttons, focus on the merits of the thoughts on the table, not what you think about the person. Otherwise you'll discolor the interaction in an unfair way.

You can't always control how you feel in a heated moment, but you can control how you respond. Do so in the right way—palms up.

Your First Small Step: Losing your temper can happen in a flash. So, the more reflexive you can make the PALMS Up exercise, the better. For certain, in the beginning, when you're all fired up, it won't be easy to stop, pause, breathe, and go through this maneuver. But it begins with your first small step of familiarizing yourself with each letter of the PALMS acronym. If it helps, make a little visual by tracing your hand and labeling each finger with the five letters/words of the PALMS acronym. (It thus becomes your "keep it cool" reminder.)

In Moments of Weakness: People lose their temper at times. It happens. When it happens to you, though, don't brush it aside. Note how unhelpful your reaction was, immediately apologize as appropriate, and immediately afterward, review the PALMS Up exercise to see how it could have helped you in that moment. Then, commit to use the exercise next time. With practice, being palms up will produce a thumbs up for how you handle future temper flare-ups.

Messaging Habit #3: Avoid Demotivating Language

Mentally strong leaders plant seeds of growth with their words, not seeds of doubt. Meaning, they're careful to use what they say as a way to build people up, not to tear them down and trigger waves of self-doubt. Instead of resorting to a flippant word or callous comment (which send any number of unproductive messages), they're disciplined and emotionally intelligent with their words. I asked three thousand respondents what were the most demotivating things their manager ever said to them at work. What I discovered led to what follows.

Habit-Building Tool #3: The Eight to Eliminate are eight of the most demotivating things you could say to an employee. You'll want to flex your messaging mental muscle and eliminate them from your vocabulary. I'll go through each, and what to say instead.

1. **"It's your fault."** Mentally strong people don't pass blame on to others; they show belief in others. They don't judge, they jump to defend. If someone said to you, "It's your fault," you couldn't help but be defensive. Don't raise defenses, lower them, and move discussion forward.

Instead say, "This didn't go as hoped, what should we do next?"

2. **"I don't care."** I'm not talking about indifference toward something trivial. I mean saying these words to intentionally show no interest in a point, emotion, or circumstance of importance to someone else. It sends a message of disrespect.

Instead say, "I hear you and understand why that's important to you."

3. **"That's your problem, not mine."** Being mentally strong means resisting the temptation to dodge responsibility, while having empathy for others and their problems, and wanting to help in some way, even if it's just to let that person know they're not alone.

Instead say, "How can I help?"

4. **"I'll do it myself."** You can't say this without sounding frustrated and condescending, as if the other person must be incompetent and only you have the skills to get the job done.

Instead say, "Is there anything I can specifically do to lend a hand?"

5. **"I don't care what anyone thinks."** Mentally strong leaders are self-aware that they can benefit from different perspectives. And they have enough self-confidence to handle disagreement, using it to make the best decision possible.

Instead say, "I have a strong point of view but am willing to get input that could change my thinking."

6. **"Because I said so."** This might work with children, but to adults it says "I'm in charge," which, if you have to say it, means you're not really in charge, and fosters resentment.

Instead say, "Here's why it's important to do this."

7. **"Failure's not an option."** Maybe not, but saying it this way kills innovation and risk taking and causes people to bury problems and the truth. It sends a message of closed-mindedness.

Instead say, "What's our backup plan in case this doesn't work?"

8. **"You failed."** I bet the person already knows they "failed" and doesn't need a harsh reminder. The mentally strong resist the temptation to lash out at failure, building up instead of tearing down.

Instead say, "Not yet." Or say, "What did you learn from this and what could you do differently next time?"

Your First Small Step: Start by determining if you say any of the above demotivating phrases at times, or if there are any other demoralizing phrases that slip into your vocabulary. The phrases are very clear cues you can spot, telling you to pick alternative language. Enroll your team to help and bravely call you out when you say any of them. The sooner you start recognizing when you're using demotivating language, the sooner you can course-correct and send more beneficial messages.

In Moments of Weakness: If you slip and say any of the Eight to Eliminate, stop, pause, redirect, and say something like, "I'm sorry, disregard that, it was my emotion talking. What I mean to say is . . ." Showing regret and redirecting to more productive language shows you're human and that you want to help in some way.

Messaging Habit #4: Avoid Ninja Negativity Traps

It's clear that caving in to unhelpful emotions in the moment (including anger), and saying demotivating things, feeds negativity, sending out the wrong energy and communicating the wrong thing (about you and the environment you foster).

But there are two stealth areas to be wary of, two things that quietly pull you down into a gloomy demeanor that obstructs positivity, with ninja-like precision and sneakiness. That is, when:

1. You get pulled into pessimism by complainers.
2. You hold on to debilitating emotions.

Both of these can subtly alter the message you send, robbing it of energy and replacing it with weariness. Let's look at how to habitually hamper each.

Habit-Building Tool #4: The Catch and Release exercise is a great way to catch when you're inadvertently getting sucked into negativity created by complainers, and to release a specific set of particularly debilitating emotions that weigh down your outlook. Let's start with the complainers.

1. *You get pulled into pessimism by complainers.* Few things are more draining than a constant complainer, someone who corners you with their "woe-is-me" tales of negativity. As a leader, you can't get caught up in it; it's hard enough to keep everyone energized (including yourself) as it is. But it's not easy to derail the Complain Train once someone's got it rolling, and it's not always easy to notice that you've hitched a ride (i.e., to catch that you're contributing to the complaining, or at least not countering it). So, the next time you're experiencing a chronic complainer, let it trigger one word in your mind, an acronym: CAUSE. As in, what's causing this person to complain? Considering *why* they're complaining helps you catch that they're doing it, and helps you react in a more productive manner, as opposed to adding to it, or complaining about their complaining, which is another form of spiraling down. Let's go through the acronym to understand the psychology behind why we complain, and what to do about it.

Can't solve the problem.

Your complainer may simply be super frustrated that they can't resolve an issue. If you sense that's the case, carefully ask if they want your thoughts on how they might solve the problem. Gently talk them down from frustration mode into solution mode.

Attention.

As in, they're seeking some. For example, they might feel alone in dealing with their problem or neglected of late in general, and are yearning for acknowledgement. If you sense their complaining is a cry for attention, give them the gift of attentiveness and careful listening (up to a point, of course). Often, the whole point of complaining is just wanting to be heard and understood.

Underlying insecurity.

Sometimes, complaining is just a way of masking discomfort about our inadequacies. For example, I'm embarrassed to admit that as a much younger leader, I'd sometimes complain about coworkers, when I was really just trying to take attention away from how talented they were (which made me feel deficient). If you sense insecurity in someone else's complaining, find reaffirming things to say to them to alter the backdrop they're working against—from one of deflection and cynicism, to self-acceptance.

Stress relief.

We've all vented before, dropping our guard to let out our frustrations. So, you know doing this can make you feel better. If you sense this is what's happening, give the person an outlet (again, within reason) to keep them from bottling up their negativity, then point out any positives in the situation to help them improve their mood.

Environment.

As in, consider the environment they're in. For instance, maybe they're surrounded by a complaining culture at work, or by complainer role-models elsewhere. In this case, find a gentle way to make them aware of the impact their complaining is having on those around them—they're probably pretty numb to it.

By the way, if it's *you* that complains a lot, you can still use the CAUSE acronym to examine why. And try this next trick for dealing with an especially acidic brand of complainer.

Pro tip: Challenge cynics. Cynics get their power when no one challenges them; their caustic comments can seem smart in the absence of any pushback. So, challenge their statements and invite them to be a part of the solution instead. If they can't suggest solutions, they lose their power.

Now for the Release part of the Catch and Release exercise. This is about the power of letting go.

2. *You hold on to debilitating emotions.* Some of the best things happen when you let go of that which no longer serves you well: old stories, beliefs, behaviors, identities, relationships, emotions. Especially true when you let go of debilitating emotions, ones that detract from

your best leadership-self. Four particularly devastating ones at that, which form a "Most-Unwanted" list (other than Self-doubt, which we addressed in chapter 4). They are:

- Regret
- Guilt
- Shame
- Self-pity

Entire books can, and have, been written about each of these. This is simply about asking you to consciously release these most unhelpful emotions the minute they make an unwanted appearance. It's about "bang for the buck," reaping the most emotional reward by targeting the few, most penalizing offenders.

To help with that, know that the first three—regret, guilt, and shame—can all be released in the same way. By countering them with *acceptance, forgiveness,* and *introspection.*

Accept that, yes, you may have made some mistakes (take accountability), but that they don't diminish who you are. You are not your mistake. Accept all your weaknesses and strengths, knowing that they add up to the unique you. *Forgive* yourself, knowing that everyone makes mistakes, again, believing that no mistake defines you. *Be introspective*, to glean what lesson you can from past circumstances, so you can now move forward, more informed.

Regarding self-pity, know that it simply cannot exist in the presence of gratitude. Period. For leaders, one of the more common forms of self-pity is feeling exhausted by your duties, not wanting to engage in the parts of the job you don't particularly enjoy, feeling victimized by all that you have to do that you don't want to do. That feeling will eventually reflect on your demeanor, which will eventually have an unhelpful, de-energizing ripple effect.

Try this trick for bringing gratitude to the foreground in this case; it's so simple, yet so powerful. The next time you're feeling down about your duties, try a one-word language change.

Don't think:
I *have* to do this.

Think:
I *get* to do this.

This magic one-word shift can reframe your entire day, filling it with more energy and joy.

For example, I was waiting to board a flight, on my way to give a keynote address. But I found myself stuck in my general distaste for travel (it's the only downside to my job). The gate was overcrowded, the flight delayed, the throng growing ruder by the moment, a five-hour trip still ahead. It all had me feeling down about my day, not looking forward to going through it. But then I remembered that subtle power-shift. I went from thinking, "I *have* to do this," to "I *get* to do this." It changed my entire mindset. Yes, there was some inconvenience to trudge through, but it was secondary. I focused on the fact that I'd get to be in front of an audience, sharing inspiration and insight. I was reminded what a privilege and honor it is to have this as my occupation, how lucky I am. It put into perspective how the good in my day would outweigh anything less palatable. I carried this reframed positivity directly over to the stage when giving the keynote (talk about a place where your outlook/demeanor has an outsized impact on your audience!).

I hope you *get* the power of doing this too.

Your First Small Step: Regarding the "Catch" part of this exercise, grab an index card and write down each step of the CAUSE acronym. Keep it handy and refer to it the next time you realize you'll be with a chronic complainer. For the "Release" portion, ask yourself, "Which of the four debilitating emotions do I fall into from time to time?" Or is there another one you want to release? It's an important first step to pinpoint the disproportionate source(s) of emotional drain in your life, so you're ready to release it when the emotion surfaces. It's about generating a broad, positive impact, with narrow focus. So, set yourself up for that.

In Moments of Weakness: It's easy to get pulled down by a chronic complainer, and pulled into their negativity. It's just as easy to quietly try to avoid them altogether. Neither is good, so when you find yourself engaged in either, own up to it, and commit to better understand/respond to the complainer (via use of the CAUSE acronym). Remind yourself in the moment that losing your patience with them won't get them out of pessimistic mode. And regarding the four debilitating emotions to release, if you find yourself in their insidious grip, acknowledge it, remind yourself of the cost of staying trapped, and put the remedies in place offered above. While you're working to let go of these emotions, don't forget to let go of your dismay at feeling them. All four are all too common to experience.

PROACTIVE POSITIVITY

Messaging Habit #5: Choose to Stay Positive

Some days, it's hard to keep a positive outlook. Frustrations at work, current events, things going wrong in your life; negativity can be everywhere, weighing down your perspective, presence, and potential. Still, in the face of it all, as a mentally strong leader, with the intent to send advantageous messages to the organization, you can foster ongoing positivity. Not by chance, by choice.

Habit-Building Tool #5: The Plus Sign tool outlines four fundamental choices you make that trigger positivity as a default, and one important "central" behavior. To help you remember the four choices (and centerpiece), visualize a plus sign, like so:

Fig. 6.3 The Plus Sign

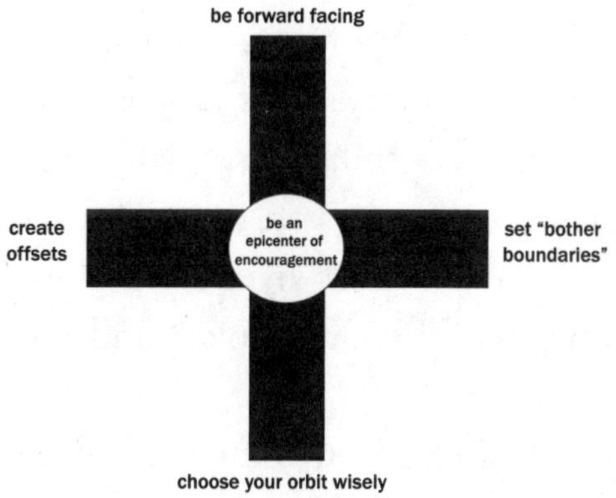

be forward facing

create offsets   be an epicenter of encouragement   set "bother boundaries"

choose your orbit wisely

The Plus Sign asks that you:

Be forward facing. It's human nature to feel bad or sad at times, but even when things aren't going well and you feel you're going backward, you must keep moving forward. No matter what. Positivity fuels all forward progress, even small steps forward. It's not always easy, but this will help. When struggling in the face of setbacks, say to yourself, "Big picture, small step." Meaning, to motivate yourself, visualize your big picture again, the big thing you're aiming for, the vision of the life you want to live; whatever is hard to see at that moment. Then ask yourself, what's the smallest step I can take to start moving toward my big picture again? Just making that first move is powerful because it triggers progress, which positivity flows from.

For example, say you really wanted that job in your dream industry. But someone else (not as qualified as you) got it. The setback could throw you into a negative spiral, or you could say, "Big picture, small step." You visualize the big picture, working in that industry, and identify the first small step you can take to get back on track, like asking the interviewer how you could do better for the next opportunity.

Pro tip: Being forward facing also requires watching your language. Meaning, incredibly, the language you choose to use, how you *verbalize* things (especially negative thoughts), actually influences the way you think and see the world. It's known as the Sapir-Whorf hypothesis,[5] and it underscores the relationship between our choices and our ability to stay positive-minded.

To illustrate, say you encounter an unexpected setback. You can say, out loud, "This is devastating!" or you can say, "This is a challenge." Say a pile of new tasks gets put on your plate. You can say, "This will be draining!" or you can say, "This will be a learning opportunity."

Set "bother boundaries." These are lines you draw on what you will, and won't, worry about. It keeps you from getting sucked into things you can't control, which only makes it harder to be proactively positive. For example, you set "bother boundaries" regarding who gets promoted at work. You simply refuse to get upset when someone gets a promotion who didn't deserve it, or who got it ahead of normal timing for a promotion, or who got one before you. It's outside the boundary you've set, you can't control it, so you won't be bothered by it.

Choose your orbit wisely. Meaning, be intentional about who you spend your time with; whose "gravitational pull" you draw toward and circulate within. The more positive the orbit, or people you're connecting with, the better. You already know you should cut toxic people out of your life, to make more time for interactions with positive-minded people. But you'd be surprised just how powerful it is. A seventy-plus-year study at Boston University found that *the single biggest contributor* to living a happy, positive-minded life is surrounding yourself with happy, positive-minded people.[6]

It's that simple, and that hard. I know you can't just cut some people out of your life altogether. But at a minimum, you must set boundaries (there's that word again). The truth is, negative people often don't understand the impact they have when they suck others into their negative orbit. So, make them aware of the impact it's having on you (as hard as that might be), and establish a boundary that you won't engage in the gloom. Access perspective from those who give you energy rather than those who drain your energy. Author Jim Rohn said, "You're the average of the five people you spend the most time with."[7] So, choose wisely.

Create offsets. You always have the option, at least in your little corner of the world, to offset negativity you encounter with little acts of positivity elsewhere. It doesn't have to be huge acts of volunteerism, for example, or switching to a career focused on serving others (although those things are wonderful, of course). It could be as simple as choosing to live your values very day (more on that in the last habit/tool of this chapter). For example, maybe a core value is showing kindness. Despite a negative experience you just had at work, you choose to extend kind words to the coffee shop barista, or tell a coworker what a great job they're doing. Creating offsets like this gives you your power back.

Now for the center of the Plus Sign.

Be an epicenter of encouragement. Plenty of people, everywhere, are having a hard time of it, for all kinds of reasons (insert your best guess here, and you'll be right). But what if you emanate encouragement, spread support, radiate the rah-rah? I'm not talking about being superficial, or a Pollyanna. Just the opposite. I'm asking you to look for every opportunity to give *informed encouragement*. It's a special brand of encouragement where you provide positive feedback, optimism, and affirmation, along with well-informed, thoughtful, specific reasons for your positivity. The specificity gives your encouragement credibility, which makes it meaningful. For example, not only do you tell your IT person they did a good job, you give detail on the positive impact of their efforts, how it made you *feel*, what others said about it, how it delivered on some crucial company objectives, and why their effort classified as "above and beyond," something to celebrate.

It's far more effective than general cheerleading. There's nothing wrong with you giving a "You can do it!" but it's so much more powerful when that other person understands specifically *why* you believe they can do it.

Pro tip: You can also *spread positive gossip*. Meaning, make it a point to share positive things about people and their accomplishments; when they're in the room, of course, but also when they aren't. Just as negative gossip travels quickly and has a devastating effect in so many ways, so can positive gossip have an opposite, uplifting impact. Especially when word of your praise makes it back to the recipient; it's something they won't soon forget and a foundation of trust-building. To build this mini-habit, institute *The Positive Gossip Game.* At your next team meeting or group gathering, break everyone into pairs. Have one person in the pair take two minutes to tell the other person something positive about someone in the room, but someone that's not within earshot. Then, the other person in the pair takes their turn doing the same. After everyone has shared, each person must then, later on, go find the person they heard positive gossip about, and tell them what they heard. You'll be surprised at how energizing this exercise is. Not only does it feed a culture of spreading positive gossip, it sends the message that the opposite is unwelcome.

Your First Small Step: Re-create the simple (but powerful) Plus Sign visual on anything you can keep handy. Negativity has a way of surrounding us at times, and little reminders can be of great use in trying to counter it all.

In Moments of Weakness: Recognize when you drift into negativity. Pause in that moment and consider the ripple impact it has on those around you, especially as a leader. Say to yourself, "My pessimism permeates," to remind you of that echo. Use that moment as a clear cue to then tip the balance back toward persistent positivity (with the Plus Sign as your aid).

QUALITY OF PRESENCE/INTENT

Messaging Habit #6: Be an Active Listener

Few things are more noticeable in a leader (and in anyone) than when they're not really listening, they're distracted or uninterested, less than fully engaged. You can tell. And it happens all the time; a Harvard study showed that our minds are not focused on what's happening right in front of us a whopping *47 percent of the time.*[8] How can we listen if we're not even present in the moment half the time?

Think of all the unintended things you're saying to someone, the unwanted messages you're sending, when they know you're not listening. What does it say to *you* when you know someone's not listening?

We can do better. And mentally strong leaders do. They send a message that those they work with are *heard*.

Habit-Building Tool #6: Listening, truly listening, like so much else with mental strength, requires intention, structure, and discipline. The Peak Listening model helps you make a habit of all three.

Fig. 6.4 The Peak Listening model

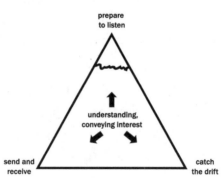

Let's go through the model, and you'll see how the three points lead to peak listening. We'll start in the center. Harvard research indicates that the listener in any conversation has two goals; to understand what the other is communicating, and to convey interest in so doing.[9] To truly accomplish these goals requires three distinct tasks (the three points of the model).

Prepare to listen. Preparing to listen forces you to be present in the moment and ready to listen. This draws people to you and encourages them to share more with you, creating a *connection* (which is the point of active listening). To illustrate, ever notice how much people are drawn to babies? And babies don't say a word. Psychologists say it's not because of their magnetic personality, which isn't fully formed yet, or their cuteness, which is only part of it. It's because of how present they are in the moment: wide-eyed, curious, fully engaged in everything right in front of them. It's hard not to be drawn to, and connected with, that.

To establish an active listening presence, try the Wet Sponge method. Before engaging with someone, picture your brain as a dry-erase board. Take an imaginary wet sponge across it to wipe it free of distracting thoughts. If you need a moment to do that before engaging, let the other person know. Now you're ready for focused listening. This tactic acknowledges that we often enter a conversation with multiple thoughts floating around in our mind. It commits you to starting that conversation with a clean slate, so you can better focus. For instance, you're about to start a one-on-one with an employee, but you're still thinking about a bad meeting you just had. Stop, pause, breathe, picture that dry-erase board, wipe it clean, *then* engage in that one-on-one.

Two other ways to prepare for focused listening. Right before engaging with the other person, ask yourself, "What has my attention right now?" If it isn't the person in front of you, redirect.

Or, remind yourself *why* you want to listen. It's either for understanding, or for conveying interest in some form (to show compassion, to smooth over an argument, to make someone feel validated). Establishing your purpose for listening reminds you why it matters, and helps you lock into the task at hand, just like reviewing the agenda for a meeting before you start focuses you on what's to follow.

It's important to note that preparing to listen requires *cutting off multitasking*. Multitasking is the biggest barrier to being present (and thus able to listen), and, by the way, you're not accomplishing what you think you are by doing it. Research shows multitaskers lose an astonishing 40 percent of their productivity, yet feel more emotionally satisfied while multitasking, thus creating an illusion of productivity.[10] In fact, MIT neuroscience has proven that doing two cognitive things at once doesn't work, no matter how good you think you are at it—the mind simply doesn't work that way.[11] That's why the National Transportation Safety Board reports that texting while driving is the equivalent of driving with a blood alcohol level three times the legal limit.[12] What you can do is what's called task-switching; shifting your focus from one thing to the next with astonishing speed. But in so doing, your brain is forced to use the same exact part of the brain, which slows down the time it takes to complete the tasks you're switching between, and causes more errors than when focusing on doing one task at a time.[13]

In other words, if you actually want to comprehend what the other person is saying and respond accordingly, you'll have to single-task (which includes placing your biggest attention skimmer, your smartphone, out of reach/sight).

Send and receive. Listening is both sending *and* receiving. I'll explain. Let's start with what it takes to truly *receive*. It's about laser-focus listening, tuning in as if nothing else in the world matters. You do that by:

- Defaulting to silence (giving them the space to say what's on their mind)
- Putting yourself in their shoes, identifying with their feelings and emotions
- Paying attention to their nonverbals (like facial expressions, hand gestures, or posture)
- Picking up on what's not being said

It's also vital to *send* signals that you're listening, using tactics that help you listen better to begin with. You do that by:

- Using physical cues (like eye contact, nodding, or taking notes)
- Contributing rather than commandeering (i.e., giving your thoughts and reactions, but without hijacking the conversation)
- Asking questions and follow-ups to those questions
- Repeating their last few words back to them from time to time (which shows you're listening and processing, and gives you a simple task to do that further enhances your listening)
- Using "interest indicator" phrases like "Tell me more," or "Then what happened?"

- Mirroring their emotions and gestures (for example, if they're excited about their topic, you show excitement too, while subtly mimicking their body language/gestures, facial expressions, and vocal qualities)
- Acknowledging versus discounting

The last two require explanation. Mirroring, also known as the Gauchais Reaction, works because it subconsciously helps the other person see themselves reflected in you, which creates a connection. It makes them feel heard and valued and builds rapport. Research broadly proves just how effective the technique is, even showing that waitresses who mirror get higher tips, and sales clerks who mirror achieve higher sales and better evaluations.[14] But don't think of it as manipulative; it's quite natural, actually. Case in point: Ever been in a conversation with a friend, and catch yourself mimicking their vocal patterns, their gestures, or even their accent? It's about absorbing yourself into the conversation so much that the natural tendency to mirror comes out, which you help along, rather than entering the discussion with a calculating plan to copy everything the other person does.

Regarding acknowledging as opposed to discounting, keep in mind that when we listen to someone's frustrations or worries, we want to help—it's human nature. But instead of acknowledging what they're saying, we can end up unintentionally discounting it. We do this with dismissive language like "it'll be okay," or "well, at least you . . .," or "it's not as bad as you think," which undermines the importance of what the person is saying and feeling. We do this to make ourselves feel better when the other person just wants to feel like they're not alone.

Better, validating language to use includes "I see," "Yes, of course," "I hear you," and "I see why you'd feel that way." Using language like this also helps them get past emotions, to express feelings, which opens up discussion on why they feel that way (thus enabling understanding). Since people tend to show their emotions *before* they explain their feelings, validating language thus serves as a good bridge to being understood/understanding what the other is saying.

Pro tip: If you tend to interrupt people, remember WAIT, which stands for "Why Am I Talking?" (As opposed to listening right now.) If you find yourself starting to interrupt, like before a colleague is finished explaining an idea, this acronym should flash in your mind's eye.

Catch the drift. By this I mean make a point to notice when your attention is drifting. Excuse yourself and admit where you are mentally if you have to—faking it is frustrating and people will see through it. You do that by:

- Using listening mantras (i.e., writing down simple reminders, even placing them where you can see them, to stay present in the conversation, like, "Don't zone out, zone in," or "Be mindful, not mind full," or, "Run your mind, don't let it run you")
- Monitoring your emotions (i.e., not letting emotional responses sidetrack you and compromise your listening, like when the other person says something you strongly disagree with)
- Resisting the 4:1 Rule

A bit of explanation for this last one. This rule acknowledges research that shows we think four times faster than others talk—the 4:1 Rule.[15] So how do we fill that space while our brain is waiting for the other person to catch up? Most often by formulating what we're going to say in response. That does not lend itself to high-quality listening. To help here, breathe slowly while listening. This helps still the mind and keeps it focused on what's being said as opposed to what you want to say.

Your First Small Step: Objectively recognize that you very likely have opportunity to improve your listening skills. Research shows 96 percent of us believe we're good listeners, and yet we can only retain half of what people say to us—and that's *directly after they say it.*[16] This is important because working on listening skills is something so many blow off, because they (a) again, think they don't need to, or (b) cringe/scoff at listening exercises. So, take the Peak Listening model to heart, and people will know your listening comes from the heart. In fact, review the model before engaging in the next ten conversations. You'll be amazed at how fast you can build this critical Messaging habit.

In Moments of Weakness: If you realize you weren't listening well in a conversation, return to the Peak Listening model thereafter and review it once again, reminding yourself of the stakes (fewer things are more visible, or vulgar, then when you know someone isn't listening). If you catch your attention wandering in the middle of the conversation, get back on track by leaning on the insight and approaches from the "Catch the drift" element of the Peak Listening model.

Messaging Habit #7: Be Transparent.

Ever notice how transparent it is when someone's not being transparent? (We human beings are savvy creatures.) And it comes with a steep price: a lack of transparency sends a message that you can't be trusted. Mentally strong leaders have the courage to share truth and transparency, and the self-discipline to resist manipulating either. They understand that to achieve, to push to something exceptional through something challenging, is hard enough; why add to the angst by giving people a reason to doubt them? You'll give no such reason, instead proactively enhancing trust, by following what follows.

Habit-Building Tool #7: The Window of Transparency is a simple visual model that frames five key ways to be transparent, in a manner people can clearly see. See Figure 6.5.

Fig. 6.5 The Window of Transparency

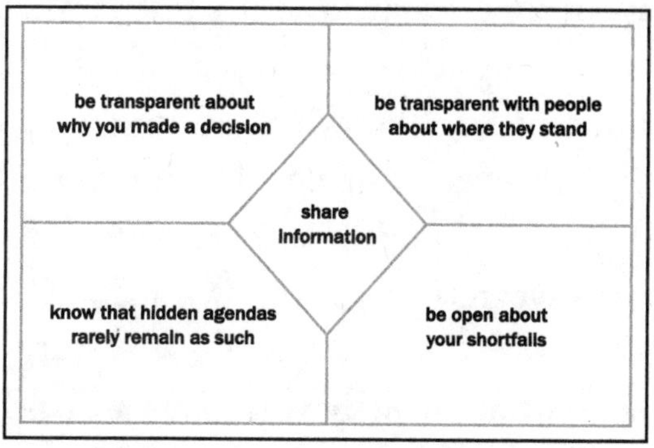

Failing on any of these window "panes" will cause you pain, so let's go through each, starting in the center.

Share information. Unfortunately, some leaders believe the more information they withhold, the greater their power. But they aren't exerting control, they're just keeping people from doing their jobs, and creating distrust (if their information withholding is discovered). They're even hurting creativity, as research shows hoarding information denies people stimulus that helps them better create and keeps the hoarder working in a vacuum.[17] Why would anyone give their all for a boss who hides, hoards, or won't take the time to share information?

For certain, it takes work to share information and communicate what that information means. But I can tell you from personal experience that putting in the effort to do so, with proper context and framing, repeatedly pays dividends via a more engaged, solutions-oriented organization. Of course, sometimes there is truly sensitive information that you can't share as a leader. We're talking here about investing the time it takes to form a habit of information-sharing as a default.

Pro tip: Think of information-sharing on the same importance level as strategy. The truth is, it's just as worthy of your time. Start by writing down two pieces of information your team would benefit from knowing (like the outcome of that board meeting, or what your decision was on a key issue). Then take the time it takes to share it, with proper context and framing, in whatever form (a town hall, an email, face-to-face, etc.).

Be transparent about why you made a decision. When it comes to explaining your decisions, don't be evasive, don't worry about hurting feelings (but be respectful), and don't hide underlying motivations; those motivations have a way of eventually showing themselves.

Just as important, don't assume you can just make decisions in a vacuum without giving context and reasoning for them. I learned this the hard way early in my career when I was in a failing business that required a rapid turnaround. I was using the need to move fast as justification for making decisions in a vacuum and not taking time to explain anything to anyone. I soon learned I wasn't bringing the organization along to execute and improve the quality of the very decisions I was so rapidly making. Again, I'm not talking here about disclosing confidential reasons for a decision (such as revealing that the decision links to a future pending plant closing and mass staff reduction). I'm talking here about caring enough to take the time to enroll, educate, and explain why you decided what you did.

We'll dive much deeper into decision-making in the next chapter.

Be transparent with people about where they stand. On the positive side here, don't hold back telling someone how good they are because of whatever imagined downside to doing so that you're conjuring. On the more difficult side, it's never easy to tell someone something they won't enjoy hearing about their performance, or how they're perceived. But it's a core responsibility as a leader; you owe them the truth, and they'll be better off for it in the long run. You'd want to know where you stand, right? It might sting in the moment, but if you communicate the message with compassion, respect, and a clear desire to be of service, they'll be better able to hear, process, and ultimately accept the message. They'll respect that you're willing to share the good and the "bad." Mentally strong leaders work toward this with bravery.

Be open about your shortfalls. Be honest about what you're not good at, ask for help improving on that front, and surround yourself with people who offset your weaknesses. Don't pretend to know everything and be everything. For example, say you share you're not good at noticing when people are feeling burnout. You ask your team to help by identifying when they are (feeling burnout), and you ask your HR partner to do periodic sensing to help you assess when it's happening. Everybody wins from your vulnerability. Yes, even you.

Know that hidden agendas rarely remain as such. Having a hidden agenda, or a desire to accomplish something through manipulation (that's different than the agenda on the table), usually doesn't stay hidden. It only takes one little slip for the true intent of someone's actions to come out. And that one slip sends a toxic message that can undo the power of a thousand other positive messages sent beforehand. Don't play this game. The most toxic organization I've ever been a part of had a leader who always had hidden agendas—you were just waiting for the thing he really wanted to be revealed. Most often, eventually, it was. Not surprisingly, commitment to him was nonexistent.

So, look to the Window of Transparency to ensure people are seeing the right things about you, rather than seeing right through you.

Your First Small Step: Commit to transparency as a standard operating procedure. Look for, or create, opportunities to share information, talk with people about where they stand, or explain a decision, and even schedule these occasions on your calendar.

In Moments of Weakness: Given that a lack of transparency leads to a lack of trust, you'll have to be extra careful when you stumble here. If you do make a misstep, own it, explain why you weren't transparent (unless it's something truly confidential that you can't share), and get right back on the right path.

Messaging Habit #8: Set a Balanced Tone

It's a basic truth of leadership. Employees take cues from the tone their leader sets (especially in times of adversity). Mentally strong leaders distinguish themselves by carefully regulating the tone they set, the messages they send, ensuring balance, all to help achieve whatever they're setting out to achieve. For example, think of the best leaders. As they communicate, they intentionally set a balanced tone. They're:

- Demanding *and* empathetic
- Calm *yet* show urgency
- Confident *and* humble
- Candid *and* kind
- Fearless *yet* intentional
- Celebratory *yet* improvement-oriented
- They provide reality *and* hope

Being balanced matters because it accomplishes one primary thing: it *ensures you're actually motivating the behavior you want.*

To illustrate, say you've got to address very disappointing results with your group. You want to set a demanding tone that everyone needs to do better, while showing empathy for mistakes made along the way, and for what it takes to get back on track. Too much on the demanding front, with too little empathy, and you demotivate people. Too much empathy, without holding a high bar, and people aren't motivated to improve (little sense of accountability).

Or say you're sharing incredible quarterly results with your group. You want to come across as confident that the group can keep the momentum, and yet convey humility. Too much confidence with no humility means that complacency sets in (no need for improvement, after all). Too much humility, without celebrating results and expressing confidence in the group, means that people feel demotivated (like what they've accomplished has been downplayed).

It's about not being one-dimensional with the tone you set, so that you're actually encouraging the behavior you're trying to inspire. Make a habit of doing so with this next tool.

Habit-Building Tool #8: The Motivating Match exercise helps you pair the primary tone you intend to set with a "balancing partner," a complementary tone that ensures a balanced message, and thus motivates the desired behavior. See Figure 6.6, and I'll explain.

Fig. 6.6 The Motivating Match exercise

	TONE	MESSAGE
Primary	demanding	"Where we are is unacceptable, we simply must do better"
Balancing	empathetic	"I appreciate how hard it has been, and that it won't get easier"
Primary	confident	"We've been outstanding, and have the talent to keep the momentum"
Balancing	humble	"There's still so much we can learn, so much room to get better"

Look at the top half first. We'll build on the prior example that you want to set a demanding tone for better results, while balancing that with an empathetic tone. So, you plan your primary, demanding tone message of "Where we are is unacceptable, we simply must do better." But you're sure to bring an empathetic balancing tone, with a message of "I appreciate how hard it has been, and that it won't get easier." As a result, everyone is motivated to get to work.

Looking at the bottom half, let's build on the other prior example. You want to share terrific quarterly results with your group, while keeping them humble and hungry. So, you plan your primary, confident tone message of "We've been outstanding, and have the talent to keep the momentum." But you're certain to balance the tone with the humble message of "There's still so much we can learn, so much room to get better." As a result, everyone is motivated to keep driving hard.

The idea is to conduct your own version of this exercise, starting with the primary tone you want to set (and message you want to send), for whatever purpose, then identifying the balancing tone and message that ensures you'll actually motivate the behavior you want. Note that the tone pairings listed earlier (demanding *yet* empathetic, candid *and* kind, etc.) represent some of the most common primary tones that leaders seek to set (along with the balancing tone that's required). If the primary tone you're seeking to set isn't included in those pairings, just think through what the right balancing tone partner would be, and get to practicing that pairing.

Your First Small Step: Download the Motivating Match exercise template at scottmautz.com/mentallystrong/templates, add any other pairings to the list you want to focus on, and use it to plan your balanced tone setting and communications in advance.

In Moments of Weakness: The good thing about maintaining balance is that you can always adjust on the fly. If you catch yourself communicating too much of one element (like too much harsh reality, for example), you can always adjust and rebalance with more messages of hope (to complete the example).

Messaging Habit #9: Exhibit Unswerving Integrity

Ever experience a time when someone betrayed your trust by acting without integrity? You probably have. And you'll probably never forget it. The fact is, even the smallest breaches of integrity can absolutely destroy trust. (Talk about sending a self-sabotaging message!) It's extremely hard to recover and regain employees' trust when you do things like be untruthful, untrustworthy, or act with disguised self-interest. Unfortunately, especially under the pressure of adversity, these toxic behaviors can surface, in even the best-intentioned leaders.

But here's the thing. The vast majority of us probably think we have perfect integrity, even under pressure. It's others who lack it. But the truth is, we can all improve our integrity in small ways (as opposed to just avoiding gross violations of it). In fact, by applying just a little intentionality and mental strength, you can do just that with what follows.

Habit-Building Tool #9: The Integrity Audit is a four-question, self-reflective exercise you conduct to help ensure you're acting with unswerving integrity, to send an "always on" message that you're trustworthy. Periodically ask yourself:

1. **"How might I improve my invisible integrity?"** This means being certain that you're always doing what's right, even the small things, and especially when no one is looking. For example, sure, you could put that money in your pocket that you just saw the person in the elevator drop. No one would ever know. But giving it back to them feeds the habit of doing the right thing. Do that often enough, and it will feel instantly wrong to do anything else.

2. **"Do I have a high Say/Do Ratio?"** This is the ratio of things you say you'll do to the things you actually follow through and do. Ideally, you'd have a 1:1 ratio (you do everything you say you're going to). To illustrate, you tell employees that being on time for meetings is critical and that you'll role model punctuality, but then you show up late for half the meetings you attend. This hurts your Say/Do Ratio, and is clearly something to improve upon. Just examining your ratio from time to time helps you make the changes you need to, thus improving self-integrity. And, by the way, being a person who always does what they say they'll do sends a message of reliability.

3. **"Am I avoiding mistakes of motive?"** Of course, you can make mistakes; mentally strong leaders do, and they admit them and learn from them. But you absolutely should not make a *mistake of motive*, which is having questionable intent behind your actions. The next time you feel yourself about to do something out of spite, anger, jealousy, pure self-interest, etc., stop, pause, and ask, "Does my intent have integrity?" If not, rethink what you're thinking.

   For example, you catch yourself about to complain about a coworker to his boss, but then you realize your intent lacks integrity. You're doing it to get the coworker pulled off your team and make your life easier, when you should be addressing the issue face-to-face with the coworker, with the intent of helping him change/improve.

4. **"Do I act consistent with my values?"** Values are those little things you do every day that exemplify who you are. When you act in a manner inconsistent with your values, you're being fake or disingenuous, like when you violate your value of kindness by lashing out at that slow checkout cashier. The tool that follows next will help you identify your most closely held, nonnegotiable values. This point is about monitoring how you act in relation to your values; to ensure you're living each day in support of your values, not in spite of them.

Your First Small Step: Since most of us don't worry about our own integrity, the first step here is just understanding and accepting the idea that we all have room to improve on this front, even if in small ways. Consider scheduling a biannual or annual Integrity Audit on your calendar, using the four questions for reflection.

In Moments of Weakness: If you fall down on the integrity front in any of the four ways measured in the audit, acknowledge it, forgive yourself, but take it seriously. Remind yourself of what's at stake here: the erosion of hard-earned trust, or feelings of regret, guilt, or shame (emotions important to be rid of, as established earlier in this chapter). Then get right back on track to sending a message that you can, indeed, be trusted.

Messaging Habit #10: Use Your Values as Your Lighthouse

Your values serve as a lighthouse, giving you something to steer toward, through the rough seas of adversity, keeping you on course and away from the rocks. They're like your internal

GPS, guiding you, especially through dark patches, something you can return to, over and over, when you feel lost. And as a leader, living and leading according to an established set of values helps you steady the ship, giving everyone something constant and unyielding they can depend on, even when the strong winds of hardship kick up. Values are like an espresso shot of mental strength come to your aid when you most need it, turning guesses into good decisions.

Consistently, visibly, intentionally living your values sends the message to those you work with that you are principled, grounded, and predictable (in a good way). It's a way to show up authentic, show you're trustworthy, and encourage others to bring their true selves to work. Which makes it even more important that you can articulate your non-negotiable values—so you can live them, non-negotiably, each day.

However, my experience shows that when you ask somebody, "What are your most closely held values?" and give them ninety seconds to jot them down (which I've done in research many times), only half of people are able to do so. If you fall in the half that would struggle with this (or even if you don't), the tool that follows will help you identify and/or sharpen exactly what your values are.

Habit-Building Tool #10: The Values Vault is a self-questionnaire, consisting of six proven steps that will unveil your values (as outlined in the text box). The "Your First Small Step" section that immediately follows will indicate how to get the complete questionnaire so you can take it for yourself.

The Values Vault

Step 1: The Foundation. There's a reason why only half of all adults can readily list their values—it's not like they automatically spring to mind for everyone. It requires laying a foundation to start, to get in the right mindset. Answer the five prompts that follow to get you warmed up:

1. Think of a peak experience or meaningful moment in your life. What was happening? What values were you honoring at the time?
2. Think of when you were the happiest, most proud, or most fulfilled in your life. What was happening during those times? What factors were contributing to your happiness, pride, or fulfillment?
3. Think of a time when you were particularly upset or frustrated. What was happening? What values were being suppressed or violated?
4. Think of someone you love or admire. What values do they embody?
5. If you had to write your epitaph (what's written on your headstone), what would you like it to say about you? About how you chose to live your life?

Step 2: Inspiration. Below are a set of common values, intended to help stimulate what yours might be. Circle any word that stands out as being extra important to you. Don't overthink it—just react. For example:

Accountability
Candor
Humility
Kindness
Selflessness
Etc. (see the Values Vault template for the complete list of
    common values)

Step 3: Look for central themes. With the first two steps in mind, write down any central themes.

Step 4: List your top five values. Write them down. As a check, ask yourself, "Is this truly a core value of mine that I live by, or just one that *should be* a core value?" The idea is to list your true, core values, most important to you, not what's expected of you.

Step 5: Pick the top two driving values in your life. To narrow down from the list of five, consider these questions:

- What values are *essential* to your life?
- What values are primary drivers of your behavior/how you strive to behave?
- What values represent your *primary way of being*?
- What values are essential to supporting your inner self?
- What *must* you have in your life to experience fulfillment?

Now, write those top two values below.

CORE VALUE #1:

CORE VALUE #2:

Step 6: Share your top two core values with your team/group. How will the values show up at work?

(*Note: It's powerful when you share your values with teammates, and vice versa. You learn things about each other that you wouldn't have otherwise known. It creates bonds *with* and deeper understanding *of* one another. Knowing your teammates' values informs you on how best to interact with them.)

Your First Small Step: Download the complete Values Vault template at scottmautz.com/mentallystrong/templates, print it, and answer all the questions contained within. With a little self-reflection, you'll soon have articulated your most closely held values. Then you can get to living them, each day, with discipline, sending messages of authenticity, centeredness, and trustworthiness.

In Moments of Weakness: You stumble here by not knowing your values, and yet deciding to carry on not knowing. The little time it takes to complete the Values Vault questionnaire is well worth it; knowing your values helps you know yourself, and gives you another steadying hand at the wheel of leadership when you need it most. You also fall down here when you know your values, but violate them anyway. It happens. Just acknowledge when it does, register how it feels in the moment (which surely won't be good), then get back to thinking of your values as your lighthouse (and using them as such).

NOTES

1. Ito, T. A., J. T. Larsen, N. K. Smith, and J. T. Cacioppo. 1998. "Negative information weighs more heavily on the brain: The negativity bias in evaluative categorizations," *J Pers Soc Psychol.* 75(4): 887–900.

2. Troy, A. S., A. J. Shallcross, A. Brunner, R. Friedman, and M. C. Jones. February 2018. "Cognitive reappraisal and acceptance: Effects on emotion, physiology, and perceived cognitive costs," *Emotion* 18(1): 58–74.

3. Mayo Clinic Staff. April 14, 2022. "Anger management: 10 tips to tame your temper," mayoclinic.org.

4. Schacter, D. L., D. R. Addis, D. Hassabis, V. C. Martin, R. N. Spreng, and K. K. Spzunar. November 21, 2012. "The Future of Memory: Remembering, Imagining, and the Brain," *Neuron* 76(4): 677–94.

5. "Sapir-Whorf Hypothesis," sciencedirect.com/topics/psychology/sapir-whorf-hypothesis.

6. The Framingham Heart Study, National Institutes of Health, framinghamheartstudy.org.

7. Jim Rohn quotes, goodreads.com.

8. Bradt, S. November 11, 2010. "Wandering Mind Not a Happy Mind," *The Harvard Gazette*, news.harvard.edu.

9. Abrahams, R., and B. Groysberg. December 21, 2021. "How to Become a Better Listener," *Harvard Business Review*, hbr.org.

10. "Multitasking: Switching Costs—What the Research Shows." March 20, 2006. American Psychological Association, apa.org/topics/research/multitasking.

11. Hamilton, J. October 2, 2008. "Think You're Multitasking? Think Again," NPR, npr.org.

12. Formica, M. June 14, 2011. "5 Steps for Being Present," *Psychology Today*, psychologytoday.com.

13. Hamilton.

14. Van Edwards, V. "Mirroring Body Language: 4 Steps to Successfully Mirror Others," scienceofpeople.com.

15. Spataro, S. E., and J. Bloch. 2018. "'Can You Repeat That?' Teaching Active Listening in Management Education," *Journal of Management Education* 42(2): 168–98.

16. Drinko, C. August 4, 2021. "We're Worse at Listening Than We Realize," *Psychology Today*, psychologytoday.com.

17. Černe, M., C. Nerstad, A. Dysvik, and M. Škerlavaj. January 7, 2013. "What Goes Around Comes Around: Knowledge Hiding, Perceived Motivational Climate, and Creativity," *Academy of Management*.

7 The Decision-Making Habit

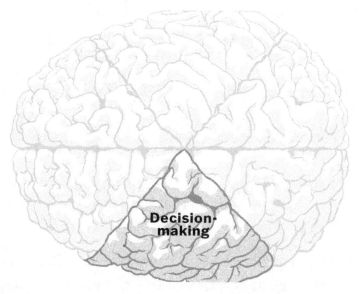

We all make decisions, all day long, an impossible number of them. Heck, Cornell research found we make 221 decisions a day just on food.[1]

And while we all make decisions, all day long, not everyone is equally skilled at making them.

The best draw on their mental strength and self-regulation skills, for the discipline, courage, and conviction it takes to make better decisions more decisively. That's particularly important for the leader, as few constituents make as many decisions, with as much pressure, or with as broad an impact, as leaders must. It's the decisions leaders make that move the organization to something worth achieving. It's why decision-making is so clearly one of the six vital tests of leadership, requiring powerful habits of self-regulation to support and excel at it (like all the tests).

Vijay, the CEO/founder from chapter 1, who effectively changed the business model of his company using disciplined decision-making along the way, benefited from the emotion/ thought/behavior-regulating habits and tools in this chapter. From avoiding decision-making biases, to developing a data-based, analytical approach with a clear decision-making process, meeting, and testing structure, to outright decisiveness, and more, you'll find it all in the menu that follows. Everything you need to create your own tailored set of habits that will consistently lead to better decisions (and to you being more decisive).

Decision-Making Habit #1: Avoid Decision-Making Biases

According to Gartner research, over 60 percent of employees cherry-pick (selectively choose) data to support the decision they actually want to make. Fifty percent make the decision, then seek data afterward to support their decision.[2] It's called confirmation bias, the tendency to search for, interpret, and favor information that confirms your beliefs, or a decision you want to make. It's the most common of many biases that can distort the decision-making process. But if you want to be a great decision-maker, you need the mental strength to notice, and resist, biases like this. That's where this next tool comes in; it offers help on overcoming confirmation bias, and eleven other common decision-making biases.

Habit-Building Tool #1: The next time you have to make a substantive decision, pull out the Bias Buster sheet (Figure 7.1) and place a checkmark next to any decision-making bias you

Fig. 7.1 The Bias Buster

If you want to be a mentally strong decision maker, you must be aware of, and resist, biases that can distort decisions–like the twelve most common ones below. Get into the habit of referring to this sheet when you have to make a decision. At that time, review each bias below, and mark an "X" in the "Yes, this could be me" column next to any bias you worry could surface in that decision-making scenario. Wherever you marked an "X," refer to the solution column for help in avoiding that bias.

Bias	Yes, this could be me (mark "X" for all that apply)	Solution
Confirmation bias—the tendency to search for, interpret, and favor information that confirms your beliefs, or a decision you want to make.		Invite people in to challenge your point of view, to try to disprove what you're inclined to decide. Accept inevitabilities sooner (stop looking for data to support what you want, and accept facts and data that may be pointing you towards an obvious decision).
Sunk cost bias (the IKEA effect)—when you over-value something as a result of having put effort into it.		Look at resources you've put into something—time, money, effort, people-hours—as a non-recoverable cost. Your job isn't to recover your investment, just to make the best decision possible with the data you have.
Availability bias—when you make a decision based on the most immediate information available to you (including recent, dramatic examples), as opposed to gathering further information that could bring greater clarity to a situation.		Pay attention when you're drawing on a recent piece of information. A little flag should go up in your mind saying, "Do I have other information I can draw from to create a well-rounded perspective here?"
Loss aversion—the tendency to protect against loss, more than seeking to gain.		Ask, "What might we gain?" vs. just focusing on "What could we lose?" Put things in perspective by asking, "How painful is the downside here, really?"
Bandwagon effect—doing, or believing, things because many other people do, or believe, the same.		Separate what's right in that situation from what others are doing. Go back to the data, ignore the crowd.
Status quo bias—the preference towards alternatives that keep things the same, even when better alternatives exist.		Ask yourself, "Does my decision move things forward, in a positive way, or hold things constant?" Be honest if you're trying to maintain status quo, and question why.
Authority bias—when you favor authority figures' input over others, despite there being information and opinions that are more informed and relevant to the decision you're trying to make.		Put all input on equal ground. Remember that the collective wisdom of a group is better than the position power of an individual.
Self-serving bias—making decisions that benefit yourself over other employees, customers, clients, partners, or the organization and its goals.		Ask yourself, "Have I made a decision, or a "deciision"? Meaning, does your decision have too many "i's" in it—is it too focused on how "I" will benefit vs. the greater good.
Similarity bias—the tendency to prefer that which is like you, vs. what is different (most obvious in people decisions—who to hire, promote, etc.)		Actively find common ground with people who appear different.
Overconfidence bias—overestimating or having excessive confidence in your ability to predict/foresee future events.		Identify the risk you're introducing by being so "certain." Balance that risk with humility and an understanding that each event is independent of the other, and deserves data as its primary guide.
Imbalance bias—the tendency to focus only on the benefits of a decision, without weighing the potential downsides. Happens most often in a time crunch, when limited information is available, or when one option is favored over another.		Ensure an objective analysis of the pros and cons. If time or information is limited, at least spend some time brainstorming what potential downsides could be. Resist looking at only the positives of a favored option.
Anchoring bias—the tendency to fixate on a single, initial piece of information when deciding, and failing to adjust for subsequent information as it's collected.		Commit to a breadth of data collection. Treat that first piece of information as equal to the other information you must go and collect.

could see yourself falling into. Then, follow the solution to avoid them. Make a habit of referring to this sheet for every substantive decision, and before long, your biases will go bye-bye.

Let's go through the top four biases to get you warmed up to this powerful exercise.

To overcome *confirmation bias*, invite people in to challenge your point of view, to try to disprove what you're inclined to decide. You may also have to accept inevitabilities sooner. In other words, stop looking for data to support what you want, and accept facts and data that may be pointing you toward an obvious decision. For example, you know you must decide to let a very poorly performing employee go, but you keep looking for reasons to keep them, because you like them.

Another common cognitive bias that affects decision-making is the *sunk cost bias*, also known as the IKEA effect. This occurs when you overvalue something as a result of having put effort into it (a reason why many people like build-it-yourself IKEA furniture so much). For example, say a product you worked really hard on doesn't do well in test market. But you decide to launch it anyway, influenced by the fact that it's hard to admit a mistake or walk away from something you're so invested in.

To overcome this, look at the resources you've put into something—time, money, effort—as a non-recoverable cost. Your job isn't to recover your investment, just to make the best decision possible with the data you have.

Availability bias is also common. This happens when you decide based on the most immediate information available, rather than gathering further data that would better inform the decision. For example, say you decide not to hire a talented marketing executive for that sales job, because you just lived through an example where a marketing person was a disaster in a sales role. You drew that conclusion based on recent, superficial information. Had you dug deeper, you would have found the candidate had actually been quite successful in sales roles earlier in their career. Recent examples often drive availability bias because you're inherently more likely to recall those examples, because they're recent. And the more dramatic the recent example, the more likely you are to recall it and base a decision on it. Not good.

Key to overcoming this bias is to notice when you're drawing on a recent piece of information. A little flag should go up in your mind saying, "Do I have other information I can draw from to create a well-rounded perspective here?"

One more common bias to highlight—*loss aversion*. This is based on the tendency to protect against loss, more than seeking to gain. For example, multiple studies show we prefer not to lose money even more than we like to gain money.[3] This causes us to make bad decisions, like bypassing the opportunity for a clearly good financial investment, because of our aversion to loss.

Bypassing this bias requires asking "What might we gain?" not just zeroing in on "What could we lose?" It also helps to put the potential loss in perspective, by asking, "How painful is the downside here, really?"

Your First Small Step: Download the Bias Buster template at scottmautz.com/mentallystrong/templates, and start familiarizing yourself with the biases that can warp your decision-making. Warm up to using the template to its full effect with the next substantive decision you have to make. (Then make using the template a habit, to keep any biases at bay.)

In Moments of Weakness: It's hard work to make a habit of exposing your biases, let alone resisting them, so forgive yourself when you fall victim to one. At the same time, remind yourself of how biases are the silent enemy—sitting quietly in wait to manipulate and distort your next decision. Then double down on not letting that happen again. Anytime you anticipate having a meaningful decision to make, mark it on your calendar, along with a reminder note to pull out the Bias Buster template at that time.

Decision-Making Habit #2: Stop Bad Habits That Lead to Bad Decisions

Forty percent of our daily activity is driven by habits; most often, habits we don't even think about.[4] It's vital to gain better awareness of your bad habits, because bad habits lead to bad decisions.

As a more extreme example of this, think of a young, professional athlete who has a bad habit of surrounding himself with people who aren't a good influence, which leads to poor decisions. While this likely isn't you, there's still a good chance you're making some poor decisions because of your bad habits. For example:

- Maybe you stare at your phone screen in bed, right up until you close your eyes, so you wake up tired and irritable, causing you to make less-than-optimal decisions the next morning (not a good choice).
- Maybe you have a habit of catastrophizing whenever something goes wrong, drawing your focus and energy away from finding a productive way to move forward (also not a good choice).

- Maybe you have a bad habit of always starting out late, so you drive well over the speed limit to make up for it (never a good choice).

The point is, one of the most fundamental ways to get better at making good decisions is to not set yourself up to make bad ones. The tool that follows will help.

Habit-Building Tool #2: Cutting off bad habits that lead to bad decisions starts with becoming more aware of what those bad habits are, and what impact they have. That's why it's so helpful to periodically take a Bad Habit Inventory. Here's how it works. Draw a simple table like the one in Figure 7.2 (or download the template), with three columns and multiple rows. Mark the left column "Bad Habit," the middle column "Impact on Decisions," and the right column "New Habit."

Fig. 7.2 Bad Habit Inventory

Bad Habit	Impact on Decisions	New Habit
Chewing my fingernails	—	—
People-pleasing	Self-neglect	Think of the youniverse, vs. the universe
Perfectionism	Working too long on something, vs. choosing to work on something else more important	Being good at good enough (making better decisions on how I spend my time)
Etc.		

We'll walk through each row momentarily. The idea here is to create an inventory of your bad habits. Pair the time(s) of year you take the inventory with when you step back and take stock of yourself and your goals for some time frame ahead (like at New Year's resolution time, or when you're doing a "spring cleaning" of unhelpful things in your life). Regarding the inventory, don't overthink it, don't beat yourself up. Just reflect, be honest with yourself, and list your bad habits—we all have them. Be brave and ask coworkers, friends, and family what your bad habits are. Then, evaluate whether or not the impact of each bad habit is such that it's actually driving bad decisions (which won't be the case for all of them). In fact, as you're evaluating each habit, say to yourself, "Has this habit led me to make choices I wish I hadn't?" After careful consideration, if the answer is "yes," then write down the new habit you'll replace it with.

Now let's look at each row. Say you list your bad habit of chewing your fingernails. That would be great if you stopped, but that doesn't drive bad decisions, per se, so that's not the focus of this exercise.

Now, say upon reflection, you know your bad habit of people-pleasing leads you to choose, too often, to neglect taking care of yourself and what *you* need to do. As was shared in chapter 4, you decide to replace this bad habit with a new habit: to "Think of the *you*niverse, not the universe" (take care of you first, so you're better energized to serve others in a more authentic way, rather than making a default decision to engage in people-pleasing behavior).

Let's also say that you list your bad habit of perfectionism. Upon reflection, you see that it leads to you working on something for way too long, rather than choosing to work on something else more important. You commit to replacing that bad habit with a habit of "being good at good enough," which will lead to better decisions in the future on how you spend your time. (By the way, we'll go much deeper into curing perfectionism in chapter 8.)

The power of this exercise is that it forces awareness of the unhelpful chain of events that *you* create, allowing you to recognize when a bad habit later leads to a bad decision. In this way, you interrupt the cycle of bad decisions you make on autopilot. And don't skip past that step of actually writing down the new replacement habit, as psychology research from Dominican University of California shows you're an astonishing 42 percent more likely to achieve your goals when you write them down.[5]

Your First Small Step: Download the Bad Habit Inventory template at scottmautz.com/mentallystrong/templates. Schedule the inventory to coincide with a time when you plan to step back and do some reflection. As you prepare the inventory, don't be afraid to get input from people who know you well.

In Moments of Weakness: Whoever you've enrolled to help you identify your bad habits, ask them to call you on it when you fall back into that old, unhelpful way. When they do, be kind to yourself, but remember the power of stopping bad habits that lead to bad decisions. It's like eliminating some competitors in a race before you even get started.

Decision-Making Habit #3: Clarify the Who, What, and How of Decision-Making

Decisions go wrong quite often before they're ever made. A lack of discipline in the earliest stages of the decision-making process can create chaos and lack of clarity and doom a decision from the get-go. The next tool helps you avoid all this.

Habit-Building Tool #3: You can dramatically set yourself up for far more efficient decision-making by being disciplined enough to ask the Who, What, How Questions of Decision-Making. It's simple: ask three questions every time you identify a decision to be made.

1. **Who makes the decision?** Don't underestimate the importance of clarifying who makes the decision. There are four choices. You:
- decide on your own
- decide with input from others (others weigh in, but it's still your call)
- decide jointly (decision by committee, you work to a consensus outcome everyone can support)
- delegate the decision (usually with some parameters)

If it's your decision, make sure it really is your decision, that you have decision space. The stress of not being certain can impact the quality of your decision. For example, you make a more conservative decision than you would otherwise, because you're not 100 percent sure it's your call to make.

On the other hand, if others think it's their decision (when it's not), or believe they get to input or vote on the decision (when they don't), chaos ensues. Lack of role clarity in decision-making burns time, causes frustration and confusion, and muddies the decision-making process, leading to poorer decisions altogether. Note that the habit that follows, "Hold disciplined decision-making meetings," will help you pinpoint everyone's role in the decision-making process.

2. **What (exactly) are you deciding?** Being clear here avoids what's known as *decision drift*. This is where you're deciding things outside the scope of what the original decision to be made was intended to accomplish. For example, you're supposed to decide whether or not to build a new manufacturing plant, but you drift into arguments of where to build the plant if

you do. Different decision, with different criteria, requiring different data.

3. **How will you decide?** Meaning, it's important to communicate if you're going to make the decision on gut (which often isn't ideal, by the way), or aided by easily accessible data, or expert opinion, or a full-blown test market, for example. In other words, what inputs are needed to enable the output of a good decision? The clearer you are on this, the sooner, and more thoroughly, or expertly, the conditions for decision-making are met. Everyone knows what will trigger a decision, and so can work diligently on providing what's needed for the best quality decision to be made.

Your First Small Step: Share with your team that these three questions must be answered, up front, for every substantive decision to be made (i.e., start setting the expectation for it). Appoint a "decision deputy" on your team to ensure these three questions habitually get asked (or assign yourself to this role).

In Moments of Weakness: Hold your "decision deputy" accountable to get the group back on track in adhering to the Who, What, How questions—both in asking them, and staying true to implications of the answers. Remind the group how painful an unclear decision-making process is for the organization.

Decision-Making Habit #4: Hold Disciplined Decision-Making Meetings

Ever been in a meeting where a decision was supposed to be made, but it turns into a free-for-all? The discussion goes in circles, people jump in with irrelevant information or opinions, while others drag out the meeting with inarticulate arguments. Still others weigh in too aggressively as they think it's their decision (when it isn't). The poorly run meeting ends with a less-than-optimal decision, or worse yet, no decision.

Mentally strong decision-makers run disciplined decision-making meetings. You can too, with what follows.

Habit-Building Tool #4: Run a tight decision-making meeting with the Decision Meeting Dictates, three things you must do if you want to ensure a meeting yields a decision. (Use this in conjunction with Decision-Making Habit #3 above.)

1. **Define everyone's role in the decision-making process.** This is an add-on to the "Who decides" question in Habit #3 above. Here, you drive clarity of *everyone's* role in the decision-making process, defining and assigning specific roles.

Multiple models exist to help you with this—one I like is McKinsey's DARE framework.[6] It asks you to assign the following roles within a decision-making group (those that will be in a decision-making meeting). The roles are:

D—Decider. You're the one, or one of only a few, who actually gets to make the decision—you get a "vote," or are *the* vote.
A—Advisor. You have a voice in the decision. You can input your opinion and try to influence the decision.
R—Recommender. You identify and explore options, sharing the pros and cons of each, presenting data

and analysis, and making a recommendation. The Recommender's role is about *organizing, simplifying,* and *clarifying* the context in which the decision is made.
E—Executor. You carry out and execute or implement the decision. You ask questions to clarify the decision, as needed. As part of executing, you inform whoever needs to be informed of a decision.

The point is, when everyone understands their role in a decision/decision-making meeting, you get better, faster decisions, with higher-quality execution.

2. **Control the discussion flow.** This is about owning the decision-making meeting, or assigning an owner (the "decision deputy"). The task here is to keep the meeting moving, to rein people in where necessary, to make sure every stakeholder feels heard, and to ensure all the information, options, and *honest* points of view are on the table.

This last point is especially important—we've all been a part of "polite" decision-making meetings where most attendees are silent, or silently head nodding, but aren't actually in agreement with the decision. It yields a decision by default, rather than through debate, which usually doesn't lead to the best decision.

3. **Send decision-meeting agendas in advance.** Include any necessary pre-reading, like details of the decision to be made, the recommended option and alternatives on the table and supporting data for each, and even the

expected roles of each person in the meeting. Sending out an agenda, say, twenty-four hours in advance, gives people time to think and develop a clearer point of view for the decision-making meeting itself. It also helps those who process more slowly, or just like to reflect longer, to get more comfortable, so they, too, can share their point of view in the decision-meeting. Again, a "decision deputy" can help ensure this gets done, every time.

The bottom line here is that sharp discussions net sharp decisions. Now, you can have both.

Your First Small Step: Establish a powerful, desired identity for your team: to be seen as a decisive group that makes excellent decisions in a timely manner—nothing is more enabling for an organization. This will provide the backdrop and motivation for the disciplined, detail-oriented approach to decision-making that you're asking for from your group.

In Moments of Weakness: Your "decision deputy" can help get you back on a disciplined track when things go astray. And again, remind the group of the cost of an inefficient, ineffective decision-making process to the organization.

Decision-Making Habit #5: Know When to Decide and When Not To

Guess what aspect of great decision-making is most often overlooked?

Knowing *when* to decide, and *when not to*. Mentally strong leaders make better decisions, time after time, by deciding at the right time. Now, you will too.

Habit-Building Tool #5: Use the Decision Timing Table in Figure 7.3, and you'll decide to decide when the time is right. Refer to it whenever you know you'll have a substantive decision to make. There are two columns, "Do Decide When," and "Don't Decide When," and five sets of reminders.

Fig. 7.3 The Decision Timing Table

DO Decide When...	DON'T Decide When...
your *realistic deadline* arrives	the deadline has passed
your energy is highest	you're exhausted
you've taken time to reflect	you're emotional
focused	multi-tasking
you add unique perspective to the decision	you can delegate

Let's go through the table, one row at a time.

Do Decide When "your realistic deadline arrives," Don't Decide When "the deadline has passed." Realistic deadlines are the key here—not too short, or too long, a time frame. Too short, you might rush a decision. Too long, you might fall victim to Parkinson's Law, which says "work expands to fill the time allotted."[7] For example, you set a deadline to make a decision in thirty days, knowing it's more than enough time. You end up needlessly expanding the scope of work, filling that time with too much potentially distracting analysis, possibly even pushing you past your decision deadline. Or, having so much time you procrastinate, forcing a rushed, last-minute decision. Neither scenario helps decision quality.

To overcome Parkinson's Law, assess how long it should realistically take to make a decision (and do the supporting work needed), then set a deadline and stick to it. Regularly drifting past decision deadlines feeds an unhelpful lack of discipline.

Do Decide When "your energy is highest," Don't Decide When "you're exhausted."

High-priority decisions should be made at high-energy times—most often in the morning, when, research shows, we make our best decisions.[8] This avoids the trap of "decision fatigue," when you're mentally worn down from an extended period of making decisions, and just decide with far less thought. The result is, at worst, a terrible decision; at best, a decision distorted by default.

For example, a famous study showed deserving prisoners were more likely to have parole rightfully granted if their parole meeting was in the morning, as opposed to the afternoon (when deciders were worn down from multiple hearings).[9]

You further counter decision fatigue by standardizing things to reduce the number of decisions you have to make. For instance, one former US president wore only gray or blue suits so he wouldn't have to choose his wardrobe every day. It freed up mental decision-making space. You can too, by standardizing the time you go to sleep, wake up, exercise, etc.

Do Decide When "you've taken time to reflect," Don't Decide When "you're emotional." Think about any time you chose to "sleep on it" before making a decision—to get some distance, clear your head, consider past decision-making mistakes, and reflect in general. I'll bet it led to a better decision, every time.

Now think of times when you decided while emotional. I'm betting the opposite resulted. Emotions can cause you to gloss over facts, or skew your perception of what really needs to happen—not good ingredients for the decision-making soup. Mentally strong decision-makers are aware of their emotions (and thoughts and behaviors) and regulate them so they don't hijack their decision-making process.

By the way, it's okay to go with your heart or a bit of emotion as a tiebreaker for making the call. Just keep the heart and head balanced when deciding.

Do Decide When "focused," Don't Decide When "multi-tasking." This is about simply focusing when making a decision, ignoring the constant flow of email, social feeds, and other interruptions. If you must, hide away somewhere to think things through, free of distractions. Great decisions come from intentionality as much as intelligence.

Do Decide When "you add unique perspective to the decision," Don't Decide When "you can delegate." If you're best suited to decide, do so. If others can make the decision, or if it's an unimportant decision, delegate it. Remember, fewer decisions to make means more energy for important decisions. For example, say you determine that of the next several decisions you're slated to make, only one of them actually requires your specific perspective. The rest can be delegated. So, you delegate them.

Pro tip: To delegate effectively, create an Agreement for Autonomy, which is a document or discussion that spells out the operating rules for the handover of power. It helps ensure that the giver of the autonomy (you) and the receiver (the employee) are clear and comfortable with the delegation of work. The agreement has three parts:

- *Construction*—You clarify what's being delegated (the scope), why (the objective), and how it will be measured (success criteria and measurements). This ensures the employee feels like you're delegating work and empowering, rather than dumping work and running.

- *Communication*—You create a communication loop to keep you, the delegator, informed along the way, and for you to share information as needed. For example, say you gave your team autonomy to achieve an important objective as they see fit. They should still keep you in the loop on progress and issues so you're able to answer questions from the chain of command, and to back up their decisions if necessary. It also gives you the opportunity to share any pertinent information.

- *Consultation*—You identify circumstances that will require your consultation. For example, back to that important objective you granted autonomy to your team on. You indicate you must be consulted if, along the way, the team feels they must overspend their budget. While the team has autonomy, in special instances like this, it requires they consult you first. The idea is to still be brave in liberally granting autonomy, but to have this mechanism in place should you truly need to be enrolled on something.

Your First Small Step: Start internalizing that there are times to make a decision and times not to. Start familiarizing yourself with the "Dos" and "Don'ts" of decision timing. Make it easy to refer to the Decision Timing Table when you know you'll have a pending decision of importance (by writing those decision dates down on the calendar, for example, with a reminder note to check the Decision Timing Table at those times).

In Moments of Weakness: The "decision deputy" mentioned previously can help hold you accountable for deciding at the right time, or getting you back on track when timing is off (share the Decision Timing Table with the decision deputy). If you end up making a decision under "Don't Decide When" conditions, like when you're exhausted or emotional, notice that you've done so, and what it felt like in the moment (it won't feel good). Then, commit to making the next decision under better conditions.

Decision-Making Habit #6: Collect Data Wisely, Analyze It Critically

Research from the Kellogg School of Management showed that in the typical meeting, an average of three people do over 70 percent of the talking.[10] That makes it hard to get a diversity of input to aid decision-making, especially if there are several introverts you'd like to hear from. But a breadth of input is critical for making great decisions. Otherwise, you risk working in an echo chamber, a vacuum, with only a few vocal opinions shaping an incomplete point of view.

Of course, just collecting data to broaden your point of view isn't enough. Potentially great decisions turn into misguided ones when that data isn't properly analyzed.

What follows will help you avoid each of these traps.

Habit-Building Tool #6: You increase your conviction to gather perspective-broadening data, in the right way, and to properly honor/respect that data by analyzing it critically, when you invoke the Collect and Respect Credo. The credo centers on three fundamental points to keep in mind when collecting, and analyzing, data. Let's look at the "collect" aspect first.

When Collecting Data

1. *Force fresh perspective.* This simply means to gather data from sources outside of your typical circle. For example, encourage introverts at that meeting to share their point of view. Or get an informed outsider's point of view—someone in the industry, but not close to the decision. As an example of this, say you're struggling to decide which vendor should supply a key component. So, you bring in outsiders from other companies, all of whom have experience with each vendor, and who can share pros and cons of each. It's about being curious, not complacent.

It also helps to seek out others to contradict your opinion, not validate it. Ask someone to play devil's advocate and challenge assumptions. Of course, this isn't about gathering so much data that you overwhelm yourself or unduly delay a decision, but about expanding your point of view selectively and wisely.

2. *Beware the danger of familiarity.* Being super knowledgeable in an area can be just as dangerous as helpful. When making a decision on a familiar topic, it's easy to cut corners and just rely on what you already know to make the call. But when you do, you lose objectivity and may miss important, fresh perspectives. For example, say you have to hire someone for a role on your team, a role you've personally occupied in the past. So, you cut the hiring process short and hire someone like you (since you did the job so well

and know what it takes). But in so doing, you miss interviewing candidates who might be very different from you, and who would bring a much-needed new perspective to the table. The net here is to keep challenging what you know and recognize when you're too close to be objective.

3. *Revisit your values.* While collecting a variety of data, don't forget one constant. Your values. Revisiting your values can make it clear what to decide. As detailed in chapter 6, values can turn guesses into good decisions. For example, if a core value is risk taking, your decision should probably push some boundaries.

When Analyzing Data

1. *Be mindful of how data is presented to you.* Every piece of information you receive from someone else has been structured, represented, or filtered in a way intended to influence your opinion. Be careful to avoid what neuroscientists call the *framing bias* (another bias in addition to the ones covered in the Bias Buster exercise earlier in this chapter). This bias occurs when your decision is influenced not by *what* information is presented, but *how* it's presented.

As a simple example to illustrate, a team shows a chart visually indicating a high growth rate for a product (Figure 7.4, Chart A on the left), for the period from April through May.

Fig. 7.4 Data Representation

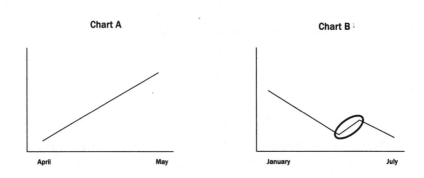

At a glance, the overall visual impression is one of high growth. But when you change the scale of the chart, and examine the same data over a longer time period, from January through July (Chart B), you see it's a modest short-term spike amid an overall alarming decline. How data is presented can shape the decision you make; so it's important to keep a critical eye.

Now, some framing of information is often helpful, to help make different decision options clearer, for example. Just keep the motivations in mind behind the information or argument presented. Be clear on what is fact and what is opinion. Watch for potential distortion or exaggeration of facts or data. And surround yourself with people who can help break down and interpret the data you have access to (in this instance, and in general), and who can help course-correct any of your misperceptions about the data.

2. *Listen carefully to what's said and not said.* Actively listen when people are sharing data or their point of view. Ask lots of questions. Don't get swayed by emotion.

And pay attention to what's not being said. For example, you're trying to decide whether or not to buy that new car. And while the salesperson goes on about the fantastic mileage, they're not answering your question about safety ratings. There's often something behind what's not being said.

3. *Analyze versus paralyze.* Meaning, invest the time you've allotted to carefully analyze the data you've collected. But don't drown in the data, getting paralyzed by it all, unable to discern what to do next.

Look for patterns in data, or discrepancies and inconsistencies. Of course, keep an open mind, but at the same time, question data sources and apply some healthy skepticism. If it's a big strategic decision, take time to analyze, up until the point you worry the opportunity will pass you by (like when acquiring a key competitor or investing in a start-up).

Again, though, avoid analysis paralysis. Equipped with the best information and perspective you have, just *make the call.* And don't look back. Except, possibly, to later evaluate that decision and learn from it.

You can also overcome analysis paralysis by following the advice of Google's first chief decision scientist, Cassie Kozyrkov, who says this of critical analysis: *commit to your default decision up front.*[11] Meaning, pick a decision among your emerging options, up front, using your best judgment of the pros and cons of the options at that time. Ask yourself, "If I see no additional data, or more influential data, beyond what I've already seen, what will I do? Which decision would I make if I had to choose right now?" Then, have the discipline to stick to your default choice if the data doesn't clearly tell you otherwise. This keeps you from swimming in the data for too long or relying on it too much.

Your First Small Step: Mark deadlines for upcoming substantive decisions on your calendar. Also mark a window of time before each deadline for data collection and analysis (reviewing the Collect and Respect Credo principles for each at that time). We often don't gather the data we need for an informed decision because we feel rushed for time, not able to wait for the data. So, plan for it. Pair this with Habit #3 (clarifying the who, what, and how of decision-making), as the habit of collecting data wisely is part of discerning *how* you will decide. And keep in mind that the data is only as good as your disciplined analysis of it. Being careless in the process here is as unhelpful as never having collected the data to begin with.

In Moments of Weakness: Sometimes you have to rush to a decision or just make the call, and that's understandable. But when you feel like you've skipped the data collection and analysis steps, and it could have affected the quality of the decision, commit to upping your discipline next time around. Remember the decision you made without proper analysis, and compare it to the one you made where you did due diligence. You'll surely see a difference in the quality of decision that will reinforce the importance of getting back on track here for future decisions.

Decision-Making Habit #7: Explore a Better Third Option

An interesting phenomenon happens in the decision-making process, known as the Pairing Paradox. We're drawn to having just two options to decide from; our brain is wired that way, to compare and contrast A versus B, this one to that one. It feeds our comparison instinct, and makes it easier to do so because, after all, it's just comparing one thing to the other—we do that all the time.

But there's a downside to this. In an effort to simplify the decision-making process and choose from just two options, you can end up accepting way too many trade-offs with the option you choose.

Habit-Building Tool #7: That's why mentally strong decision-makers have a habit of *exploring if a better third option exists*, perhaps one that's a blend of the two options on the table, and that minimizes the trade-offs of either option.

For example, say you're choosing between buying a home that's close to the city where you work, but is expensive, or one that's far more affordable, but is quite a distance from your work. You're eager to get on with making a decision, so you choose the expensive home near the city.

But you could have allotted more time in the decision-making process up front for the potential identification of a better, third option. Had you done so, you would have discovered a lovely home for sale in the first suburb out from the city, an option that splits the difference between distance and affordability, minimizing the trade-offs of your other two options.

Former CEO of Procter & Gamble David Taylor made a habit of leveraging this decision-making approach, at a much higher, strategic level, particularly when there wasn't a clear best choice between two options.[12]

And that's an important distinction, here. I'm not talking about making the decision-making approach more complex—simpler is better. If there are two options, and one is not only better than the other, but has very few trade-offs altogether, by all means, proceed with that option. I'm just talking about weighing the pros and cons of each decision option equally, and making sure there's not a better "other" option that minimizes substantial trade-offs. The minimization of those trade-offs, of course, has to be worth any complexity you're adding to the decision-making process.

Your First Small Step: Start ingraining the thought that any time you're carefully considering two options, it should automatically trigger your curiosity as to whether or not there's a better third option. Start by avoiding the Pairing Paradox (boiling things down too quickly into just two options).

In Moments of Weakness: It's easy to forget that a better third option might be available, especially when, in your evaluation of the two current options, you begin to mentally minimize the trade-offs and are increasingly drawn to the positives of one of the options (and you just want to move forward). If you fail to look into a possible better third option, commit to do so the next time a decision rolls around, carving out enough time for more extensive consideration. Imagine the power of being known for always making the best decisions with the fewest trade-offs (without taking too long to decide, of course).

Decision-Making Habit #8: Maximize Decision Confidence

What are three of the most important words in decision-making?
Debate. Decide. Commit.

People often miss the importance of this last one—fully committing to a decision made. It's easy to doubt your decision, not fully committing to it because you're not really convinced it's the right decision. To feel more certain about what you decide, run some tests, as follows.

Habit-Building Tool #8: More specifically, use the Decision Confidence Test, shown in Figure 7.5; it provides four overlapping ways to test if the decision you're about to make is indeed a good one.

Fig. 7.5 The Decision Confidence Test

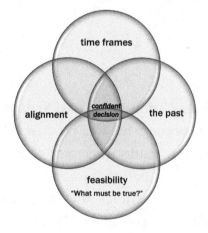

Pass all four tests, and in the center, you'll have a decision you can be confident in. Let's go through each test.

Test 1

Evaluate based on **time frames**: near-term, mid-term, and long-term. For example, you're trying to decide on accepting that new job offer. Ask yourself, is it a decision I'll feel good about immediately (fifteen minutes from now), tomorrow (fifteen hours from now, after sleeping on it), or longer term (fifteen years from now)? Doing so helps you take emotion out of the decision and ensures that you consider your most deeply held goals.

You don't have to answer yes to all three time frames, by the way. Taking that job might not feel great for the short and mid-term, but you know it will help your career in the long run. Or the opposite—you might be really excited about the job, but you know, deep down, it takes you off track from your long-term goals.

The point is, consider the near, mid, and long term of your decision as a filter, and evaluate any trade-offs or benefits accordingly.

Test 2

Test your decisions against **the past** (i.e., previous similar decisions). There's no teacher like the past. How did the last similar decision you made work out? What can you learn from it? Even if the situation wasn't exactly the same, what drove you to that past decision—all the right things, or all the wrong things? Analyze, and apply to your current decision.

Test 3

Test for **feasibility**. Ask, "What must be true for this decision to be a good one?" You're trying to avoid making a decision that depends on everything going right. For example, say you're on the fence about whether or not to launch that new product next month, despite poor early test results. You realize that for this to be a good decision, too many things have to be true: the product has to be redesigned drastically better, the marketing must be fixed, the pricing has to be exactly right. Too much must be true, too fast, so you opt not to launch. Probably a good decision.

Asking "What must be true?" also helps identify the minimum the decision must satisfy. For example, maybe to launch that new product you just need the redesign done well, and you can accept having to keep working on everything else as you go. If you're confident about the redesign, launching becomes a good decision.

Test 4

Test your decisions for **alignment**—ensuring they align with and support your business model, strategies, or vision. For example, before you decide to commit all that effort to that one customer, is growing your business with that particular customer consistent with your business model or growth strategies? It's about evaluating how your smaller-scale decision fits in with the broader picture.

By the way, when you do make the call, do so with confidence—even if it's a complex decision with uncertain outcomes. The troops want to know that you believe in what you decide—they don't want to be led based on probabilities. And, research shows, showing confidence in your decision boosts others' faith in you as a leader and makes them believe you have a good path forward, which actually helps the group be more successful.[13]

Your First Small Step: Refer to the Decision Confidence Test as you're solidifying/finalizing a decision. Write decision deadlines on your calendar, along with a reminder note (a day or two prior) that says, "Run the test, make the call."

In Moments of Weakness: When you forget to conduct these tests and end up making a decision with less-than-optimal confidence, remember that uncomfortable feeling. Use it as a reminder to use the Decision Confidence Test tool next time.

Decision-Making Habit #9: Elevate Your Predictive Ability

Guess what some of the most difficult decisions are to make? Ones you have to make in the face of adversity. In such times, you're likely already stressed enough with enough to do in a short amount of time. Anything that makes decision-making better and easier at these times is of great value. Especially the strategy that follows.

Habit-Building Tool #9: You get out ahead of poor decision-making that happens in adversity when you habit-ually elevate your predictive ability. Meaning, when you learn to anticipate issues and events by identifying patterns, and taking time to scenario plan, you dramatically improve the quality of decisions that get made. To do this, regularly commit time to study your industry, your competition, and your organization. Literally schedule time to do so, and pro-tect that time to look for trends and identify what triggered past struggles.

And spend time engaged in planning scenarios for the big-gest problems your business or organization could face. Do so with a diverse group of experts, and include modeling for what you think competitors might or might not do in the face of the expected challenge. Plot out specific courses of action for each scenario and get preapproval for resulting actions so that you can move fast when the time comes.

As an example, I've been involved with one company, many times, on scenario planning (in case raw material costs spiked, forcing a price increase). We'd assemble a team to think through a variety of competitive response scenarios. This improved our adaptability as we were more prepared for however the competitor actually ended up responding to a price increase. If their response created problems for us, we could then quickly make good counter-decisions and adjustments to our plans.

The reality is, adversity *will* happen. Might as well be prepared for it when it does. The decisions you make will be all the better for it.

Your First Small Step: Schedule the first block of time on your calendar for elevating your predictive ability. Label the time block GASP (groundwork and scenario planning), remembering that it also refers to the reaction you'll have (gasp!) when this work reveals a major emerging issue or opportunity.

In Moments of Weakness: It's easy to fall into a pattern of assuming you know enough to head off most issues. When an issue (or opportunity) surfaces that you see should have caught earlier, let that frustration trigger a recommitment to strengthen your predictive abilities.

Decision-Making Habit #10: Default to Being Decisive

What's one of the worst things you can decide as a leader?

To not decide.

Indecision is a lack of self-regulation (of emotions, thoughts, and behaviors) in one of its most damaging forms.

It paralyzes an organization. It kills a sense of certainty and completion, sapping an organization's energy. Multiple options can linger too long, bloating costs and timelines, putting you or your organization in a corner. Clearly, choosing not to decide is a choice with consequences. When occasional indecision escalates to the status of a bad habit, fewer things are more destructive for an organization.

The other habits in this chapter help you be more decisive simply because they make you better at making decisions. But let's address the bad habit of indecisiveness directly now.

Habit-Building Tool #10: To decisively end indecision, use the Cornering Indecision visual, a simple figure of a square with four pinpointed reminders for overcoming indecision, one tucked in each corner, all to prevent you from getting cornered by your own indecision.

Fig. 7.6 The Cornering Indecision visual

evaluate the cost of a wrong decision and indecision	set timebound parameters for deciding
be willing to make the tough, unpopular calls	accept inevitabilities sooner

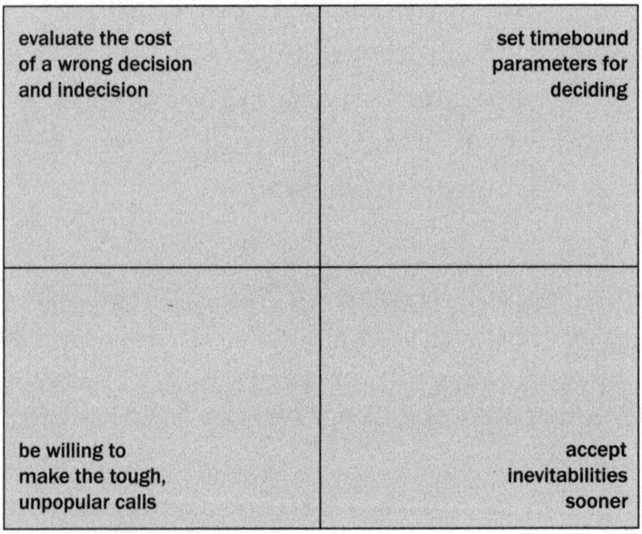

Let's keep you from cornering yourself, one pinpointed preventative at a time.

Evaluate the cost of a wrong decision and indecision. Step back and ask, "What's the worst thing that could happen in the long run if this decision is wrong?" Consequences likely aren't as dire as you're assuming (so resist catastrophizing). The point is, getting comfortable with the possibility of being wrong helps the right decisions happen faster.

Also consider the risks/costs of *not deciding*. Doing so creates awareness of pitfalls that would otherwise be glossed over. For example, it becomes obvious that putting off a decision will cause budget overruns or keep resources from working on other priorities.

You can also step away from the decision you're having a hard time making for a bit, then return to it with renewed perspective and commitment to just make the call. It works. How often have you "slept on a decision" to then find the clear choice emerge?

One other trick here. Ask yourself, "Who do I least want to disappoint with this decision?" Let that drive what you decide. Overthinking and indecision can take hold when you worry about trying to please every stakeholder—which is often impossible to do.

Set timebound parameters for deciding. It's natural to take as much time as possible to decide; time that only ends up expanding the amount of work you do (I mentioned Parkinson's Law earlier in this chapter). So, create tension by setting time limitations to deciding—concrete, timebound parameters, with teeth to them. For example, one client of mine communicated a date they'd announce the location of a new manufacturing plant. Not deciding by that date would have tax incentive implications and make them look disorganized—not good.

When the time comes, make the best decision with the information you have, with confidence. Then let it go, even if that decision doesn't work out. Even if people don't agree with the decision, they'll appreciate that a decision was made, so everyone can just move forward. And by the way, revisit decisions only when you have new information.

Accept inevitabilities sooner. This idea was mentioned earlier in this chapter (as part of a solution for *confirmation bias*). Sometimes, you *know* you have to decide in a certain way, but you're reluctant to do so. So you stall, by gathering more data, holding more meetings, etc. Building on the example used earlier, you know you must decide to let an unproductive employee go (a painful thing to do), but keep putting it off to see if they'll suddenly improve. Instead, you should ask yourself, "Am I putting off deciding a course of action I *know* I must take?" If so, you know what to do.

Be willing to make the tough, unpopular calls. Difficult decisions, ones that won't be liked by at least some faction of people, are often the kind that drag on the longest. Why? Because you dread the "blowback" you'll get. It won't feel good. For example, you might keep putting off the decision of whether or not to kill that project because so many people put so much work into it and still believe in it. If your indecisiveness stems from your attempt at avoidance, it's a clear signal to step up and make the call you know you have to.

Note that making tough calls may also require you to have the mental strength to delay gratification. For example, say that if you decided not to kill that project, it would have helped you hit your sales figures this year—quick gratification.

But by giving up the short-term sales bump, you gained an important, longer-term benefit (you avoid the profit drain the project would ultimately have created on your business).

Your First Small Step: Refer to the Cornering Indecision visual when you feel undue indecision putting you in a corner, wreaking havoc. And enroll an accountability partner to call you on it when you've gone beyond reflection, consideration, and analysis and crossed over into indecisiveness.

In Moments of Weakness: When you find you're having difficulty just making the call, don't despair. Reflect on the identity of being seen as decisive—it's one of the most mentally strong, leader-like attributes you can embody. And remember how poorly the opposite reflects on you. Keep coming back to the cost of not deciding, to create tension and motivation to move forward.

NOTES

1. Lang, S. S. December 22, 2006. "'Mindless autopilot' drives people to dramatically underestimate how many daily food decisions they make, Cornell study finds," *Cornell Chronicle*.

2. Ganeshan, A., and G. Herschel. September 15, 2021. "Innovation Insight for Decision Intelligence," gartner.com.

3. Ruggeri, K., A. Alí, M. L. Berge, et al. 2020. "Replicating patterns of prospect theory for decision under risk," *Nat Hum Behav* 4: 622–33.

4. "How we form habits, change existing ones." August 8, 2014. Society for Personality and Social Psychology, sciencedaily.com.

5. "Goals Research Summary," www.dominican.edu/sites/default/files/2020-02/gailmatthews-harvard-goals-researchsummary.pdf.

6. De Smet, A., C. Hewes, and M. Luo. July 25, 2022. "The limits of RACI—and a better way to make decisions," mckinsey.com.

7. Parkinson, C. N. November 19, 1955. "Parkinson's Law," *The Economist,* economist.com/news.

8. Leone, J. M., D. F. Slezak, D. Golombek, and M. Sigman. January 2017. "Time to decide: Diurnal variations on the speed and quality of human decisions," *Cognition* 158: 44–45, sciencedirect.com.

9. Danziger, S., J. Levav, and L. Avnaim-Pesso. April 11, 2011. "Extraneous factors in judicial decisions," *PNAS* 108(17), pnas.org.

10. "The Introvert's Guide to Mastering Meetings," nextbigideaclub. com.

11. Kozyrkov, C. June 25, 2019. "The First Thing Great Decision Makers Do," *Harvard Business Review,* hbr.org.

12. Based on working for, and with, David for many years.

13. Anderson, C., S. Brion, D. A. Moore, and J. Kennedy. 2012. "A Status Enhancement Account of Overconfidence," *Journal of Personality and Social Psychology* 103(4).

8 The Goal-Focus Habit

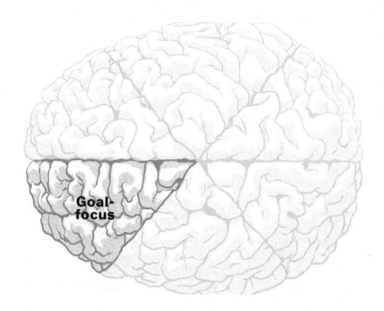

Goal-focus

It would seem we're almost genetically predisposed to have poor goal-focus, i.e., we have difficulty staying focused on our goals—one of the more self-evident tests of leadership that correlates directly with achievement. Case in point: one of the least pessimistic studies I could find regarding the percent of New Year's resolutions that fail was from a psychology study at the University of Hertfordshire, which reported a 78 percent failure rate.[1] Another clinical psychologist reported an 80 percent failure rate, *by the second week of February.*[2]

The low success rate isn't that surprising. Because with the discipline and conviction required, and the never-ending parade of distractions, staying goal-focused is *hard*. It takes persistent, deliberate steps, and grit, as a famous study from the University of Pennsylvania's Angela Duckworth[3] has shown. That's the point of this chapter; to create "grit fortifiers": habits of self-regulation with supporting tools, systems, and routines to drive goal-focus (and goal-achievement).

To reinforce that such tools work in maintaining goal-focus, other research[4] shows the small group that succeeds with their New Year's resolutions "employ significantly more stimulus control, reinforcement, and willpower." In other words, they self-regulate their emotions, thoughts, and behaviors (as was also shown among the small group of "resolutioners" in the Hertfordshire research).

Also know that many of the same habits and tools in this chapter were used by Javier, our goal-focused sales leader from chapter 1, who kept his team laser-focused on achieving an astounding 25 percent sales increase in a stagnant category.

You'll keep goal-focus on your own targeted achievement by learning how to set intrinsically motivating goals, visualize the work it will take, set a thorough collection of specific expectations, focus on what you can control (and focus more sharply in general), avoid distractions, drive accountability, leverage the power of small wins, eliminate procrastination and perfectionism, and more.

Let's get to the toolbox, so that focus on regulating your emotions, thoughts, and behaviors quickly leads to goal-focus.

Goal-Focus Habit #1: Set Intrinsically Motivating Goals

One of the most powerful ways to keep people focused on a goal is to set goals they care about achieving in the first place. When you do, motivation is "baked in," generated from doing the work itself, as opposed to doing the work for the sake of hitting some stretch goal.

Said another way, that big numerical goal of reaching a billion dollars in sales, or doubling profit margins, or achieving the number one share position in the category, while great, isn't enough by itself to maintain people's focus over time. The key is to embed those numerical targets within a goal people care about, further encased in a system that taps into intrinsic motivation along the way. What follows does just that.

Habit-Building Tool #1: If you want to set stretching goals that people care about and will stay focused on, use the Cascading Goal System. Its power comes from the fact that *it encourages the expenditure of discretionary focus and energy.* Here's how it works.

Fig. 8.1 The Cascading Goal System

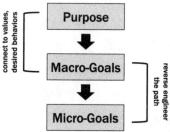

I'll explain the system, using an example to illustrate as we go.

Start with the purpose behind the goal—the why. To identify it, ask, "Why should people work so hard to achieve this goal, spending so much time away from their loved ones in so doing, taking on so much pressure and potential stress along the way? What's the higher-order reason for achieving the goal that *gives it meaning*, that makes it clear *why what we do matters?*" You can also ask, "Who do we ultimately serve, in what way?" Or "How might we integrate who we are with what we do?

For example, say you've been charged with turning around an underperforming portfolio of health-care products. In fact, you must transform the business and turn it into a reliable growth engine for the company. You could simply set a goal of "Transforming the business into a growth engine, reaching $1 billion in sales by date xyz."

Or you could start from a place of purpose: to "Be the everyday heroes empowering consumers everywhere to live unimpeded by their condition."

Note, I'm not saying forget any numerical targets (we'll get to that shortly). Starting with purpose maintains focus on the goal because it reminds people of what they're fighting for. It gives them something to return to, over and over, when they feel lost. Invoking the purpose inspires them to renew their commitment and stretch even further.

Ah, but you say. Our organization isn't in an industry inherently rich with meaning, like health care. We just sell widgets, or provide service for a mundane category, and so on.

But there's always something about the work that people can find meaningful and inherently motivating, even if it's just the pursuit of learning and mastery (articulating what you can be the absolute best at). Former CEO of Dunnhumby USA (a data science company) Stuart Aitken told me that his company's purpose was "Learn to become the best in our field at doing things *for* the customer, not *to* the customer."

As Harvard Business School professor Max Bazerman says, "There is a growing set of research that shows 'learning or mastery' goals have much more positive effects on performance and internal motivation than 'performance' goals."[5]

From the compelling purpose flow the macro-goals—the few biggest objectives or business goals that ensure everyone is working toward the same end. The best macro-goals feed directly into the purpose, and are cooperative in nature. Meaning, they're lofty enough that everyone realizes the only way to achieve the goal is by everyone working together (not in silos). Note, not every macro-goal will directly relate to the purpose, but more often than not, they should.

Back to the health-care products example. With the purpose in mind, two macro-goals might be to (a) reignite the innovation portfolio, fueling $1 billion in sales (there's that hard, stretch number), and (b) expand sales and distribution overseas for the first time.

Now it's time to further fuel the sense of intrinsic motivation required to maintain focus on the goals. You do so by breaking the macro-goals down into smaller micro-goals. This makes the associated work feel more manageable, and gives the opportunity to celebrate small wins along the way. As a classic study of top swimmers[6] showed, the athletes that focused on small wins and progressing toward their goal in small increments enhanced both their skills and confidence in their abilities. And greater confidence means more focus on the very goal you're becoming increasingly confident you can hit.

Once more, let's return to the health-care example. Say to achieve the macro-goal of reigniting the innovation portfolio and fueling $1 billion in sales, it requires the micro-goals of (a) launching five new products a year and growing disproportionately with the current top three customers. And to accomplish the macro-goal of expanding sales globally, it requires the micro-goals of (b) hiring a top-notch new sales force and building an overseas headquarters.

If you're thinking, "Yeah, but some of those micro-goals feel more like macro-goals to me," don't get hung up on that—the relative scope of each is certainly subjective. The critical point here is that goals need to be broken up into interconnected, smaller pieces, to generate the intrinsic motivation required to keep employees focused on those goals.

Two more intrinsic motivators to build into the system are seen in Figure 8.1. The first happens as you're meshing the purpose with the macro-goals. It's at this point you ensure that the purpose and macro-goals connect to the organization's values and the desired behaviors you want to see along the way. This helps prevents the phenomenon of "goals gone wild," as Harvard's Bazerman describes them, "stretch goals that produce serious side effects: shifting, (unhealthy) attitudes toward risk, promoting unethical behavior, and triggering the psychological costs of goal failure."[7]

Applying this insight, the health-care group dictates that all goals must be delivered in alignment with the organization's core values of kindness and integrity, while demonstrating the core desired behaviors of ownership and collaboration, for example.

Finally, when you've established the macro-goals, reverse engineer the path it will take to get there (listing all the big tasks, milestones, and micro-goals required along the way). Said another way, start with your macro-goal and work backward, as opposed to starting from where you are now and trying to plot out, with greater uncertainty, all the steps it will take to achieve the macro-goal. Research from the Korea University Business School and the University of Iowa found that starting with the macro-goal and planning backward yielded greater goal-motivation and goal-performance, due to the fact that "backward planning allowed people to think of tasks required to reach their goals more clearly."[8]

Here's how the Cascading Goal System looks (with the example we've been using plugged in).

Fig. 8.2 The Cascading Goal System

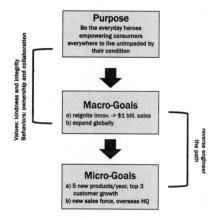

Your First Small Step: Refer to the Cascading Goal System when it's time to set a goal. Begin discussion with your team about the purpose behind a goal you want to set, by starting with the Why/Who/What questions: Why will this goal matter? Who do we ultimately serve by achieving this goal? What can this group do better than anyone else that's reflected in accomplishment of the goal?

In Moments of Weakness: The three most common mistakes made here are skipping past the purpose part, failing to break the big goal into smaller pieces, or failing to communicate the purpose/goals often enough. If you stumble on any of these, stop to consider how much more difficult it will be to achieve the goal, as a result. Then, simply commit to getting it right next time. After all, there are always more goals to be set with each new challenge you face.

Goal-Focus Habit #2: Visualize the Work It Will Take

As established in the last chapter, just writing down your goals makes it much more likely you'll achieve them.

Doing so feels like low-hanging fruit then, no? It is, and here's a big cherry on top.

Habit-Building Tool #2: If merely writing down your goals can have that kind of impact, imagine the power of visualizing those goals and *the work it will take to achieve them*. You do so with a GRAB, a goal realization and action board. It's a board (either physical or digital) you create by finding images and key phrases that represent your goals and, more importantly, the specific work it will take to achieve them. Note that I'm not talking about a popular tool known as a vision board (visualizing just the goals), which I believe, on its own, is an incomplete approach to maintaining goal-focus and aiding goal-achievement. In fact, psychology research from the University of California showed that a group of students who were asked to visualize *studying* for an exam scored better than students asked to visualize *getting a great grade* on that exam.[9] Why? Visualizing doing the work it takes to score well prompted students to do more of that very work.

Here's what a goal realization and action board (GRAB) looks like.

Fig. 8.3 Goal Realization & Action Board (GRAB)

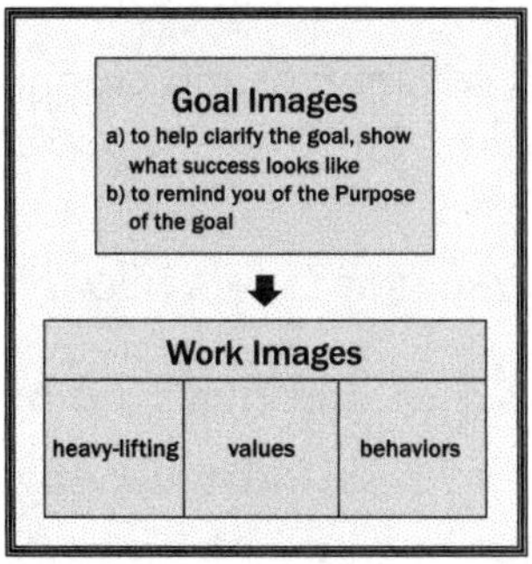

The board starts with Goal Images, selecting images/supporting phrases that represent your goals and achievement of them. Doing so helps you clarify your goal and articulate what success looks like. It helps make your ambitions more tangible. And it reminds you of your "Why," the purpose behind the goal, further reinforcing positive intentions for achieving the goal.

But as mentioned, just visualizing goals isn't enough. To understand why, let's examine the positives of doing so, and the limitations.

Benefits of Visualizing Goals (Goal Images)

Neuroscientist turned executive coach Tara Swart indicates that the brain engages in "value tagging," assigning a higher value to images than it does to written words on a to-do list. The more you look at those images, the more those images move up in importance; this is helpful for staying goal-focused.

Additionally, goals often involve trying something new, which can be scary. But when you repeatedly look at images related to your goals, your brain no longer sees them as new. As Swart says,

"The process (visualizing goals) reduces the physiological fear response to any new situation or person, making you more likely to take healthy risks, collaborate and embrace opportunity."[10]

Limitations of Visualizing Goals (Goal Images)

However, Swart also indicates that your brain can't distinguish between visualizing success and achieving it, which can create issues. More specifically, research from New York University shows that fantasizing about an ideal future state, especially one that is more pressing to achieve, decreases the energy people have for pursuing that state.[11] Why? Again, your brain can't distinguish between visualizing success and achieving it, so you subconsciously "take your foot off the gas," as mental strength expert Amy Morin describes it.[12]

The key here then, is to mentally "keep your foot on the gas" by also visualizing *the actual work it takes to achieve your goal.* We do that in the next part of the GRAB, the Work Images (as shown in Figure 8.3). It's here that you find images (and perhaps a few key supporting phrases) to visualize three things in particular: (a) the specific heavy lifting that must be done along the way, (b) the values that need to be adhered to while doing the work, and (c) the behaviors expected in the pursuit.

Science, once again, further supports how powerful Work Images can be. A study from the National Institute for Brain and Rehabilitation Sciences shows that, incredibly, people who simply imagine themselves flexing a muscle (i.e., just part of the work it takes to lift something), achieve *actual physical strength gains.*[13]

Let's walk through a simple example of a GRAB, using the scenario described in Goal-Focus Habit #1 (set intrinsically motivating goals). Say we want to visualize the macro-goal of expanding sales and distribution overseas for the first time, as well as the micro-goals of hiring a top-notch new sales force and building an overseas headquarters.

The Goal Images might include pictures of an impressive-looking, inviting new HQ building and a smiling, sharp-looking group of salespeople, along with a catchphrase that's been gaining steam in the c-suite: "Building growth through a world-class building."

The Work Images might include pictures of the hardest tasks (heaviest lifting), like an excavator digging, construction workers high up on a beam, and a room full of people waiting to be interviewed. The point of these images is not to demotivate but to help the viewer visualize going through the motions of what it will take (while making "scary" tasks seem more familiar). Research from the University of Western Australia shows enabling such mental rehearsal is helpful, even when things are going well, as it prevents people from complacency and toughens them up mentally for the work ahead.[14]

Images here might also include some that depict kindness and collaboration, a key value and desired behavior (also from the previous example).

With a GRAB completed, it's about sharing it broadly so it has its intended effect (perhaps digitally as a PDF document, or as a visual stapled to every meeting agenda, for example).

Your First Small Step: Pick someone creative to own the process of developing a GRAB, and turn them loose.

In Moments of Weakness: It can be tricky to visually represent the hard work ahead, or the values and behaviors expected (or even the goal itself, for that matter). If you're struggling, just select the images that best represent the feeling behind the goal and the most important things you want the viewer to mentally rehearse; the images don't have to be picture-perfect.

Goal-Focus Habit #3: Set Expectations—Thoroughly

A goal, of course, is an expectation. Quite often, it's a hard number expectation; increase sales by 10 percent, profits by 8 percent, reduce costs by 15 percent. Nothing wrong with hard number goals/expectations—it gives organizations a clear performance metric to aim for. But the problem arises when that hard number expectation is *all* the leader focuses on, when it's the only expectation they set (which happens all too often).

In truth, there's a much broader collection of expectations that mentally strong leaders set, to ensure the troops know exactly *what* is expected of them and *how* they're expected to deliver it. The tool that follows illuminates that collection of standards for you to set.

Before we get to that though, it's worth illustrating just how much employees need more comprehensive expectation setting. Case in point, I conducted research with hundreds of pairs of bosses and subordinates. In the study, I asked the employee, "What do you think your boss expects from you?" Then I compared what the employee said to what their boss said about expectations. In 81 percent of the cases, there were material breaches in the employee's understanding of even some of the most basic expectations. The point is (and I say this with love), your employees are likely not as clear on what you expect as you think they are.

Let's get to that expectation-setting tool now.

Habit-Building Tool #3: Keeping an organization goal-focused requires they understand the full set of expectations underlying the goals they're being held accountable for. That happens when you use the Expectation-Setting Spectrum, a collection of standards that you set, ranging from the "hard" side (*what* numbers employees are expected to hit), to the "soft" side (*how* employees are expected to achieve those numbers along the way). See Figure 8.4.

Fig. 8.4 The Expectation-Setting Spectrum

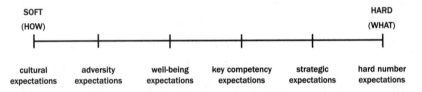

SOFT (HOW)					HARD (WHAT)
cultural expectations	adversity expectations	well-being expectations	key competency expectations	strategic expectations	hard number expectations

Let's work our way through this spectrum, from left to right.

On the far left, you establish *cultural expectations* about how you expect employees to behave, and what values they must uphold, as they work toward the organization's goals. What are the team norms you want them to adhere to? For example, say you establish that a collaborative spirit is expected at all times, while upholding the organization's core values of respect and inclusion. Establishing cultural expectations keeps employees goal-focused in the right way, and away from bridge-burning and toxicity just to hit the number they're expected to hit.

Moving to the right, you establish *adversity expectations*. Meaning, you spell out what you expect from your organization in times of adversity and crisis, which at some point, you'll likely go through. For example, you establish that focus, calmness, urgency, and mutual support are all expected. True character comes out in times of adversity, and you want your organization to show theirs in the best way possible. So, establish the expectation for it. You can even create an "Adversity Manifesto," as outlined in chapter 3.

Moving further to the right, you set *well-being expectations*. It's more essential than ever to do so. After all, the U.S. Surgeon General declared toxic workplaces a health hazard, and even issued guidelines for combating them.[15] So, set expectations here, but ones that aren't too personal (well-being is an individual journey, after all). For example, establish that no one is expected to return emails after normal work hours, encourage employees to take all their vacation, require managers to support employees in taking time for personal needs, and encourage participation in learning and growth programs. Just bringing up the idea that employees are expected to experience well-being will be seen as a breath of fresh air.

Next in the spectrum, you set *key competency expectations*. Pick the key competencies that you most want your organization to demonstrate, like leadership, collaboration, and smart risk taking, for example. Then, and this is critical, define what the difference between *good* and *great* looks like for those competencies. For example, you define good leadership as getting things done and great leadership as getting things done through, and in support of, your people (by delegating effectively). The tension in having to define what good looks like and what great looks like forces specificity in your language. The number one reason employees are unclear on expectations is, they say, because their boss isn't specific enough in spelling out what they really want. And of course, what you really want is great (not good), which you've now given a clear description of.

Further to the right, you set *strategic expectations*, what's expected from employees to support key strategies. This requires that you and the employees clearly understand key organizational strategies, and that you reinforce those strategies through the expectations you set. For example, your company's core strategy is to differentiate from competitors by delivering superior customer service at every customer touch point. So, you set the strategic expectation that all employee activities should support this critical priority in some way.

Finally, at the far right, you have your *hard number expectations*, which you've likely already set. But now you have a thorough, goal-focusing set of expectations to go with the numerical ones.

Your First Small Step: Embrace the need to be more thorough in the expectations you set, then start thinking through what your expectations are for each spot on the spectrum. Download the Expectation-Setting Spectrum visual at scott-mautz.com/mentallystrong/templates. When you're ready to communicate your full range of expectations, you'll find that this visual helps you frame that communication.

In Moments of Weakness: The biggest stumbling block that pops up here is that the organization becomes fixated on the number they have to deliver and loses sight of what else is expected from them in getting to that number. When this happens, leverage the power of the spectrum visual. Bring the organization back to the diagram of the spectrum to help them visualize once again the full range of expectations they're accountable for.

Goal-Focus Habit #4: Control the Controllables

Lack of control equals lack of focus.

That's generally true in life, but especially when it comes to staying goal-focused. If you feel you have little control over the ability to make progress on your goals or to overcome barriers or setbacks along the way, good luck keeping focus on that goal.

The tool that follows will put the power back in your hands, while keeping unhelpful emotions, thoughts, and behaviors productively in check (literally).

Habit-Building Tool #4: Staying goal-focused requires concentrating on things you can control, and that give you more control over goal-progress. That's where the Control Check comes in. Here's how it works.

Take a piece of paper and create two columns: label one *Setbacks,* and the other *Systems* (or use the template referenced at the end of this section). Sit down with your team, and in the *Setbacks* column, list everything that you're worried about regarding pursuit of your goal—everything that could be a setback. This is important because it's hard to stay focused on the goal when you're worried about all the barriers that could pop up preventing you from achieving it. Then, and this is the magic here, *circle only what you can control.* Research from Saint Louis University shows that doing so helps you recognize which barriers are self-imposed and which barriers to focus effort on, and indicates that the mere act of sharing such worries frees up mental space to focus on the positive.[16] In this way, you also set "Bother Boundaries," as articulated in chapter 6. The things you can't control are out of bounds, and you commit to not being bothered by them, instead focusing on what you can do something about (what's within the boundaries).

In the *Systems* column, list all the systems you'll need to have in place to help you achieve your goals. By systems, I mean the processes, procedures, and structures that will help you stay focused on (and successfully complete) the work that leads to progress. This is important because, as habit-building guru James Clear says, "Goals are good for setting a direction, but systems are best for making progress on those goals."[17] It's those systems that enable continuous small improvements and doses of forward movement that give you a sense of control. It's about "falling in love with the process, not the product."

To see examples of systems and setbacks, let's look at the Control Check in use in Figure 8.5. We'll continue to follow the scenario we've been using in this chapter (a macro-goal of expanding sales and distribution overseas, with micro-goals of hiring a top-notch new sales force and building an overseas headquarters).

Fig. 8.5 The Control Check

Setbacks	Systems
- a key competitor makes an aggressive bid for distribution	✓ have a governing body in place for quick decisions on merchandising and promotion
- initial overseas sales insufficient to maintain distribution	✓ create a standard evaluation process to make it easy for interviewers
- lack of a quality talent pool to hire from	✓ establish a procedure so that senior leaders can connect with newly offered candidates
- not closing the deal on candidates we make offers to in a competitive job market	✓ create a system for getting employee input on the HQ design
- permits for each building phase get delayed	
- HQ design doesn't compel people to come into the office	

The biggest potential setbacks have been listed in the left-hand *Setbacks* column, with only those things that the team can control, or do something about, having been circled. Referring to the three things circled: if initial overseas sales aren't strong enough to maintain distribution, many things can be done on the merchandising, promotion, and marketing front. If there's concern about getting candidates to accept their offer, many things can be done to "sweeten" the offer, or to present an even more convincing case for taking the job. Should the HQ design underwhelm, the design team can step back and make design adjustments based on employee input. By circling only the things the team can control, an instant sense of clarity, focus, and ability to influence results.

In the *Systems* column are listed all the key processes, procedures, and structures the team would need to ensure are in place to overcome the "controllable" setbacks circled (and to ensure goal progress). Listing these systems in advance gives a sense of control, confidence, and increased ability to produce the desired outcome.

And just like that, you're focused on worries you can do something about and on ensuring you have the systems in place to help you maintain focus and progress on the goal. It's a check that creates more control.

Your First Small Step: Download the Control Check template at scottmautz.com/mentallystrong/templates, and explain to your team why you want to engage in the exercise. When they start to focus on what they can control, and the systems needed for goal achievement, they'll be energized by the increased sense of goal viability.

In Moments of Weakness: It's easy to find yourself catastrophizing over imagined scenarios that you have no control over. Likewise, it's easy to work outside of helpful systems and processes in a rush to make progress toward a goal. When you catch yourself/the team doing either of these things, download a Control Check template, discuss, and get back on track.

Goal-Focus Habit #5: Avoid Distractions with Intention

The antithesis of staying goal-focused are all those times when you're inadvertently drawn to something else that *feels* more urgent or important in the moment. Goal researchers have a fancy term for these occasions.

Distractions. They're like catnip for poor self-regulation.

At least distractions are reliable; they're going to keep reappearing. It's a question of whether or not you have an intentional plan for how to handle them when they pop up. Otherwise, your ability to stay goal-focused will be inversely proportional to the number of distractions that arise.

Not to worry. The tool that follows *is* your plan.

Habit-Building Tool #5: You maintain goal-focus in the face of distractions by creating an If/Then Inventory. It's a series of if/then statements to help you anticipate distractions likely to arise and the action you'll take if they do. As a result, you keep distractions from scattering focus, responding to them with intentional, goal-oriented actions instead. Research from the University of Sheffield and the University of North Carolina supports this, indicating that forming a connection between a cue (the if) and your reaction to that cue (the then) is absolutely vital for staying focused on your goals and ultimately realizing them.[18]

Here's what an If/Then Inventory of anticipated distractions might look like, continuing on with the example we've been using throughout this chapter.

If/Then Inventory
If we get the usual flurry of inquiries/requests from upper management at the end of the quarter, **then** we'll assign one person to handle those, so the rest can focus on our overseas distribution goals.
If our interviewers are given too many forms to fill out about candidates, **then** we'll push back and reinforce the new low-touch, high-speed hiring process we're using.
If our competitors launch a burst of small innovations to divert the attention of our potential overseas customers, **then** we'll increase our marketing spending.
If we get multiple requests for upgrades in our manufacturing plants, **then** we'll be certain to prioritize review of those requests until after the HQ design is complete.

Your First Small Step: Schedule time on the calendar with your team to brainstorm potential distractions that could arise in the pursuit of any goal you're trying to accomplish (and what to do, accordingly). Intentionally increasing awareness of potential distractions is the first step to avoiding them.

In Moments of Weakness: If distractions continually arise that, in retrospect, you could have anticipated and planned for, be certain to recognize just how much productivity and focus is being drained. That should trigger a commitment to conduct an If/Then Inventory next time around. Unexpected distractions will certainly crop up. This is about making a habit of doing the hard work of anticipating and planning as needed.

Goal-Focus Habit #6: Ask for Accountability Appointments

To help keep your team (and yourself) focused on your goals, apply one of the greatest forces on earth.

Accountability.

Nothing maintains focus and fuels progress like having people feel accountable to deliver on their stated goals. In fact, say you decide to pursue a goal and that your likelihood of success is about 25 percent. Research shows that if you commit to that goal to someone who matters, your probability of success goes up to 65 percent. If you have regular Accountability Appointments, where you meet to discuss progress against the goal with the other person, the likelihood of success hits a whopping 95 percent.[19]

So, you can see where we're headed with this next tool.

Habit-Building Tool #6: Let's start here by presuming that you're committed to pair up people (or groups of people) and ask them to hold regular Accountability Appointments regarding their goals. In these meetings, one person is the "goal-pursuer," the other is the "accountability partner" (the person who holds the goal-pursuer accountable). Three questions, the Accountability Asks, constitute the agenda for the Accountability Appointment. The goal-pursuer should come prepared to discuss (regarding themselves/their team):

1. *Where are we making progress or excuses?*
2. *Where are we owning the issue or avoiding the issue?*
3. *Where are we being brave or blaming?*

The idea here is to provide an opportunity to highlight good work being done, while mitigating accountability-dodging behavior. Before we examine each question, note that they all demand two things: vulnerability and compassion. I'll explain.

Answering these questions clearly requires the goal-pursuer to be willingly vulnerable (and obviously, honest), modeling accountability in so doing. There's a social factor involved as well. When you've shared your missteps with someone, you don't want to later disappoint them by repeating those missteps. Furthermore, the tension of knowing in advance that you're expected to be vulnerable and share missteps heightens your sensitivity to making missteps in the first place.

Also, discussing these questions clearly requires compassion from the accountability partner. Of course, the act of asking the questions itself is about holding the other accountable. But the point is not to judge or scold, it's to help turn missteps into learning opportunities. The point is not to assign blame, but to lend an empathetic ear and look for ways to help. (Note: Goal-pursuers should also show compassion for themselves, knowing that things go wrong, and that it's okay, as long as you're learning and improving.)

Again, note that each question starts with the opportunity for the goal-pursuer to shine. It's very motivating to share your progress, proudly talk where you've owned an issue, or where you've been brave about something. Accountability Appointments are not meant to be something to dread.

Now let's look at each question.

1. *Where are we making progress or excuses?*

This first part of this question is for assessing progress to date. It's here that measurements in place can help gauge the level of progress. The second part of the question is meant to encourage honest, vulnerable discussion about where excuses might be predominating.

For example, you proudly give an update on how far the new software installation has come. At the same time, you admit you'd be even farther along if you/your team weren't making excuses about not having enough direction from upper management. You commit to proactively reaching out to key managers for further guidance, i.e., no longer using the issue as an excuse. And admitting and discussing the excuse heightens sensitivity to future excuse-making.

It's an important discussion to have because, as I saw painted on the lobby floor of one client's headquarters, "The opposite of progress is excuses."

2. *Where are we owning the issue or avoiding the issue?*

This one's about discussing problems that pop up along the way in pursuit of the goal. If you're owning the problem, you're taking responsibility and stepping up to address the issue. If you're avoiding an issue, you're dodging responsibility, looking the other way, not stepping up, remaining quiet, doing nothing.

In our software installation example, you eagerly share three big issues that you/your team are taking ownership of. At the same time, with vulnerability, you share that your team avoided an issue regarding software reliability, instead hoping that the software vendor would address it. Again, something that you learned from, though, and, with heightened awareness, something you feel accountable to not repeat.

3. *Where are we being brave or blaming?*

Being brave means openly acknowledging mistakes and how
they were addressed. For the second part of the question, you
discuss blaming behavior, where you've not admitted mistakes and instead pointed fingers, or even lashed out. Not
easy discussions to have. But they're like self-awareness and
accountability superglue.

In our example, you acknowledge mistakes that were made in
the physical installation of the software and share how they
were corrected. You also acknowledge that a few team members got caught up in finger-pointing over who was at fault for
the errors. With heightened sensitivity, you commit that you
won't let that happen again.

It's worth restating that Accountability Appointments are
meant to energize, foster transparency and self-awareness, and
encourage goal-focus and goal progress, not to create uncomfortable conversations.

Your First Small Step: Establish accountability partner
pairings, share the Accountability Asks to use as an agenda,
and ask the partners to schedule their first Accountability
Appointment.

In Moments of Weakness: Holding others (and yourself)
accountable isn't always warm and fuzzy work. Your team
might struggle a bit at first with the Accountability Asks,
and the forthrightness and vulnerability required in discussing them. If this happens, simply encourage them to stick to
it, reminding them that it's all in service of the goal you're
all trying to achieve. Also point out that over time, it will
become easier and more natural, if they stick to it. In fact, the

discussions can become rewarding because, remember, they also offer the chance to highlight things done well and hard-fought progress earned to date.

Goal-Focus Habit #7: Leverage the Power of Small Wins

Few things drive as much focus and commitment to a meaningful goal as making progress on that goal. It's known as the "progress principle," identified in landmark research conducted by Harvard Business School's Teresa Amabile.[20] Here's how to take advantage of it.

Habit-Building Tool #7: Drive supreme goal-focus by instituting a Circle of Perpetual Progress. It's a disciplined system for turning the encouragement of progress, small wins, into a virtuous cycle of forward movement. Here's how it works.

Fig. 8.6 Circle of Perpetual Progress

⁴ visibly aid progress

¹ communicate when progress is made

² reconnect goal progress to personal/professional progress

³ celebrate progress (especially small wins)

Start by frequently *communicating when progress is made* (even small wins), using a technique called mileage messaging. It's based on a 2008 University of Chicago study that showed to maintain an organization's goal-focus, it's vital to communicate two types of messages regarding progress to two different groups. Convey how far you've come to those less committed to the goal, and convey how far there still is to go, the tasks still to do, to the more committed.[21] (Both communications reference the distance to a goal, thus the term "mileage messaging.")

In other words, the intensity of goal commitment the audience has (or lack thereof) directly influences the message the audience needs to hear. That doesn't mean you have to discern who exactly is goal-committed to what degree (or not), and parse your message accordingly. It just means be certain to communicate both forms of mileage messaging. And in case you're wondering, "But wouldn't communicating to less goal-committed people how far there still is to go (in addition to how far they've come) demotivate them?" The answer is no, as long as you frame how far there is to go within a strong belief that they'll get there, along with a reminder of how important it is to do so.

For example, you share a small win that a group of social services caseworkers had in improving the living conditions of some at-risk constituents. You include messaging on how small steps like this just keep adding to how far the caseworkers have come in advancing their mission. At the same time, you communicate there's still plenty to do to get all the way to the ultimate goal.

Next, *reconnect goal progress to personal/professional progress*. In other words, every time you share progress or small wins, don't let the opportunity pass by—use it as a chance to reinforce the connection to people's personal and professional progress.

In our example, you make sure the caseworkers are reminded that it's small wins like these that lead to bigger government grants, increased pay, promotions, new team assignments, and rewarding new projects. It's about keeping employees focused and motivated toward goal achievement by continually making them feel personally rewarded.

The next step in this virtuous cycle is related, but worthy of its own mention. That is, *celebrate progress;* especially the small wins. The Harvard research indicated that employees were the most motivated and energized not after big celebrations of major milestones, but when celebrating the small breakthroughs along the way.[22] Not sure how small of a win is too small? Lean into it, as a study conducted by OnePoll showed that 82 percent of employees believe "there's no such thing as a win being 'too small' to celebrate."[23] Just make sure you're celebrating actual results, rather than just activity (which keeps it feeling meaningful each time you celebrate). After all, this step is about making the small wins feel like a big deal.

Back to our example: You throw a celebration dinner to honor the caseworkers and give them a moment in the spotlight, asking them to share how they achieved their result.

Finally, *visibly aid progress.* Let people see, and feel, that you're there to help them build on the hard-earned small wins. Provide more resources, or serve as a resource ("being sure to check-in versus seeming to check-up," as Amabile says[24]). This could include spending extra time helping the team problem-solve or anticipate future potential roadblocks, or removing barriers that only you can remove. There are infinite ways to be a propellant; it's simply about doing whatever you can to visibly help keep the momentum going.

Once you've done all of these steps, guess what happens then? More small wins (and certainly some big ones), which starts the productive cycle all over again. You communicate those wins, link them to personal/professional goals, celebrate them, build on the momentum with further assistance, and so on—a perpetual progress machine.

Your First Small Step: Get the virtuous cycle going by picking just one small win to highlight and communicate about. Build from there, referencing the Circle of Perpetual Progress visual as your guide.

In Moments of Weakness: The good thing about the Circle of Perpetual Progress is that if you misstep along the way and fall out of the loop, say by forgetting to link personal incentives to progress, there are other steps to lift you up and keep you moving forward (like celebrating small wins and actively aiding progress). Just jump right back onto the "flywheel," trying to move it forward until progress begets more progress.

Goal-Focus Habit #8: Stop Procrastination

You just saw how forward movement, even in small doses, yields more focus, thus more progress, and so on. So, what throws a wrench into that whole thing?

Procrastination.

In other words, delayed effort. Zero progress. Dulled focus. Self-regulation of emotions, thoughts, and behaviors, out the window.

No longer can we put it off. Let's get right to putting an end to procrastination.

Habit-Building Tool #8: To remain goal-focused and forward moving, follow the Path Through Procrastination. It has five steps. Let's take them one at a time.

Step 1: Ask: "Why am I procrastinating?" Maybe the goal-related task bores you, you don't like doing it, or you're afraid of failing at it. Find a positive to offset the negative. Bored? Make it more interesting. Don't like the task? Tie a reward to finishing it. Indifferent? Clarify the goal and find the meaning behind the task.

Step 2: Ask: "Why _must_ I get this task done?" Consider the pain of not completing the task. If there isn't any, by the way, consider eliminating the task. And consider the benefits of completing the task. Are you underestimating the importance of doing so, or how good it will feel to finish?

Step 3: Recognize the power of _just getting started._ Simply starting a task triggers what's known as the Zeigarnik Effect, named after researcher Bluma Zeigarnik.[25] Her studies showed that if you can manage to just start a task, you're far more driven to finish it. The brain registers when a task has started and when it has been interrupted. Uncompleted tasks nag at us, driving us to complete the task. That's why television shows often end their season with a cliffhanger episode. Creators know our brain remembers that last episode and the interruption in the story. Our brain wants a conclusion, so we hungrily tune in to, or stream, the next season.

Simply starting a task also stops you from overestimating how difficult or unpleasant the task will be. How many times have you started on something and wound up telling yourself, "This ain't so bad"?

And don't fall into the trap of waiting for the magic "I feel like it" moment (odds are, it won't come), or count on your willpower to kick in and get you going. In fact, studies like one from Northwestern's Kellogg School of Business show that willpower is consistently overestimated, while how quickly it's depleted is underestimated.[26] Nor should you convince yourself, "I'll wait, I work better under pressure." Research shows the opposite: people under stress make more errors. This is especially true when the stakes are high, as evidenced by a study showing that stressed doctors and nurses in an emergency department made more errors.[27]

Finally, on this front, you might think setting self-imposed deadlines will get you going, but a study from noted MIT researcher Dan Ariely shows it's far more effective to set deadlines externally, like with your boss or a friend.[28]

Step 4: Get started! Time for action. But it can still be hard to get going. Start by forgiving yourself for not starting yet. Doing so eases guilt, which causes further procrastination, as you want to avoid the uncomfortable feeling of confronting your utter lack of progress. It also helps to start with extremes. Break the task into a series of smaller steps, from easiest to hardest. Then, start on either end. Getting the stressful, hardest parts done first allows you to be more present with each of the tasks thereafter, rather than having that toughest task gnawing at you in the back of your mind. Your energy is highest at the start as well, increasing the likelihood you'll blast through the tough task. Or start with the easiest task, which feeds into your natural desire for instant gratification, and can thus get momentum going.

Step 5: Stay on track. Key here is to avoid device distractions and busywork—mindless work unrelated to the task at hand that gives you the illusion real work is being done. For example, you have to prepare for a big meeting tomorrow, but you soon find yourself rearranging the apps on your phone. (Been there, done that.) The key is to catch this distracted behavior, evaluate each task you're engaging in, and then redirect your effort to the actual work that will get you back on course. Having everything you need to complete the task in front of you can also help keep you from straying.

Your First Small Step: Procrastination is a dastardly, goal-distracting foe that requires constant vigilance to overcome. Familiarize yourself with the steps above, and identify key projects/tasks where you simply cannot afford to procrastinate. Mark on your calendar the dates you want to start work on those projects/tasks, along with a reminder note to refer back to what you've learned here about avoiding procrastination.

In Moments of Weakness: The next time you catch yourself slipping back into procrastination, give yourself a pat on the back—you noticed it! No small feat, as procrastination is a sneaky little miscreant. One study showed we lose more than two hours a day due to procrastination.[29] In the moment you realize you've slipped, forgive yourself and gently return to step 1. Just realizing you're procrastinating and asking why you're doing it starts you down the right path.

Goal-Focus Habit #9: End Perfectionism

How's this for ironic: pursuing perfection blocks you from achieving success. Frustration, disappointment, exhaustion, and feelings of being overwhelmed result instead. Self-regulation of emotions, thoughts, and behaviors gets perfectly passed over. Instead, adopt the next habit/tool to put an end to perfectionism.

Habit-Building Tool #9: When someone's engaged in perfectionism, the only thing it really accomplishes is a delay in achieving the goal they're trying so pristinely to pursue. The Perfectionism Pyramid makes a habit of breaking this habit. It has three sections: Awareness, Standards you set, and where to Focus, as labeled in Figure 8.7.

Fig. 8.7 The Perfectionism Pyramid

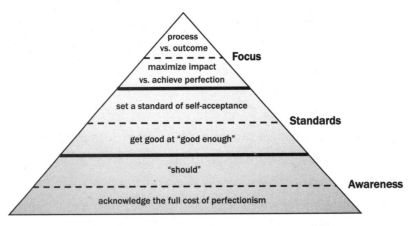

Let's go through each layer, starting with Awareness at the bottom.

First, be aware of and *acknowledge the full cost of perfectionism*. Perfectionism keeps you from spending your time in far more valuable ways, and worse. Perfectionists tend to judge and criticize not only themselves, but those around them, too. The more they see their own flaws in others, the more they pick at them. The criticism and judging push people away and isolate the perfectionist, further increasing their "I'm not good enough" belief—a vicious cycle. This cycle is broken only when the full impact of perfectionism is acknowledged.

Next, be aware of "should." Meaning, avoid using this word. To illustrate, consider these statements: "I *should* go over this again to make sure it's 100 percent right," "This *should* be a lot better than it is right now," "I *should* have done this instead of that." The very nature of the word fosters overthinking and spurs attempts to control everything (not helpful). Instead of saying "should," give yourself a reason to move on, like, "If I just finish this, I can go to the movies."

Moving one layer up the Pyramid, we get to Standards. Here, it's important to *get good at "good enough"* (as briefly mentioned in chapter 7). Chances are, nobody's holding you to the same standards you're holding yourself to. There's nothing wrong with high standards, of course; they're healthy. The problem arises when you view success as "all or nothing," all the time. Learning to say "good enough" can be liberating. It also helps here to calibrate your standards with colleagues by sharing your early work. You might find it's already plenty good enough.

Next, *set a standard of self-acceptance.* In other words, "Accept yourself before you wreck yourself!" It's easy to become a prisoner to your perfectionist tendencies, constantly trying to avoid any rejection, disappointment, or criticism. You can only break free when you learn to practice self-acceptance and self-appreciation; when you learn to forgive yourself. When you have the courage to be imperfect (like we're all wired to be) and live with vulnerability. Look to the Self-Acceptance Scale in chapter 4 to help here.

Now, the top layer of the pyramid—where to Focus. Quite simply, focus on *maximizing impact versus achieving perfection.* Recognize when your efforts are at a point of diminishing returns, and move on. If you're honest with yourself, you'll spot when your incremental efforts are no longer having an impact. Accept that sometimes just being done is a worthy goal. By the way, don't exaggerate the impact of not achieving perfection. Ask yourself, "What's the realistic cost of imperfection here? Is even the worst case really that bad?" Humorist Mark Twain said: "I've suffered a great many catastrophes in my life. Most of them never happened."[30]

Finally, focus on *process rather than outcome.* Perfectionists focus on the outcome (will it be perfect or not?), missing the richness of the process and the opportunities to learn and grow along the way. For example, consider the case shared by one of my readers, who we'll call Daniel. Daniel's perfectionism kept him from learning how to do things he was interested in because he couldn't be perfect at them right away. He wanted to learn to play guitar, but because he couldn't quickly perfect the art, he abandoned it. His perfectionism robbed him of the process of practicing, learning incrementally, and improving. The point is, learn to fall in love with the process of improvement, not perfection.

So, if you practice each level of the Perfectionism Pyramid, your ability to stay focused and move forward will improve.

Your First Small Step: It's too easy to slip unwittingly back into perfectionist mode. Familiarize yourself with each level of the Perfectionism Pyramid and identify key projects/ tasks where you simply cannot afford to be a perfectionist. Mark on your calendar the date those projects/tasks must be completed, along with a reminder note to refer back to what you've learned here about avoiding perfectionism.

In Moments of Weakness: Perfectionism is often deeply ingrained, so it takes time and patience to overcome. When you (or whoever you're coaching on this) slips and gets tangled in it, return to the Perfectionism Pyramid and start putting into practice the layer that would be most immediately relevant and helpful. By the way, starting again, right from the bottom, is always immediately impactful because you're facing head-on the cost of your continued perfectionism.

Goal-Focus Habit #10: Sharpen Your Focusing Skills

The ability to stay goal-focused (and ultimately achieve those goals) includes the ability to concentrate and focus deeply in "crunch time," when you most need to be locked in to what you're doing. If you struggle with this, even occasionally, here's help.

Habit-Building Tool #10: Here's a simple, but very effective exercise for when you need to concentrate, called the Mental Spotlight. Here's how it works.

Picture a spotlight in a dark theater shining onto a stage. The beam of light is narrow at the top, then really broadens when it hits the stage. This image (like the one in Figure 8.8) is a metaphor for how you're going to create intense focus.

Fig. 8.8 The Mental Spotlight

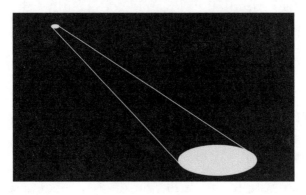

First, ensure you've created the "dark theater environment" by removing distractions. In other words, put your mobile devices in another room. In this way, you establish firm "terms of engagement" with your devices; you won't engage with them when it's time to get down to business. And no, keeping the device near you, but turning it off, or committing to not check it while you're working, simply isn't enough. A study from the University of Chicago shows that just the presence of a mobile device is a "brain drain that reduces available cognitive capacity," sapping your ability to focus.[31]

Wherever your location, go to a quiet space without traffic, or put on earphones as a signal you're not to be disturbed. On your computer, close all applications, especially email and social media, except the one you're working with in full screen mode.

With a darkened surrounding environment now, picture being at the top of the beam of light, at its narrowest part. It's narrow because this is where you decide what you need to focus on. Many of us don't have a problem focusing per se, we have a problem deciding what to focus on. We jump from task to task or try to mentally multitask (do two cognitive things at once), which we think we're great at, but we're not (as I pointed out in chapter 6). So, don't multitask, single-task, and choose what to focus on.

For example, having created your "darkened surrounding environment," you decide you must really focus on writing that recommendation, crisply, so it fits on one page. That becomes the top of the beam of light for you.

Continuing with the image of the spotlight, now tell yourself to stay within that beam of light and ride it downward, maintaining the intensity and sharpness of focus on your task. If your attention strays outside that beam of light, away from what you're trying to concentrate on, simply *forgive yourself* and move right back within that focused beam. You lose even more focus when you beat yourself up for not focusing, so resist the impulse.

Back to our example: You get distracted from recommendation writing by a coworker who pings you with a question (with the corresponding phone "ding" from the other room sucking you in). Oh, well, it happens (although turning off notifications on your phone would have helped). Then you just pull yourself right back into the focused beam of light, back to concentrating.

Now, picture moving to the end of the beam of light where it's at its widest. It's here that you're really locked in, in a state of flow, mentally surrounding your task. It's here where you successfully drive your task to completion. That's the state of mind you're aiming for with this goal-enabling exercise.

In our example, you're at the widest part of the beam of light now, fully surrounding your task, on a roll with your writing. You stay locked in and finish the recommendation.

Your First Small Step: The next several times you sit down to do focused work, work that requires concentration, let that trigger the mental image of a spotlight in a dark theater, shining onto a stage. Just learning to associate this image with the times you need to get down to business is a great start. Then you can begin really using the metaphor, following the beam of light down as described above, until you've mentally surrounded and completed the task at hand.

In Moments of Weakness: When you "fall out of the beam of light" (lose your focus and concentration), just forgive yourself, and mentally picture pulling yourself right back into the beam, continuing to ride it downward as best you can until you're in that state of flow.

Goal-Focus Habit #11: Adjust Goals as Needed

It might surprise you, in a chapter about staying goal-focused, to learn that it's also important to keep an open mind to adjusting your goals along the way—if the situation warrants. Doing so can mean your ultimate outcomes, organization, and people will be better off for it. This is also true in life, as research indicates not only does remaining goal-flexible reduce depression and aid in successful aging,[32] it leads to a better quality of life overall.[33] The key is to have a self-regulating strategy for goal adjustment, so you're not changing direction every time the wind blows.

Habit-Building Tool #11: Here's a strategic approach for guiding goal adjustment. It's called the Funnel Vision vs. Tunnel Vision framework.

Fig. 8.9 The Funnel Vision vs. Tunnel Vision framework

Goal adherence: YES   Goal adherence: NO

It's built on the principle that you shouldn't have "tunnel vision" when it comes to your goals, setting a goal in stone then stubbornly ignoring anything that might cause you to make some goal adjustments along the way (visualized on the right side of Figure 8.9). Instead, think "funnel vision" (on the left side, above), keeping your mind open (like at the top of the funnel) to various inputs along the way, as you funnel down in pursuit of your focused goal. By "inputs" I mean realities of the current circumstances, setbacks, and the environment.

As an example, let's return to one of the chapter's running examples one last time. If you have a goal of building an overseas headquarters, but that country's economy collapses, interest rates skyrocket, and building material supply dries up, should you just plow forward without considering any change to the scope or timing of that goal (i.e., have tunnel vision)? Of course not.

The key is to be clear on what exactly to allow into your field of view (at the top of the funnel) for consideration; what might warrant an adjustment to a goal. Consider adjusting a goal when:

- there have been substantive changes in circumstances or the environment you're operating in (creating a context different from the one in which the goal was originally set)

- there have been setbacks that call the validity of the goal into question
- what you want has changed
- your "why" (the higher-order reason you're pursuing the goal) has changed
- priorities have shifted
- the goal is turning out to be too easy
- the goal is turning out to be wildly unrealistic, and is now just demotivating
- resources are proving to be too slight (not enough time, money, people)

Pro tip: Regarding that last one, when resources are too slight; don't give in to this one easily. Make a habit of asking, "Are we short on resources, or on resourcefulness?"

It's important to note that the funnel image represents a willingness to stay open to changes in your circumstances, but that it does ultimately narrow. Meaning, while considering environmental changes, it's critical to still narrow your focus to a specific goal (whether or not you've decided to alter that goal). Also note that changes or adjustments to your goals can be broad in scope (a new goal altogether) or narrower in scope (same general goal, but on a different scale, or timing, for example).

Your First Small Step: Get used to thinking about the funnel shape as opposed to the tunnel shape. It's the default for most people to think that staying focused on your goals, and ultimately achieving them, requires a closed-off, tunnel-like focus on those goals. So, it will take a little mental adjustment at first to think funnel rather than tunnel.

In Moments of Weakness: The desire to achieve a goal can cause you to blow through red lights and warning signs that your goal may no longer be relevant, doable, etc. If you look up and suddenly find yourself pressing toward the wrong endpoint, step back, and know that it's never too late to adjust. Better to shift late in the game than to keep trying to win the wrong game.

NOTES

1. Sample, I. December 27, 2009. "New year's resolutions doomed to failure, say psychologists," *The Guardian*, theguardian.com.
2. Luciani, J. December 29, 2015. "Why 80 Percent of New Year's Resolutions Fail," *US News & World Report*, usnews.com.
3. Duckworth, A. L., C. Peterson, M. D. Matthews, and D. R. Kelly. June 2007. "Grit: perseverance and passion for long-term goals," *J Pers Soc Psychol* 92(6): 1087–101.
4. Norcross, J. C., and J. C. Vangarelli. 1988–1989. "The resolution solution: longitudinal examination of New Year's change attempts," *J Subst Abuse* 1(2): 127–34.
5. Silverthorne, S. January 2, 2013. "Why Setting Goals Can Do More Harm Than Good," *Forbes*, forbes.com.
6. Chambliss, D. Spring 1989. "The Mundanity of Excellence," *Sociological Theory* 7:1.
7. Ordóñez, L. D., M. E. Schweitzer, A. D. Galinsky, and M. H. Bazerman. February 11, 2009. "Goals Gone Wild: The Systematic Side Effects of Over-Prescribing Goal Setting," *Academy of Management Perspectives*.
8. Park, J., F.-C. Lu, and W. M. Hedgcock. 2017. "Relative Effects of Forward and Backward Planning on Goal Pursuit," *Psychological Science* 28(11): 1620–30.

9.   Pham, L. B., and S. E. Taylor. February 1999. "From Thought to Action: Effects of Process-Versus Outcome-Based Mental Simulations on Performance," *Personality and Social Psychology Bulletin* 25(2): 250–60.

10. Scipioni, J. November 22, 2019. "Top execs use this visualization trick to achieve success—here's why it works, according to a neuroscientist," *CNBC Make It*, cnbc.com.

11. Kappes, H. B., and G. Oettingen. July 2011. "Positive fantasies about idealized futures sap energy," *Journal of Experimental Social Psychology* 47(4): 719–29.

12. Morin, A. November 16, 2018. "Why Vision Boards Don't Work (And What You Should Do Instead)," *Inc,* inc.com.

13. Leisman G., A. A. Moustafa, and T. Shafir. May 25, 2016. "Thinking, Walking, Talking: Integratory Motor and Cognitive Brain Function," *Front Public Health* 4(94).

14. Gucciardi, D. F., S. Gordon, and J. A. Dimmock. July 24, 2009. "Evaluation of a Mental Toughness Training Program for Youth-Aged Australian Footballers: I. A Quantitative Analysis," *Journal of Applied Sport Psychology* 21(3): 307–23.

15. "The U.S. Surgeon General's Framework for Workplace Mental Health & Well-Being." 2022. The Office of the Surgeon General, hhs.gov/sites.

16. Kellogg, R. T., H. K. Mertz, and M. Morgan. 2010. "Do gains in working memory capacity explain the written self-disclosure effect?" *Cognition and Emotion* 24(1).

17. Clear, J. "Forget About Setting Goals. Focus on This Instead," jamesclear.com/goals-systems.

18. Webb, T. L., and P. Sheeran, P. March 2007. "How do implementation intentions promote goal attainment? A test of component processes," *Journal of Experimental Social Psychology*, 43(2).

19. Newland, S. 2018 (third quarter). "The Power of Accountability," *AFCPE The Standard Newsletter*, afcpe.org.
20. Amabile, T. M., and S. J. Kramer. May 2011. "The Power of Small Wins," *Harvard Business Review*, hbr.org.
21. Koo, M., and A. Fishbach. 2008. "Dynamics of self-regulation: How (un)accomplished goal actions affect motivation," *Journal of Personality and Social Psychology 94(2):* 183–95.
22. Amabile and Kramer.
23. Melore, C. December 24, 2021. "It's the little things: Average person enjoys 4 'small wins' each day," *StudyFinds*, studyfinds.org.
24. Amabile and Kramer.
25. Ciotti, G. July 11, 2012. "How Our Brains Stop Us Achieving Our Goals and How to Fight Back," blog.bufferapp.com.
26. "The Power of Temptation." August 3, 2009. kellogg.northwestern.edu.
27. Nielsen, K. J., A. H. Pedersen, K. Rasmussen, L. Pape, and K. L. Mikkelsen. March 2013. "Work-related stressors and occurrence of adverse events in an ED," *The American Journal of Emergency Medicine* 31(3): 504–8.
28. Ariely, D., and K. Wertenbroch. May 2002. "Procrastination, Deadlines, and Performance: Self-Control by Precommitment," *Psychological Science* 13(3).
29. Vaden, R. March 19, 2012. "Is Procrastination Killing You and Your Company? Author Offers Proven Distraction Busters," CNBC, cnbc.com.
30. Mark Twain quotes, goodreads.com.
31. Ward, A. F., K. Duke, A. Gneezy, and M. W. Bos. April 2017. "Brain Drain: The Mere Presence of One's Own Smartphone Reduces Available Cognitive Capacity," *Journal of the Association for Consumer Research* 2(2): 140–54.

32. Brandtstädter, J., and G. Renner, G. 1990. "Tenacious goal pursuit and flexible goal adjustment: Explication and age-related analysis of assimilative and accommodative strategies of coping," *American Psychological Association*, psychnet.apa.org.

33. Brandtstädter, J. March–June 2009. "Goal pursuit and goal adjustment: Self-regulation and intentional self-development in changing developmental contexts," *Advances in Life Course Research* 14(1–2): 52–62.

9   The MAP (Mental Action Plan)

You're now fully equipped to productively regulate your emotions, thoughts, and behaviors (i.e., wield your mental strength), to tackle all six of the leadership tests that most directly correlate with exceptional achievement—even in the face of substantive challenges. While all six tests require self-regulation skills to navigate them effectively, doing so is about to become a habit for you. Literally. In fact, you have six overall habits to build as you see fit (fortitude, confidence, boldness, messaging, decision-making, and goal-focus), and a menu of supporting habits and habit-building tools to choose from to ensure success. You're well on your way to managing internally, so you can lead externally—with brilliance.

So, it's time to create a tailored MAP (Mental Action Plan) to guide your mental strength-building regimen moving forward. You do so by using the template in Figure 9.1 (which you can download at scottmautz.com/mentallystrong/templates).

Fig. 9.1 The MAP (Mental Action Plan)

Overall Habits to Build	Supporting Habits/ Habit-Building Tools		Specific Action(s) I'll Take
The Fortitude Habit:	Habit #1: Reframe Setbacks	Tool #1: *The Lenses of Resilience*	
	Habit #2: Mind the Grind	Tool #2: *Grindfulness*	
	Habit #3: Solve Problems with Discipline	Tool #3: *The Problem-Solving Eye*	
	Habit #4: Perform under Pressure	Tool #4: *The Diamond Directive*	
	Habit #5: Shine, Don't Shrink, in Crisis	Tool #5: *The CALM Credo*	
	Habit #6: Preplan Reaction to Adversity	Tool #6: *The Adversity Manifesto*	
	Habit #7: Vanquish Victim Mentality	Tool #7: *Victim to Victor Strategies*	
	Habit #8: Foster Healthy Debate	Tool #8: *The Healthy Debate Hub*	
	Habit #9: Bravely Conduct Difficult Cnversns.	Tool #9: *Difficult Cnverstn. Consideration*	
The Confidence Habit:	Habit #1: Handle Criticism Effectively	Tool #1: *The Criticism Critical Path*	
	Habit #2: Monitor Yr. Relationship w/ Doubt	Tool #2: *The Doubt Continuum*	
	Habit #3: Monitor Relationship w/ Yourself	Tool #3: *The Self-Acceptance Scale*	
	Habit #4: Practice Two Types of Optimism	Tool #4: *Direct and Dormant Optimism*	
	Habit #5: Be Learning Agile	Tool #5: *The Figure-It-Out Figure Eight*	
	Habit #6: Engage in Deliberate Practice	Tool #6: *The Deliberate Drill*	
	Habit #7: Exude Executive Presence	Tool #7: *The Integrated Aura model*	
The Boldness Habit:	Habit #1: Think Big	Tool #1: *The Think Big Blueprint*	
	Habit #2: Change the Group Narrative	Tool #2: *Flip the COIN exercise*	
	Habit #3: Foster a Risk-Taking Spirit	Tool #3: *Right Signals/Wrong Impulses*	
	Habit #4: Inspire the Right Change Choice	Tool #4: *The TO and FOR Behavior Brief*	
	Habit #5: Lead Change with Conviction	Tool #5: *The Vision Building-Building*	
The Messaging Habit:	Habit #1: Nav. Neg. Emotions in the Moment	Tool #1: *The Redirect Rhythm*	
	Habit #2: Avoid Losing Your Temper	Tool #2: *The PALMS Up exercise*	
	Habit #3: Avoid Demotivating Language	Tool #3: *Eight to Eliminate*	
	Habit #4: Avoid Ninja Negativity Traps	Tool #4: *The Catch and Release exercise*	
	Habit #5: Choose to Stay Positive	Tool #5: *The Plus Sign*	
	Habit #6: Be an Active Listener	Tool #6: *The Peak Listening model*	
	Habit #7: Be Transparent	Tool #7: *The Window of Transparency*	
	Habit #8: Set a Balanced Tone	Tool #8: *The Motivating Match exercise*	
	Habit #9: Exhibit Unswerving Integrity	Tool #9: *The Integrity Audit*	
	Habit #10: Use Your Values as Your Lights.	Tool #10: *The Values Vault*	

The Decision-Making Habit:	Habit #1: Avoid Decision-Making Biases Habit #2: Stop Bad Habits -> Ld. to Bad Decs. Habit #3: Clrfy. Who/What/How of dec. mkg. Habit #4: Hold Disciplnd. Dcsn.-Mkng. Mtgs. Habit #5: Know When to Decd., When Not To Habit #6: Collect Data Wisely/Analyze Crtcly. Habit #7: Explore a Better Third Option Habit #8: Maximize Decision Confidence Habit #9: Elevate Your Predictive Ability Habit #10: Default to Being Decisive	Tool #1: *The Bias Buster* Tool #2: *Bad Habit Inventory* Tool #3: *Who/What/How Q's of Dec. Mkg.* Tool #4: *The Decision Meeting Dictates* Tool #5: *The Decision Timing Table* Tool #6: *The Collect and Respect Credo* Tool #7: *Explore If a Better 3rd Optn. Exists* Tool #8: *The Decision Confidence Test* Tool #9: *Elevate Your Predictive Ability* Tool #10: *The Cornering Indecision visual*
The Goal-Focus Habit:	Habit #1: Set Intrinsically Motivating Goals Habit #2: Visualize the Work It Will Take Habit #3: Set Expectations - Thoroughly Habit #4: Control the Controllables Habit #5: Avoid Distractions with Intention Habit #6: Ask for Accountability Appntmnts. Habit #7: Leverage the Power of Small Wins Habit #8: Stop Procrastination Habit #9: End Perfectionism Habit #10: Sharpen Your Focusing Skills Habit #11: Adjust Goals as Needed	Tool #1: *The Cascading Goal System* Tool #2: *Goal Realization & Action Board* Tool #3: *The Expectation-Setting Spectrum* Tool #4: *The Control Check* Tool #5: *If/Then Inventory* Tool #6: *The Accountability Asks* Tool #7: *Circle of Perpetual Progress* Tool #8: *The Path Through Procrastination* Tool #9: *The Perfectionism Pyramid* Tool #10: *The Mental Spotlight* Tool #11: *Funnel v. Tunnel Vision Frmwrk.*
Bonus Area	Bonus Habit: Ask for Help	Bonus Tool: *The Helping HANDS*

The left column lists the six overall habits to build, each of which aligns with one of the six tests of leadership. The center (split) column lists all the supporting habits and habit-building tools you can adopt in this book. The right column provides a place to write down your specific commitment about what actions you'll take (recall that writing down your goals makes it vastly more likely you'll achieve them).

Now let's go through how to use the MAP.

In the left column, circle all the overall habits you want to focus on developing, so that you can build your mental strength in a way that's tailored to you. Use your results from the Mental Strength Self-Assessment in chapter 2 to help guide you here. In the space provided in the left column, also write down detail about what specifically you want to strengthen within that overall habit. As an example, say you've done that, and decided that you want to focus on three areas:

- The Fortitude Habit
- The Confidence Habit
- The Messaging Habit

So, you circle each in the left column. Then, in the space provided in that column, you write down detail about what specifically you want to work on within each overall habit.

In the center column, you circle the supporting habits/habit-building tools you want to adopt from the book to build each overall habit area you're interested in.

In the right column, you list the specific action(s) you'll take. You number those actions in priority order, from easiest to hardest, for example, so you can do the easiest first, to help create momentum. Or number according to any priority order that suits your needs/interests.

Here's an example of what all this might look like:

Fig. 9.2 The Example MAP

(truncated for simplification - illustrates choice of three overall habits to build, supporting habits/tools to adopt)

Overall Habits to Build	Supporting Habits/ Habit-Building Tools		Specific Action(s) I'll Take
The Fortitude Habit: I need to become more resilient in the face of setbacks. I can get frazzled and off my game too easily.	Habit #1: Reframe setbacks Habit #2: Mind the grind Etc.	Tool #1: *The Lenses of Resilience* Tool #2: *Grindfulness* Etc.	**3** — We just suffered a setback on my key project. I'll apply *The Lenses of Resilience* immediately, and will continue using the tool until resilience becomes second nature, an ingrained habit.
The Confidence Habit: I need to get better at handling criticism. Too often I take it personal and it drains my confidence. I want to work on this.	Habit #1: Handle criticism effectively Habit #2: Monitor your relationship w/ doubt Etc.	Tool #1: *The Criticism Critical Path* Tool #2: *The Doubt Conundrum* Etc.	**1** — From this point forward, I commit to follow *The Criticism Critical Path* every time I receive criticism. I'll even make a habit of reviewing it before a meeting where I anticipate I'll get feedback.
The Boldness Habit:	Habit #1: Think big Habit #2: Change the group narrative Etc.	Tool #1: *The Think Big Blueprint* Tool #2: *Flip the COIN exercise* Etc.	
The Messaging Habit: I realize I'm not good in conflict or negative situations, my immediate emotions take over. I need to change this and the signals it sends.	Habit #1: Nav. neg. emotions in the moment Habit #2: Avoid losing your temper Etc.	Tool #1: *The Redirect Rhythm* Tool #2: *The PALMS Up exercise* Etc.	**2** — I'll start using *The Redirect Rhythm* every time I feel my emotions escalating in a negative situation, until using the model becomes a habit.
The Decision-Making Habit:	Habit #1: Avoid decision-making biases Habit #2: Stop bad habits that ld. to bad decs. Etc.	Tool #1: *The Bias Buster* Tool #2: *Bad Habit Inventory* Etc.	
The Goal-Focus Habit:	Habit #1: Set intrinsically motivating goals Habit #2: Visualize the work it will take Etc.	Tool #1: *The Cascading Goal System* Tool #2: *Goal Realization & Action Board* Etc.	

Now it's time to get to work on your own MAP: choosing the overall habits you're interested in (fortitude, confidence, boldness, messaging, decision-making, goal-focus), then building the supporting habits for each with the habit-building tools you adopt.

In other words, now it's time to *achieve*.

Refer back to your MAP (and this book) regularly, and by developing and sticking with the right habits, you'll soon be the mentally strong leader you set out to be.

Stay strong!

ACKNOWLEDGMENTS

The strength of this book comes from several sources, all of which I'd like to acknowledge here. Thank you to all the executives, students, and practitioners of mental strength for their contributions to this book—from granting interviews, to participating in research, sitting in focus groups, filling out surveys, sharing their stories, or letting me observe on the front lines. Thanks to all the companies that gave me the privilege of keynoting to their executives to share and shape all that I've learned. Thanks to my research partners who help me design smart, disciplined, statistically validated studies to unveil real insight. Thanks to Procter & Gamble, who served as my mental strength muse for so many years, enabling me to plant and nurture the seeds of an idea that would grow into a tree that bears wonderful fruit (much of which is low-hanging fruit, with the application of a little self-regulation). Thanks to the team at LinkedIn Learning that have supported my mission to help others become the best version of themselves, including the mentally strongest version of themselves. Thanks to the team at Indiana University's Kelley School of Business for Executive Education that continues to inspire me to be my mentally strongest. Thanks so much to Mike Campbell at Skyhorse Publishing/Peakpoint Press, whom I followed over from a previous publisher, and who has, once again, helped me shape this book into what it is today. And as always, a hearty thank-you to my friends and family, without whom I can't live, create, and be strong.

ABOUT THE AUTHOR

Scott Mautz is a popular keynote speaker, trainer, and workshopper (scottmautz.com) and just as popular a LinkedIn Learning instructor (linkedin.com/learning/instructors/scott-mautz). Scott's most popular LinkedIn Learning course to date is "Ten Habits of Mentally Strong People," a global-smash course that helped inspire this book. He's a former Procter & Gamble senior executive who successfully ran several of the company's largest multibillion-dollar businesses. He's also faculty on reserve at Indiana University's Kelley School of Business for Executive Education. Scott was named a "CEO Thought-leader" by the Chief Executives Guild, and a "Top 50 Leadership Innovator" by inc.com, where he wrote a column that drew nearly 2 million readers a month. He's the multi-award-winning, bestselling author of *Leading from the Middle: A Playbook for Managers to Influence Up, Down, and Across the Organization* (2021), *Find the Fire: Reignite Your Inspiration and Make Work Exciting Again* (2017), and *Make It Matter: How Managers Can Motivate by Creating Meaning* (2015). He's CEO/Founder of Profound Performance, a keynote, leadership training, and workshop company. Scott frequently appears in a variety of national media.